Teaching and Researching Language and Culture

APPLIED LINGUISTICS IN ACTION

General Editors:

Christopher N. Candlin and David R. Hall

Books published and forthcoming in this series include:

Teaching and Researching Language and Culture

Second Edition

Joan Kelly Hall

Routledge
Taylor & Francis Group

LONDON AND NEW YORK

First published 2002 by Pearson Education Limited
Second edition published in 2012

Published 2013 by Routledge
2 Park Square, Milton Park, Abingdon, Oxon OX14 4RN
711 Third Avenue, New York, NY 10017, USA

Routledge is an imprint of the Taylor & Francis Group, an informa business

ISBN 13: 978-1-4082-0506-8 (pbk)

British Library Cataloguing in Publication Data
A CIP catalogue record for this book can be obtained from the British Library

Library of Congress Cataloging in Publication Data
Hall, Joan Kelly.
    Teaching and researching : language and culture / Joan Kelly Hall. – 2nd ed.
        p. cm.
    Includes bibliographical references and index.
    ISBN 978-1-4082-0506-8 (pbk.)
    1. Sociolinguistics.   2. Language and culture.   I. Title.
    P40.H323 2011
    418.007–dc22
                                                                    2011014748

Set by 35 in 10.5/12pt Janson

Contents

General Editors' Preface

Applied Linguistics *in Action*, as its name suggests, is a series which focuses on the issues and challenges to teachers and researchers in a range of fields in Applied Linguistics, and provides readers and users with the tools they need to carry out their own practice-related research.

The books in the series provide the reader with clear, up-to-date, accessible and authoritative accounts of their chosen field within Applied Linguistics. Starting from a map of the landscape of the field, each book provides information on its main ideas and concepts, competing issues and unsolved questions. From there, readers can explore a range of practical applications of research into those issues and questions, and then take up the challenge of undertaking their own research, guided by the detailed and explicit research guides provided. Finally, each book has a section which provides a rich array of resources, information sources and further reading, as well as a key to the principal concepts of the field.

Questions the books in this innovative series ask are those familiar to all teachers and researchers, whether very experienced, or new to the fields of Applied Linguistics.

- What does research tell us, what doesn't it tell us and what should it tell us about the field? How is the field mapped and landscaped? What is its geography?

- How has research been applied and what interesting research possibilities does practice raise? What are the issues we need to explore and explain?

- What are the key researchable topics that practitioners can undertake? How can the research be turned into practical action?

- Where are the important resources that teachers and researchers need? Who has the information? How can it be accessed?

Each book in the series has been carefully designed to be as accessible as possible, with built-in features to enable readers to find what they want quickly and to home in on the key issues and themes that concern them. The structure is to move from practice to theory and back to practice in a cycle of development of understanding of the field in question.

Each of the authors of books in the series is an acknowledged authority, able to bring broad knowledge and experience to engage teachers and researchers in following up their own ideas, working with them to build further on *their* own experience.

The first editions of books in this series have attracted widespread praise for their authorship, their design, and their content, and have been widely used to support practice and research. The success of the series, and the realisation that it needs to stay relevant in a world where new research is being conducted and published at a rapid rate, have prompted the commissioning of this second edition. This new edition has been thoroughly updated, with accounts of research that has appeared since the first edition and with the addition of other relevant additional material. We trust that students, teachers and researchers will continue to discover inspiration in these pages to underpin their own investigations.

Chris Candlin & David Hall
General Editors

Acknowledgements

I am deeply grateful to series editors, Chris Candlin and David Hall, and the Longman/Pearson team for their enduring support and encouragement in helping me see the second edition through to completion. Their thorough attention to both substance and form has greatly enhanced the text, but, of course, I alone am responsible for the final product. I also thank Emily Rine for her able assistance with a small but important component of the project. Finally, I remain forever grateful to the JJJS cheering section: Bill, Kate, Kelly, Andrew, and Stacey. Their endless affection, patience and good humour make everything I do worthwhile.

Publisher's acknowledgements

We are grateful to the following for permission to reproduce copyright material:

Figure 6.1 from Celce-Murcia, M., Rethinking the role of communicative competence in language teaching, *Intercultural Language Use and Language Learning*, p. 45 (Soler, E. and Safont Jorda, M. (eds) 2007), Springer, with kind permission from Springer Science+Business Media B.V. and Marianne Celce-Murcia.

Introduction

The aim of *Teaching and Researching Language and Culture* is to lay out some of the major underpinnings of contemporary thought on two concepts considered to be at the heart of applied linguistics activity: language and culture. The book is organised into four sections. Section I contains three chapters in which I present some of the more significant assumptions on the nature of language and culture, and the nature of language and culture learning embodied in a sociocultural perspective of human action. In Chapter 1, I describe and trace the lineage of current perspectives on language and culture. In Chapter 2, I examine and trace the sources of current perspectives on the notion of identity and language use. In Chapter 3, I present current understandings on the nature of language and culture learning, tie them to recent findings from research on language development and discuss their implications for the development of an integrated theory of language teaching and learning.

The task of Section II is to examine how current understandings of language, culture and learning inform pedagogical practices. In Chapter 4, I provide an overview of current research revealing the vitality and richness of the culturally and linguistically diverse worlds that learners bring with them to school, and discuss some pedagogical innovations arising from this research. Chapter 5 is concerned with the sociocultural worlds of schools and classrooms. Here I present some recent research on these worlds and describe some pedagogical innovations for creating particular kinds of sociocultural communities in the classroom. In Chapter 6 I examine recent conceptualisations of language and culture as curricular content, and describe some current pedagogical approaches to teaching language and culture that have sprung from these discussions.

The purpose of Section III is to familiarise readers with current research interests in and approaches to the study of language and culture. In Chapter 7 I discuss some issues and concerns with doing research. In Chapter 8

I summarise eight approaches currently used by applied linguists to research language and culture from a sociocultural perspective, and in Chapter 9 I present a set of guidelines for planning, conducting and evaluating research projects. Chapter 10 presents a framework for conceptualising research contexts to give readers a sense of how current undertakings in the field are connected. In the discussion I include plans or blueprints for several research projects, using the framework set out in Chapter 9, that readers can try by themselves. It is hoped that the discussion of possibilities will help readers to develop and carry out their own ideas for doing research.

Section IV (Chapter 11) provides additional sources and resources to help readers in their explorations. The chapter contains an annotated list of some of the main journals in the field that publish studies on language and culture. It also includes a list of some of the major professional organisations for applied linguists. Finally, it includes an annotated listing of web-based resources that provide useful information and links related to the researching and teaching of language and culture. Following the chapter is a glossary of the terms used in the text that readers may find of assistance.

Postscript

Over the past decade, the depth and scope of the field's understandings of and research on language and culture have been transformed by the continued rising tide of globalisation and the ever-increasing digital means for communicating across geographical boundaries. This second edition of *Teaching and Researching Language and Culture* has been thoroughly revised and updated in an effort to capture some of the major theoretical and empirical developments taking place worldwide arising from these changes. Because of the vastness of the literature, my treatment of contemporary activity remains partial and broad-brushed. New routes and related activities are surely a part of this larger landscape but are not included here. Alternative routes and different sorts of activities are also taking place in the field that, while different from the world presented here, are worth exploring. I hope that the conceptual mappings provided in this text are useful to the readers in orienting them to some current theoretical and practical activities taking place in applied linguistics. At the same time, I hope readers' travels through this text propel them to begin charting their own explorations in the teaching and researching of language and culture.

Defining language and culture

A sociocultural perspective on language and culture

This chapter:

- describes current perspectives on the nature of language and culture in the field of applied linguistics;
- traces the lineage of some of the more significant assumptions on which current understandings are based;
- offers a list of additional readings on the topics covered in this chapter.

1.1   Introduction

Few would disagree that the study of language use is the central concern of applied linguistics, but opinions differ in how such study is to be conceptualised. Some have argued (see, for example, Pennycook, 2001, and Widdowson, 2000) that, until recently, much of what has taken place in applied linguistics is better understood as 'linguistics applied', a subset of the field of linguistics in which knowledge about language is used to address language-related concerns such as language teaching and language policy decisions. From the 'linguistics applied' perspective, language is considered to be a set of abstract systems whose meanings reside in the forms themselves rather than in the uses to which they are put. The contexts from which data are taken are considered useful places from which to locate and extract linguistic elements. But, at the same time, they are treated as ancillary to the analysis.

Investigations taking a 'linguistics applied' approach involve overlaying linguistic forms on instances of language use and interpreting their meanings in light of the structural frameworks. That is, concern is not with the concrete act of using language but rather with the forms themselves as objects of analysis in their own right. As Widdowson (2000: 22) notes: 'The process whereby these forms interrelate co-textually with each other and contextually with the circumstances of their use is left largely unexplored.'

> ### Quote 1.1 On the nature of *linguistics applied*
>
> So long as linguistics was defined along traditional and formal lines, as the study of abstract systems of knowledge idealized out of language as actually experienced, the task of applied linguistics seemed relatively straightforward. It was to refer such abstract analysis of idealized internalized I-language back to the real world to find ways in which externalized E-language could be reformulated so as to make it amenable to benevolent intervention.
>
> Widdowson (2000: 4)

In recent years, as concerns with the limitations of this approach for understanding language experiences have grown, the field of applied linguistics has become far more interdisciplinary, extending its purview to other disciplines, such as communication, cultural psychology, linguistic anthropology, linguistic philosophy and social theory, in search of new ways to address concerns with language use. These explorations have been fruitful, yielding theoretical and methodological insights into the nature of applied linguistics activity that differ fairly substantially from those embodied in the more traditional 'linguistics applied' approach typical of earlier applied linguistics research.

Current views consider the fundamental concern to be the 'pragmatically motivated study' (Bygate, 2005: 571) of social action – the use of language in real-world circumstances – with the dual goal of advancing our understanding of how language is used to construct our sociocultural worlds and using this understanding to improve our worlds. Analytic primacy is not language *per se*, but the ways in which language is used in the accomplishment of social life. Central to the transformation of applied linguistics activity is the reconceptualisation of two concepts, *language* and *culture*, considered fundamental to the task. While current understandings of these concepts derive from an assortment of scholarly interests, they are bound together by a sociocultural perspective on human action. We look more closely at some of the more significant assumptions embodied in this perspective in the following sections.

1.2 Language as sociocultural resource

A sociocultural perspective on human action locates the essence of social life in communication. Through our use of linguistic symbols with others, we establish goals, negotiate the means to reach them, and reconceptualise those we have set. At the same time, we articulate and manage our individual identities, our interpersonal relationships, and memberships in our social groups and communities.

A great deal of research on communication makes it apparent that much of what we do when we communicate is conventionalised. In going about our everyday business, we participate in a multiplicity of recurring communicative activities in which the goals, our roles, and the language we use as we play these roles and attempt to accomplish the goals, are familiar to us. On a daily basis, we give and take orders, request help, commiserate, chat with friends, deliberate, negotiate, gossip, seek advice and so on. We participate in such routine activities with relative ease and can easily distinguish one activity from other. For example, we can usually tell when the utterance 'What are you doing?' is meant as a prelude to an invitation and when it is meant as a reproach. Likewise, if we hear the utterance 'That's a great pair of shoes', we can anticipate with some accuracy the communicative event that is taking place, and construct an appropriate response.

The knowledge we use to help us navigate through our communicative activities comprises sets of **communicative plans**, that is to say, 'socially constructed models for solutions of communicative problems' (Luckmann, 1995: 181). These plans lay out for us the expected or typical goals of an activity, the typical trajectories of social actions and the prosodic, linguistic and interactional resources comprising the actions by which such goals are realised. They also lay out the role relationships that are likely to obtain among those involved in the activity. The plans are constructed and shared by the members of the sociocultural groups to which we belong, and are maintained and modified in our uses of them as we engage in the activities constituting our daily lives. Because we share the plans with other members of our sociocultural groups and communities, they provide some common ground for knowing what we can each appropriately, or conventionally, say and do. In other words, the plans help us to synchronise our actions and interpretations with others and to reach a mutual understanding of what is going on (cf. Levinson, 2006b; Luckmann, 1995). It is through such everyday, conventionalised communicative activities, or **language games** (Wittgenstein, 1963), that we experience the world. Thus, they constitute dynamic, vital forms of life.

In this view of language as social action, language is considered to be first and foremost a sociocultural resource constituted by 'a range of possibilities, an open-ended set of options in behaviour that are available to the individual in his existence as social man' (Halliday, 1973: 49). Options for taking action in our communicative activities include a wide array of linguistic resources such as lexical and grammatical elements, speech acts and rhetorical structures, and in the case of oral language use, structured patterns for taking turns and phonological, prosodic and paralinguistic resources such as intonation, stress, tempo and pausing.

Concept 1.1   **Ludwig Wittgenstein's notion of** *language games*

The term **language games** is commonly attributed to the Austrian philosopher, Ludwig Wittgenstein, whose views on language are best captured in *Philosophical Investigations* (1963). According to Wittgenstein, language games are established, conventionalised patterns of communicative action. These patterns, which are agreed upon and shared by members of a culture group, embody particular definitions of the situation and meanings of possible actions and, more generally, particular ways of knowing, valuing and experiencing the world.

More formalist views of language consider these resources to be fixed, invariant forms that we take from stable, bounded structural systems. In contrast, a sociocultural perspective considers them to be fundamentally social, their essence tied to their habits of use. That is, rather than a prerequisite to individual use, the shape or structure of our resources is an emergent property of them, developing from the resources' locally situated uses in activity. Structures, then, do not precede use, but arise as a consequence of use.

This view is captured most clearly in the notion of **emergent grammar**, originally proposed by Paul Hopper (Hopper, 1987; Hopper and Thompson, 1993). According to Hopper, rather than being fixed units enabling communication, language structures are more appropriately understood as dynamic, mutable by-products of it. It is through their frequent, routinised uses in specific sociocultural contexts that the symbolic means by which we take action develop into 'a minimally sorted and organized set of memories of what people have heard and repeated over a lifetime of language use, a set of forms, patterns, and practices that have arisen to serve the most recurrent functions that speakers find need to fulfill' (Ford *et al.*, 2003: 122).

At the same time, while the various shapes of our linguistic resources develop from past uses, the specific forms they take at particular points in time are open to negotiation. However, the degree of negotiation that is possible at any communicative moment is dependent on at least two factors: the frequency of the resources' past uses and the amount of institutional force behind them. The more frequently the linguistic resources are used, or the more institutional force there is behind their use, the more systematised or codified their shapes become. The more systematised the resources are, the more invisible their sociohistorical roots are. The system is then treated as if it had a life of its own, existing apart from any context of use, and apart from its users. Any individual language use becomes measured against this universal yardstick with the assumption that there is an inherent correctness to the shape the forms take.

Quote 1.2 Emergent Grammar

The notion of *Emergent Grammar* is meant to suggest that structure, or regularity, comes out of discourse and is shaped by discourse as much as it shapes discourse in an on-going process. Grammar is hence not to be understood as a prerequisite for discourse, a prior possession attributable in identical form to both speaker and hearer. Its forms are not fixed templates, but are negotiable in face-to-face interaction in ways that reflect the individual speaker's past experience of these forms, and their assessment of the present context, including especially their interlocutors, whose experiences and assessments may be quite different.

Hopper (1987: 142)

1.2.1 Dialogue as the essence of language use

As the structures of our linguistic resources emerge from their real-world uses, so do their meanings. That is, the linguistic resources we choose to use do not come to us as empty forms ready to be filled with our personal intentions; rather, they come to us with meanings already embedded within them. These meanings, however, are not derived from some universal, logical set of principles; rather, as with their shapes, they are built up over time from their past uses in particular contexts by particular groups of participants in the accomplishment of particular goals that, in turn, are shaped by myriad cultural, historical and institutional forces.

The linguistic resources we choose to use at particular communicative moments come to these moments with their conventionalised histories of meaning. It is their conventionality that binds us to some degree to particular ways of realising our collective history. However, while our resources come with histories of meanings, *how they come to mean* at a particular communicative moment is always open to negotiation.

Thus, in our individual uses of our linguistic resources we accomplish two actions simultaneously. We create their typical – historical – contexts of use and at the same time we position ourselves in relation to these contexts. Our locally situated uses of our linguistic resources are what Bakhtin (1981, 1986, 1990) calls **utterances**, double-sided acts, which respond to the conditions of the moment and anticipate what is to come. It is in our utterances that we fill the linguistic resources with our own voices, negotiating their conventional meanings in light of the communicative task at hand. Together their conventional meanings and our uses of them exist as inseparable parts of a **dialogue**, and are in a continually negotiated state of 'intense and essential axiological interaction' (Bakhtin, 1990: 10).

Concepts 1.2 and 1.3   **Mikhail Bakhtin's notions of dialogue and translinguistics**

The concepts of **dialogue** and **translinguistics** are central to the linguistic philosophy of the Russian linguist Mikhail Bakhtin. According to Bakhtin, meaning is located neither solely in our linguistic resources nor in each individual's mind. Rather, it resides in between these two interdependent spheres, in the interaction, the dialogue, that is realised in our lived moments of social action. Translinguistics is the name Bakhtin gives to the study of the dialogue obtaining between our linguistic resources and the ways in which we use them to respond to real-world circumstances. Of particular significance in translinguistics, Bakhtin argues, is the study of our everyday, mundane communicative actions, since they are the source of individual innovation and social change.

From this perspective, then, the meaning of language does not reside in the system of linguistic resources removed from their contexts of use and communities of users. Nor does it reside in our individual use of them as we engage in activities particular to our sociocultural worlds. Rather, language meaning is located in the dialogic relationship between the historical and the present, between the social and the individual. We come to understand the conventional meanings of the resources only in terms of how they are used at particular moments of time. Conversely, our understandings of the concrete, here and now uses of language are developed only in terms of the positioning of the resources against their conventional. Bakhtin's notion of **dialogicality** captures well this relational character of meaning.

Quote 1.3 The relation between language use and meaning

There are no 'neutral' words and forms – words and forms that belong to 'no one'; language has been completely taken over, shot through with intentions and accents. For any individual consciousness living in it, language is not an abstract system of normative forms but rather a concrete heteroglot conception of the world. All words have the 'taste' of a profession, a genre, a tendency, a party, a particular work, a particular person, a generation, an age group, the day and hour. Each word tastes of the context and contexts in which it has lived its socially charged life; all words and forms are populated by intentions.

Bakhtin (1981: 293)

The excerpt below, taken from Hall (1993a: 209), illustrates the dialogic, or relational, nature of meaning.

Husband: Take these shirts to the cleaners tomorrow, will you?

Wife: (*stands and gives military salute by raising hand to forehead*) Yes, sir.

As noted by Hall, the military salute and verbal utterance used by the wife to respond to her husband's request are typically used together in a military context by someone in a subordinate position to mark the other as a superior. If we bring their expected meanings to this context, we may conclude that the woman is using them to create a similar military-style, hierarchical relationship with her husband and thereby mark or index her understanding of this subordinate position. Alternatively, she can be using the conventional meaning of the salute and verbal utterance not to recreate their conventional context of use, and her role in it, but to mark her stance towards an utterance that she considers inappropriate. It might be, for example, that she hears the utterance as a directive instead of a request. She may regard a request as more suitable to the situation, and so uses the salute and verbal response to convey at the same time both her interpretation of her husband's utterance and her offense towards it.

Either way, there is a dialogue between the meaning conventionally associated with the salute and verbal response and their use by the woman in this particular communicative moment. Only by examining the dialogue obtaining between the conventional meanings of the linguistic resources used by the husband and wife, and their uses of them at this particular time, can we derive a full understanding of the activity – of the shapes and meanings deriving from the locally situated uses of the resources, of the participants and their relationships to each other, and of how each views his or her place within that particular communicative moment – and of the role that language plays in constructing one's social worlds.

In positing dialogue as the core of language study and the utterance as the fundamental unit of analysis, Bakhtin erases any *a priori* distinction between form and meaning, between individual and social uses of language. Just as no linguistic resource can be understood apart from its contexts of use, no single utterance can be considered a purely individual act, 'a completely free combination of forms of language' (Bakhtin, 1986: 81), whose meanings are created on the spot. Rather, it can only be understood fully by considering its history of use by other people, in other places, for other reasons. Thus, rather than being considered extraneous to the study of language, dialogue in its encounter between historical meaning and individual motivations at a particular moment of action is considered its essence.

1.2.2   Single- and double-voiced utterances

Important to understanding this dialogic relationship obtaining between the personal and social meanings embodied in our language use is the degree of authority attached to the conventional meanings of our linguistic resources. As we noted previously, our linguistic resources come to us already laden with meanings that have been developed in their histories of use. These histories of meanings determine in part the degree of force that our voices will have in using the resources towards our own ends.

Useful for understanding the links between the historical meanings of our resources and our individual uses of them are Bakhtin's concepts of **single-voiced utterances** and **double-voiced utterances** (Bakhtin, 1981; Morson and Emerson, 1990). According to Bakhtin, single-voiced utterances consist of resources whose meanings are unquestioned, non-negotiable and thus resistant to change. The more institutionalised the meanings of the resources, the more authoritative their voices are likely to be. The more authoritative their voices, the more invisible their histories become, and the more resistant they are to individually motivated innovations. Instead, the resources take on a life of their own, and become defined as a distinct, internally coherent, logical system of meanings and values. When we use the resources to take action in our worlds, they come not only with their authoritative, decontextualised meanings, but their values as well. As their users, we become defined by the values thought to be inherent within them.

For example, cross-cultural research has shown that although the pattern of turn-taking across languages is universally constructed as one-speaker-at-a-time, there are in fact slight differences in gap length between turns across languages. These differences lead to subjective perceptions 'of dramatic or even fundamental differences' (Stivers *et al.*, 2009: 10587) of those whose turn transition timing is different from the mainstream. Even very slight variations to the timing of turns can lead to perceptions of the turn takers as 'quiet' or 'noisy', and even 'rude' and 'uneducated'. Similar stigmatised evaluations are made of users of other linguistic resources that are considered different from mainstream use.

What is invisible is the fact that such institutionalised versions of linguistic resources are social facts, 'not inherent and universal, but local, secondary, and projected' (Hymes, 1980: 112). In other words, mainstream uses of linguistic resources, and the values associated with them, are the construction of particular groups who historically have had a considerable amount of sociopolitical authority behind them. It is their unquestioned use over time by groups with such authority by which resource meanings are institutionalised. In addition to propagation of the resources through their continued and unquestioned use by such groups, written documents such as dictionaries, grammar books, style manuals and etiquette guides serve as primary means for institutionalising resource meanings.

Concepts 1.4 and 1.5   **Single- and double-voiced utterances**

According to Bakhtin, **single-voiced utterances** are those with authority, those whose sociohistorical meanings are invisible to the speaker. The individual speaks as if the words she uses had a life of their own apart from any context of use. In contrast, in **double-voiced utterances** the sociohistorical meanings of words are visible to the speaker, and she can choose to use the words in two ways. In **passive double-voiced utterances**, the individual chooses to use the words as others before her have used them, that is, with their conventional meanings. In **active double-voiced utterances**, the individual uses the words not as they are meant to be used, but for her own purposes. That is, she uses the conventional meanings in such a way as to assert her own voice in their use.

It is not the case, however, that the meanings of our resources always go unquestioned. Rather, we often make conscious choices about the language we use and, in so doing, we decide on 'a particular way of entering the world and a particular way of sustaining relationships with others' (Duranti, 1997: 46). Utterances in which we acknowledge the conventional meanings of our resources, and use them with volition to respond to the conditions of the moment, are what Bakhtin calls **double-voiced utterances**. On the one hand, we can consciously choose to use the conventional meanings associated with the resources in predictable ways; that is, we use our resources in such a way as to create their typical contexts of use. If we come across an individual in a public area, for example, and we wish to establish some kind of interpersonal contact with that person, we can create such a context with the utterance 'Hi, how are you today?' This utterance is typically associated with a greeting among friends or acquaintances and its use at that time with that person helps to create such a context. Bakhtin calls these **passive double-voiced utterances**.

We can also choose to use our resources in unexpected ways. Bakhtin calls these **active double-voiced utterances**. In such utterances, we use our resources not so much to create the particular set of conditions typical of them, as to use their histories of meaning to create our unique positioning towards a particular communicative moment. The following, taken from a public billboard displayed shortly after the acts of terrorism experienced by the USA in New York City and Washington, DC in autumn 2001, is an example of an active double-voiced utterance.

Don't make me have to come down there.
                                                    – God

For many social groups, the utterance 'Don't make me have to come down there' evokes a typical role-relationship between a parent and a child, and a typical situation in which one or some children are misbehaving. The utterance by the parent serves to admonish the children for their behaviour. While the consequences for ignoring the warning are not stated, it is implied that they will be dire if the actions do not stop. In the billboard message, the attribution of the utterance to a divine being, believed by many to be the supreme protector of all humanity, evokes a similar context of use. In this case, the utterance ascribes to God the role of scolding parent to a world filled with badly behaved children. One does not have to be a believer in the existence of a higher presence to appreciate how the conventional meanings embedded in language can be used to create a unique stance towards any locally situated communicative moment. It is important to note that what makes an utterance passive or active depends not just on the user's intentions. It also includes the response it engenders, the relationships existing among the particular participants and the history of intentions embedded in the resources themselves.

Quote 1.4 The nature of voice

Each large and creative verbal whole is a very complex and multifaceted system of relations ... there are no voiceless words that belong to no one. Each word contains voices that are sometimes infinitely distant, unnamed, almost impersonal, almost undetectable, and voices resounding nearby and simultaneously.

Bakhtin (1986: 124)

In sum, in a sociocultural perspective on human action, language is viewed at one and the same time as both an individual tool and a socio-cultural resource, whose use on a day-to-day basis is conventionalised, shaped by the myriad intellectual and practical communicative activities that constitute our daily lives. In using language to participate in our activities, we reflect our understanding of them and their larger cultural contexts and, at the same time, create spaces for ourselves as individuals within them. The meanings that our individual uses of language assume at those moments draw from their historical, conventional meanings in relation to their situated, immediate contexts of use. Hence, different uses of language embody different meanings.

This perspective rejects the idea that literal or decontextualised meaning exists apart from the use of a linguistic resource. There is no word, no use of a resource that can be considered unprejudiced, independent of its users or contexts of use. Instead, our words come to us already used, filled with the evaluations and perceptions of others. Their meanings emerge from the juxtaposition of their past uses with our locally situated uses of them in the present. Thus, when we use language to act in our social worlds, it cannot be said that we 'use our own words'. Rather, in our actions we make use of available meaning-laden resources to construct our worlds as we would have them be at that moment.

Wittgenstein (1963: 12) captures the contextualised character of our linguistic resources when he states: 'If you do not keep the multiplicity of language-games in view you will perhaps be inclined to ask questions like: "What is a question?" – Is it the statement that I do not know such-and-such, or the statement that I wish the other person would tell me . . . ? Or is it the description of my mental state of uncertainty?' Here, in linking language meaning to its contexts of use, Wittgenstein makes apparent the interdependence of meaning in the here-and-now and historical meaning, of individual meaning and meaning based in community. 'Not what one is doing now, but the whole hurly-burly, is the background against which we see an action, and it determines our judgment, our concepts and our reactions' (Wittgenstein, 1980, no. 629).

One final point needs to be made. As noted earlier, there is nothing essential to our linguistic resources themselves that makes their meanings more privileged or authoritative. Rather, their authority develops from their past uses. It follows then that language is inherently ideological. As Bakhtin argues, in the language we choose to use at any particular moment we make visible our attitudes and beliefs towards the communicative moment, towards those with whom we are communicating, and towards what we believe our social positioning is within our sociocultural worlds. Only by examining our language use at particular moments of time in relation to its history can we reveal the varied ways in which we create our voices in response to the larger social and political forces shaping our worlds.

1.3   Culture as sociocultural practice

The notion of culture has always been considered an important concept in applied linguistics. However, in studies taking a more traditional 'linguistics applied' approach it is often treated as its own logical system of representational knowledge, located in the individual mind, and existing independent of language, when it is treated at all. The basis of the system is assumed to be an abstract, universal structure for organising and generating the knowledge. When exposed to culture-specific data, provided by the physical world, the mind is thought to generate systems of knowledge that are specific to a particular culture group. Hence, while the underlying formal structures of culture are assumed to be universal, the actual substance generated by the formal structures is considered to be fairly homogeneous static bodies of knowledge consisting of accumulated and classifiable sets of thoughts, feelings, values and beliefs. By virtue of their group membership, and their innate possession of the formal structures needed to process culture-specific data, individual members are assumed to have full and equal possession of these sets of knowledge. Thus, any pattern detected across individuals is automatically assumed to reflect their cultural affiliations (cf. Sarangi, 1994).

In addition to an assumption of cultural homogeneity, the more traditional perspective assumes knowledge acquisition to be unidirectional, transmitted by, but fundamentally unrelated to, language. That is, while language may be used as a way to uncover the culture-specific bodies of knowledge, it is not deemed to have any influence on their development or, more generally, on the abstract structures by which the information is organised. Thus, the primary, if not only, role that language is thought to play is representational. In other words, language can only *reflect* cultural understandings; it can not *affect* them (Goodenough, 1964; cf. Williams, 1992).

A sociocultural perspective of culture stands in marked contrast to this more traditional view. Rather than viewing culture as systems of fixed bodies of knowledge possessed equally by all members of well-defined culture groups, current understandings view it as 'recurrent and habitual systems of dispositions and expectations' (Duranti, 1997: 45). More concretely, culture is seen to reside in the meanings and shapes that our linguistic resources have accumulated from their past uses and with which we approach and work through our communicative activities. As noted earlier, in our activities with others, we rely on these expectations to make sense of the moment and work towards the accomplishment of our communicative goals.

Because we are members of multiple groups and communities, we take on and negotiate multiple cultural identities, and in our roles, participate in myriad cultural activities. At any communicative moment, through our linguistic actions, we choose particular ways to construe our worlds, to induce others to see our worlds in these ways, as we create and sustain particular kinds of relationships with them and thus make relevant some as opposed to other identities.

Quote 1.5 Culture as embodied action

In fact, there is not much point in trying to say what culture is. What can be done, however, is to say what culture does. For what culture does is precisely the work of defining words, ideas, things and groups. We all live our lives in terms of definition, names and categories that culture creates. The job of studying culture is not of finding and then accepting its definitions but of discovering how and what definitions are made, under what circumstances and for what reasons. . . . Culture is an active process of meaning making and contest over definition, including its own definition. This, then, is what I mean by arguing that *Culture is a verb*.

Street (1993b: 25; emphasis in the original)

To locate culture one must look not in individual mind, as an accumulated body of unchanging knowledge, but in the dialogue, the embodied actions, 'discursively rearticulated' (Bhabha, 1994: 177) between individuals in particular sociocultural contexts at particular moments of time. This perspective of culture as a dynamic, vital and emergent process located in the discursive spaces *between* individuals links it inextricably to language. That is to say, language is at the same time a repository of culture and a tool by which culture is created. In making visible the mutual dependency of language and culture, current understandings overcome the analytic separation of the 'linguistics applied' approach. Because culture is located not in individual mind but in activity, any study of language is by necessity a study of culture.

1.4   Linguistic relativity

Current views of language and culture as mutually shaping forms of social life owe a great deal to ideas found in linguistic anthropology, and in particular, to the idea of **linguistic relativity** as found in the work of American linguistic anthropologist Edward Sapir (1985[1929]) and, more prominently, in that of his student Benjamin Whorf (1956). Sapir's ideas came mainly from his study of different American indigenous languages, which led him to posit a dynamic relation between language and culture.

Whorf also studied Native American languages, in particular Hopi. Influenced by Sapir's work as well by his experiences as a claims agent for an insurance company in the first half of the twentieth century, Whorf's work on language and his ideas on linguistic relativity are encapsulated in what has come to be called the **Sapir–Whorf hypothesis**. This hypothesis proposes that patterned, structural components of specific languages regularly or habitually used by members of culture groups contain particular meanings that are systematically linked to the worldviews of the groups whose languages they are. Thus, they influence the way group members view, categorise, and in other ways think about their world. Since different culture groups speak different languages, individual worldviews are tied to the language groups to which individuals belong. To state it another way, if individual thought is shaped by language, individuals with different languages

are likely to have different understandings of the world. A significant contribution of the Sapir–Whorf hypothesis is that it links individual thought
to larger, culturally based patterns of language and thus posits an interdependent relationship between language and culture.

Quote 1.6 The relationship between language and culture

Human beings do not live in the objective world alone, nor alone in the world
of social activity as ordinarily understood, but are very much at the mercy of
the particular language which has become the medium of expression for
their society. It is quite an illusion to imagine that one adjusts to reality essentially without the use of language and that language is merely an incidental
means of solving specific problems of communication or reflection. The fact of
the matter is the 'real world' is to a large extent unconsciously built up on the
language habits of the group. No two languages are ever sufficiently similar
to be considered as representing the same social reality. The worlds in which
different societies lie are distinct worlds, not merely the same world with
different labels attached.

Sapir (1985[1929]: 162)

Quote 1.7 Benjamin Whorf's view on linguistic relativity

We dissect nature along lines laid down by our native languages. The categories
and types that we isolate from the world of phenomena we do not find there
because they stare every observer in the face; on the contrary, the world is
presented in a kaleidoscopic flux of impressions which has to be organized
by our minds – and this means largely by the linguistic systems in our minds.
We cut nature up, organize it into concepts, and ascribe significance as we
do, largely because we are parties to an agreement to organize it in this way
– an agreement that holds throughout our speech community and is codified
in the patterns of our language.

Whorf (1956: 213)

1.5   A socially constituted linguistics

A similar connection between language and culture can be found in the
work of Dell Hymes (1962, 1964, 1971, 1972a, b, 1974), another linguistic anthropologist. Hymes developed a conceptualisation of language

as context-embedded social action in response to linguist Noam Chomsky's (1957, 1965) theory of language. In keeping with a formalist perspective, Chomsky conceptualised language as a fixed, universal property of the human mind containing internalised sets of principles from which language-specific grammatical rules could be derived, and thus describable in context-free, invariant terms.

Hymes regarded this view of language as too restrictive in that it did not, in fact could not, account for the social knowledge we rely on to produce and interpret utterances appropriate to the particular contexts in which they occur. He noted, 'it is not enough for the child to be able to produce any grammatical utterance. It would have to remain speechless if it could not decide which grammatical utterance here and now, if it could not connect utterances to their contexts of use' (Hymes, 1964: 110). It is this social knowledge, Hymes argued, that shapes and gives meaning to linguistic forms. Because involvement in the communicative activities of our everyday lives is usually with others who share our expectations, these links are often difficult to see. However, although it may be difficult to perceive their vitality, they cannot be considered insignificant to the accomplishment of our everyday lives. Thus, Hymes called for a more adequate theory of language that could account for the sociocultural knowledge that we draw on when using our linguistic resources so that they are considered structurally sound, referentially accurate and contextually appropriate within the different groups and communities to which we belong.

Quote 1.8 Socially constituted linguistics

The phrase 'socially constituted' is intended to express the view that social function gives form to the ways in which linguistic features are encountered in actual life. This being so, an adequate approach must begin by identifying social functions, and discovering the ways in which linguistic features are selected and grouped together to serve them.

Hymes (1974: 196)

1.5.1 A socially constituted approach to the study of language and culture

Arguing for a **socially constituted linguistics** in which social function is treated as the source from which linguistic features are formed, Hymes developed an approach to the study of language he called the **ethnography of speaking**. In contrast to more formal descriptions of language as inherently coherent systems, the focus of Hymes's approach is on capturing the conventional patterns of language used by members of particular sociocultural groups as they participate in their everyday communicative activities, with the goal of such research being not to seek 'the replication of uniformity, but the organization of diversity' (Hornberger, 2009: 350).

A great deal of research, particularly in the fields of linguistic anthropology, communication, and education, has used this approach to investigate a wide range of communicative events and activities of many different groups and communities. These have included descriptions of the conventional patterns of language for enacting such mundane activities as service encounters (e.g. Bailey, 2000), gossiping (e.g. Brison, 1992; Hall, 1993a, b), leave-taking (e.g. Fitch, 2002), dinner-time talk (e.g. Blum-Kulka, 1997) and television talk shows (e.g. Carbaugh, 1988). Also subjects of investigation are institutional activities such as classroom teaching and learning (e.g. Cazden *et al.*, 1972; Foster, 1989), professional communication (e.g. Duchan and Kovarsky, 2005) and other workplace activities (e.g. Sarangi and Roberts, 1999).

Quote 1.9 The conceptual base of an ethnography of speaking

Now it is desirable . . . to take as a working framework: 1. the speech of a group constitutes a system; 2. speech and language vary cross-culturally in function; 3. the speech activity of a community is the primary object of attention. A descriptive grammar deals with this speech activity in one frame of reference, an ethnography of speaking in another. So (what amounts to a corollary, 3b), the latter must in fact include the former.

Hymes (1962: 42)

Concept 1.6   **Ethnography of speaking**

As proposed by Hymes, an **ethnography of speaking** is both a conceptual framework and a method for conducting language study. Presuming a systematic link between language use and context, this approach considers the communicative activity, or what Hymes termed the **communicative event**, a central unit of analysis. Analytic attention is given to describing the components of communicative events and the relations among them that participants make use of to engage in and make sense of their social worlds and, in turn, to link their use to the larger social, cultural, political and other institutional forces giving shape to them. More recent formulations of this approach to the study of language refer to it as **ethnography of communication** to capture a more encompassing understanding of the variety of resources, in addition to language, that are used in communication. Leeds-Hurwitz (1984) provides a useful summary of the history of both terms.

Literacy activities of various groups and communities have also been the subject of ethnographies of communication. Ahearn (2000), for example, studied the literacy practices of young Nepali women, focusing in particular on their use of love letters in courtship. Radway (1984) explored the role that reading romance novels played in the lives of a group of women. Taking more of a wide-angle ethnographic approach, McCarty and Watahomigie (1998) studied both home and school literacy activities in American Indian and Alaskan native communities. Similarly, Torres-Guzman (1998) investigated literacy activities in Puerto Rican communities, Dien (1998) looked at similar activities in Vietnamese American communities, and Barton and Hamilton (1998) explored the activities constituted in the everyday lives of a group of adults in England. More recently, Ivanič and Satchwell (2007) investigated the academic literacy practices of college-level students and how these practices interacted with literacy practices in other domains of the students' lives. Findings from these and other studies have shown that literacy activities do indeed vary, in some cases considerably, from community to community. As these groups differ – and as the social identities of the readers and writers differ within the groups – so does the value that is placed on literacy activities and the communicative conventions used to engage in them.

The differences in literacy practices notwithstanding, the principal assumption of literacy underlying the various strand of literacy studies remains the same. Literacy is defined not as 'a technology made up of a set of transferable cognitive skills, but [as] a constellation of practices' (Ivanič, 1998: 65), each made up of particular arrangements of skills and ways of reading and writing that are tied to their contexts of use. Likewise, the ethnographies share the goal of making visible the linguistic resources and communicative plans shared by group members and used to engage in their socioculturally important communicative activities. In addition to adding to our knowledge of cultural groups, studies taking an ethnography of communication approach to the study of language and culture have contributed a great deal to current educational practices. These practices are discussed more fully in Section II. Chapter 8, in Section III, provides more details on the ethnography of communication approach to the study of language and literacy practices.

1.5.2   The recent turn in studies of communicative activities

In the past decade or so, applied linguistic studies of communicative events, particularly those realised through face-to-face interaction, have moved beyond general descriptions of the linguistic resources needed to engage in them to more detailed descriptions that show the moment-to-moment inter-actional coordination by which the communicative context is created. This move has come about in part by the incorporation of methods for analysing conversation developed by the discipline of **conversation analysis** (CA). CA began in the field of sociology over forty years ago as an offshoot of **ethnomethodology**, an approach to the study of social life that considers the nature and source of social order to be grounded in real-world activity rather than regulated by universal standards of rationality (Garfinkel, 1967; Heritage, 1984). That is, social order is a local achievement, mutually produced by participants as they engage in activity with each other. Asserting a fundamental role for interaction as 'the primordial site of human sociality' (Schegloff, 2007: 70), CA takes as its main concern the study of talk-in-interaction, and more particularly, 'the analysis of competence which underlies ordinary social activities' (Heritage, 2004: 241). More details on this particular approach to language study are given in Chapter 8.

For our purposes, it is sufficient to note that findings from CA-inspired studies have been useful in revealing the multitude of interactional methods such as turn-taking patterns and repair strategies that we have at our disposal for sense-making in our communicative activities. Examples of recent studies include Mori's (2002) analysis of the resources used by a pair of university learners of Japanese to accomplish an instructional activity, Mondada's (2004) study of the multilingual resources drawn on by participants in an international medical setting and Hellermann's (2008) study of the social actions occurring in and around instructional tasks in an adult ESOL classroom.

In addition to drawing out the shared understandings that members rely on to make sense of each other's actions in talk-in-interaction activities, interest has developed in uncovering the *variability* of resource use. A criticism of early ethnographies of communication noted that ethnographic descriptions of communicative events often gave the impression that individual members' participation was always consensual, always orderly. Assuming a more dynamic understanding of community and language use, more recent studies have examined how individual members use the resources of their communicative activities to challenge the *status quo* or to reinforce particular ideologies. In terms of challenging existing conditions of language use, Hall's study (1993c) revealed how one Dominican woman was able to manipulate the conventional opening to the activity of gossiping as practised among her peers in such a way as to positively transform the nature of her involvement in the activity. Typically, the opening of the gossiping event was signalled with the utterance 'tengo una bomba' (I have a bomb), the purpose of which was to inform the others that a story about the scandalous behaviour of another was about to be told. When this particular woman used it, however, what often followed was not a story about someone's impropriety, but a humorous anecdote in which she was the central figure. Her unconventional use of the utterance to take the stage, so to speak, generated a great deal of humour among the other participants, and thus helped to raise her status within the group. At the same time, it solidified her identity as a knowledgeable insider to her peers. In terms of reinforcing ideologies, the study by Blommaert *et al.* (2006) of three Belgian classrooms for newly settled immigrants revealed how teachers' instructional activities served to disqualify rather than to capitalise on students' uses of linguistic and literary resources that the teachers perceived to be non-standard.

As for literacy practices, the term **New Literacies Studies** has been coined to refer to studies that take a more critical stance towards practices constituted not only in educational settings but also in social and professional groups and communities outside of schools across a range of geographical contexts (for examples, see the edited volumes by Martin-Jones and Jones, 2000, and Street, 2004). The studies go beyond Hymes's basic ethnographic approach in that they seek to make visible the power relations embedded in and across the various practices, by asking '"whose literacies" are dominant and whose are marginalized or resistant' (Street, 2003: 77).

Also included in this strand of ethnographic research are studies of the multimodal literacy practices engendered by the continuing expansion of information and communication technologies. Of particular interest are the skills and strategies by which individuals use these technologies to make sense of and participate in their communities both within and across geographical boundaries. The study by Lam and Rosario-Ramos (2009) is one such example. They examined how teenaged immigrants in the United States used digital media to engage in social networking and to design and share information on local, national, and transnational events with peers and others living in their countries of origin. They found that these digitally based, multilingual literacy practices situated the youths in a 'transnational circuit of news and ideas' (p. 186) that exposed them to narratives, experiences, values, and expectations from different social communities. This exposure, in turn, helped to foster in the youths an ability to see things from multiple perspectives. The pedagogical significance of the findings from the various strands of research inspired by Hymes's ethnography of communication is discussed in Section II.

1.5.3 From linguistic relativity to sociolinguistic relativity

Without a doubt, Hymes's theory of language and his approach to the study of language use have made significant contributions to our understanding of the pragmatically based, mutually constitutive nature of language and culture. A less visible but equally significant contribution of his work is the advancement of our understanding of the concept of linguistic relativity. Like Whorf, Hymes sees language and culture as inextricably linked. However, by giving primacy to language use and function rather than linguistic code and form, Hymes transforms Whorf's notion of linguistic relativity in a subtle but significant way. More to the point, in asserting the primacy of language as human action, the source of relativity becomes located in language *use*, not language *structure*.

Quote 1.10 The priority of *sociolinguistic relativity* relative to the notion of *linguistic relativity*

With particular regard to the Sapir–Whorf hypothesis, it is essential to notice that Whorf's sort of linguistic relativity is secondary, and dependent upon a primary sociolinguistic relativity, that of differential engagement of languages in social life. For example, description of a language may show that it expresses certain cognitive style, perhaps implicit metaphysical assumptions. But what chances the language has to make an impress upon individuals and behavior will depend upon the degree and pattern of its admission into communicative events. . . . Peoples do not all everywhere use language to the same degree, in the same situations, or for the same things; some peoples focus upon language more than others. Such differences in the place of a language in the communicative system of a people cannot be assumed to be without influence on the depth of a language's influence on such things as world view.

Hymes (1974: 18)

Recent crosslinguistic research in cognitive linguistics (e.g. Levinson, 2003; Slobin, 1997, 2003) provides compelling empirical support for the notion of **sociolinguistic relativity** by revealing substantive links between thought and language use. For example, differences across languages in terms of how spatial relationships are described have been linked to different cognitive styles among speakers of these languages (Majid *et al.*, 2004). Encapsulating these findings is cognitive linguist Dan Slobin's concept, which asserts that languages afford users with preferred perspectives for encoding their lived experiences. That is, the language one uses helps shapes one's conceptual understandings about the world. The link between language use and cognition is discussed in greater detail in Chapter 3.

Quote 1.11 Thinking-for-speaking

The language or languages that we learn in childhood are not neutral coding systems of an objective reality. Rather, each one is a subjective orientation to the world of human experience, and this orientation *affects the ways in which we think while we are speaking*.

Slobin (1996, p. 91, emphasis in the original)

1.6   Systemic functional linguistics

One last source to note from which a notion of language as context-embedded social action draws is the work of British-Australian linguist Michael Halliday (1973, 1975, 1978; Halliday and Matthiessen, 2004). Like Hymes, Halliday views language not as a system of abstract, decontextualised rules but rather as fundamentally social, constituted by a set of resources for meaning-making. He thus locates the meanings of language forms in their systematic connections between the functions they play and their contexts of use. Also like Hymes, Halliday considers the essential role of a theory of language to be to explain the social foundations of the language system. Thus, his work has been concerned primarily with the development of a **systemic functional linguistics** (SFL) theory of language, the specific aim of which is the articulation of 'the functionally organised meaning potential of the linguistic system' (1975: 6). That is, it seeks to describe the linguistic options that are available to individuals to construct meanings in particular contexts or situations for particular purposes.

> **Quote 1.12**   Halliday's theory of language
>
> The key claim in SFL is that the system itself is functionally organized to address the highly complex social need to make and exchange meaning. That is, in this perspective, the linguistic system realizes culture because it is a social semiotic modality that functions in and through social processes to enable socially constituted subjects to exchange meanings.
>
> Williams (2008: 62)

To make these connections between language use and context visible, Halliday proposed an analytic framework consisting of a set of three inter-related functions. The first function is the **ideational**, which is concerned with the propositional or representational dimensions of language. The second is the **interpersonal**, which is concerned with the social dimensions of language, and more specifically how interpersonal connections are made and sustained. The third function is the **textual**, which is concerned with the construction of coherent and cohesive discourse. According to Halliday, all languages manage all three functions. Also part of the framework is a set of three components for describing situation types. The first component, **field**, refers to the setting and purpose. **Tenor**, the second component, pertains to the participants' roles and relationships and the key or tone of the situation. The third component, **mode**, refers to the symbolic or rhetorical means by which the situation is realised, and the genre to which it is most appropriately related.

According to Halliday's theory, meanings of the linguistic resources used by individuals in particular situations can be linked to the conventionalised, or systematic interactions between the three components of the situation and the three language functions: field interacts with ideational, tenor with interpersonal, and mode with textual. This knowledge comprises the communicative plans with which individuals approach their communicative activities, and they use their shared understandings of a situation in terms of field, tenor and mode to anticipate the language forms and meanings likely to be used.

Quote 1.13   On the explanatory value of systemic functional linguistics

Given an adequate specification of the situation in terms of field, tenor and mode, we ought to be able to make certain predictions about the linguistic properties of the text that is associated with it: that is, about the register, the configurations of semantic options that typically feature in this environment, and hence also about the grammar and vocabulary, which are the realizations of the semantic options.

Halliday (1975: 131)

Like Hymes's approach to the study of language, SFL has engendered much empirical research. The directions taken, however, differ somewhat in that the focus of studies from the perspective of SFL is on describing functions of particular linguistic features as they are realised in a variety of texts. For example, Young and Nguyen (2002) employed SFL analytic methods to compare the linguistics features used to present a scientific topic in a 12th grade (high school) physics textbook with those in a teacher discussion of the topic. Their findings revealed some striking contrasts in how scientific meaning is constructed across the two modes.

SFL also differs from ethnographies of communication in that, although there has been some consideration of oral communicative activities, as shown in the study by Young and Miller, up until recently, much of the analytic attention has been on written genres. With the increasing recognition of the multimodal nature of literacy, and the fact that 'language alone cannot give us access to the meaning of the multimodally constituted message' (Kress, 2003: 35), contemporary SFL research has extended its analytic focus to include a range of modes such as, for example, images, gestures, and animated movements in addition to the more traditional oral and written modes. SFL as an approach to research is addressed in Chapter 8.

Despite differences in the approaches and analytic foci, findings from myriad investigations using theoretical frameworks that draw on the work of both Hymes and Halliday make apparent in empirically interesting and compelling ways the socially constituted nature of language. Pedagogical implications of current research from these perspectives are addressed in Section II.

A last point to make is that a sociocultural perspective of language and culture does not draw the same distinction between competence and performance as the traditional Chomskyan perspective does (cf. Crowley, 1996). In the latter perspective, competence and performance are considered to be two distinct systems: the formal and the functional. A sociocultural perspective makes no such distinction. Rather it takes as fundamental the existence of one system, a system of action, in which form and meaning – knowledge and use – are two mutually constituted components.

Quote 1.14 Differences between traditional 'ahistorical' and sociocultural approaches to the study of language

... it is clear that the decontextualised, ahistorical approach to language must be called into question by a method which does not seek for an abstract structure but looks instead for the uses, and their significance, to which language is put at the micro- and macro-social levels. And this is not just a question of turning away from *langue* to *parole*, or from competence to performance, since that would be to accept the misleading alternatives on offer in the established models. The new approach would seek and analyse precisely neither abstract linguistic structure nor individual use but the institutional, political and ideological relationships between language and history. . . . In short, it would consider the modes in which language becomes important for its users not as a faculty which they all share at an abstract level, but as a practice in which they all participate in very different ways, to very different effects, under very different pressures, in their everyday lives.

Crowley (1996: 28)

1.7 Summary

Incorporation of developments in fields historically considered outside the main purview of applied linguistics has helped the field to reconceptualise two essential concepts: language and culture. In contrast to traditional views, which consider language to be structural systems transcending their users and contexts of use, sociocultural conceptualisations see language as dynamic, living collections of resources for the accomplishment of our social lives. These collections are considered central forms of life in that we use them not only to refer to, or represent, the world in our communicative activities. They are also forms of action by which we bring our cultural worlds into existence, maintain them, and shape them for our own purposes.

Current understandings have also transformed the way we view language meaning. While we can and do use our resources to realise personal intentions, our intentions alone do not give them their meaning. Nor is meaning inherent in the forms themselves. That is to say, we cannot pull resources from their contexts, dust off any contextual residue, and then claim to know their meaning. Doing so only renders them lifeless. Instead, the meanings that reside in our linguistic resources are dynamic, emerging from the dialogic interaction between our uses of them at particular moments in time, and their conventional meanings, determined by their prior uses by other individuals, in other communicative activities, and at other times. The specific components of language then are considered to be fundamentally communicative, their shapes arising from their uses by individuals to construct and enact certain social identities as they engage in activities particular to their sociocultural worlds.

Also transformed is our understanding of what it means to know language. From a sociocultural perspective, to know language does not mean to know something *about* it. It is not a body of information about forms and meanings that we first accumulate and then use in our communicative activities. Rather, to know a language means 'knowing how to go on, and so is an ability' (Shotter, 1996: 299). Tying language knowledge to social action in this way makes visible its mutually dependent, inextricable link to culture. It is through the ways we live our lives, and through our social actions, that culture is made and remade.

Quote 1.15   The study of language use

We must study how, by interweaving our talk with our other actions and activities, we can first develop and sustain between us different, particular *ways* of relating ourselves to each other . . . And then, once we have a grasp of the general character of our (normative) relations both with each other and to our surroundings . . . we should turn to a study of how, as distinct individuals, we can 'reach out' *from within* these forms of life, so to speak, to make the myriad different kinds of contact with our surroundings *through* the various ways of making sense of such contacts our forms of life provide. Where some of the contacts we make, perhaps, can elicit new or previously unnoticed reactions and responses from us, to function as the origins of entirely new language games. And it is these fleeting, often unremarked responses that occur in the momentary gaps between people as they react to each other – from within an established form of life – that must become the primary focus for our studies here, for it is in these reactions that people reveal to each other what *their world* (their 'inner life') is like for them; and can also, perhaps, initiate a new practice.

Shotter (1996: 299–300; emphasis in the original)

Ultimately, then, from a sociocultural perspective on language and culture, what we pursue in our research endeavours is not a theory of linguistic systems. Neither is it a theory of universal culture. Rather, the aim is the development of a theory of social action that is centrally concerned with how we live our lives through our everyday communicative activities, through our language games. To do this requires our attention to the explication of 'the relationships between human action, on the one hand, and the cultural, institutional, and historical situations in which this action occurs on the other' (Wertsch *et al.*, 1995: 11). A discussion on research possibilities made possible by this perspective is taken up more fully in Section III. In the next chapter, we examine current understandings of the concept of identity and its link to language use, and in Chapter 3 we review current theoretical insights and empirical findings on language and culture learning.

Further reading

Coiro, J., Knobel, M., Lankshear, C. and Leu, D. (eds) (2009) *Handbook of Research on New Literacies*, New York: Routledge. The aim of the volume is to provide direction to new literacies research by making visible the significant issues, theoretical perspectives and methodological frameworks guiding current research on new literacies. Chapters are written by leading scholars from such areas as social semiotics and multimodality, ethnographies of new literacies, multimedia studies, and computer-mediated communication.

Joseph, J., Love, N. and Taylor, T. (2001) *Landmarks in Linguistic Thought II: The Western Tradition in the Twentieth Century*, London: Routledge. The text presents the contributions of key twentieth-century scholars such as Wittgenstein, Chomsky, Sapir and Whorf to the development of thinking about language and communication.

Linell, P. (2009) *Rethinking Language, Mind, and World Dialogically*, Charlotte, NC: Information Age Publishing. Linell provides a comprehensive overview of dialogical theories of communication, examining topics such as self and others in the social construction of meaning, utterance, interactions and texts. Although the concepts are complex, the text is eminently accessible.

Young, R. (2008) *Language and Interaction: An Advanced Resource Book*, London: Routledge. This book offers an up-to-date synopsis on a view of language as social action. It brings together key readings and materials to cover a range of pertinent approaches and methodologies for the study of language and interaction. It also offers a variety of tasks to help readers further develop their understandings.

Voloshinov, V.N. (1986) *Marxism and the Philosophy of Language*, New York: Seminar Press. Although there is some dispute over the author of this text – some claim that the book was written by Bakhtin, others claim it was constructed as part of the 'Bakhtin Circle', a group of contemporaries of Bakhtin that included P.N. Medvedev and V.N. Voloshinov – the ideas presented here form a large part of the core assumptions on language and mind from a sociocultural perspective.

Language and identity

This chapter:

- describes current perspectives on the concept of identity and its connection to culture and language use;
- explores some of the more relevant theoretical insights and empirical findings on which current understandings are based;
- offers a list of additional readings on the topics covered in this chapter.

2.1   Introduction

Consistent with its view of language as universal, abstract systems, the more traditional 'linguistics applied' approach to the study of language use views individual language users as stable, coherent, internally uniform beings in whose heads the systems reside. Because of their universal nature, the systems themselves are considered self-contained, independent entities, extractable from individual minds. That is, while language systems reside in individual minds, they have a separate existence and thus remain detached from their users.

Although individuals play no role in shaping their systems, they can use them as they wish in their expression of personal meaning since the more traditional view considers individuals to be agents of free will, and thus, autonomous decision-makers. Moreover, since this view considers all individual action to be driven by internally motivated states, individual language use is seen as involving a high degree of unpredictability and creativity in both form and message as individuals strive to make personal connections to their surrounding contexts. As for the notion of identity, a 'linguistics applied' perspective views it as a set of essential characteristics unique to individuals, independent of language, and unchanging across contexts. Language users can display their identities, but they cannot affect them in any way.

Language use and identity are conceptualised rather differently in a socio-cultural perspective on human action. Here, identity is not seen as singular, fixed, and intrinsic to the individual. Rather, it is viewed as socially constituted, a reflexive, dynamic product of the social, historical and political contexts of an individual's lived experiences. This view has helped to set innovative directions for research in applied linguistics. The purpose of this chapter is to lay out some of the more significant assumptions embodied in contemporary understandings of identity and its connection to culture and language use. Included is a discussion of some of the routes current research on language, culture and identity is taking.

2.2 Social identity

When we use language, we do so as individuals with social histories. Our histories are defined in part by our membership in a range of social groups into which we are born such as gender, social class, religion and race. For example, we are born as female or male and into a distinct income level that defines us as poor, middle class or well-to-do. Likewise, we may be born as Christians, Jews, Muslims or with some other religious affiliation, and thus take on individual identities ascribed to us by our particular religious association. Even the geographical region in which we are born provides us with a particular group membership and upon our birth we assume specific identities such as, for example, Italian, Chinese, Canadian, or South African, and so on. Within national boundaries, we are defined by membership in regional groups, and we take on identities such as, for example, northerners or southerners.

In addition to the assorted group memberships we acquire by virtue of our birth, we appropriate a second layer of group memberships developed through our involvement in the various activities of the social institutions that comprise our communities, such as school, church, family and the workplace. These institutions give shape to the kinds of groups to which we have access and to the role-relationships we can establish with others. When we approach activities associated with the family, for example, we take on roles as parents, children, siblings or cousins and through these roles fashion particular relationships with others such as mother and daughter, brother and sister, and husband and wife. Likewise, in our workplace, we assume roles as supervisors, managers, subordinates or colleagues. These roles afford us access to particular activities and to particular role-defined relationships. As company executives, for example, we have access to and can participate in board meetings, business deals and job interviews that are closed to other company employees, and thus are able to establish role-relationships that are unique to these positions.

Our various group memberships, along with the values, beliefs and attitudes associated with them, are significant to the development of our social identities in that they define in part the kinds of communicative activities and the particular linguistic resources for realising them to which we have access. That is to say, as with the linguistic resources we use in our activities, our various **social identities** are not simply labels that we fill with our own intentions. Rather, they embody particular histories that have been developed over time by other group members enacting similar roles. In their histories of enactments, these identities become associated with particular sets of linguistic actions for realising the activities, and with attitudes and beliefs about them.

> **Quote 2.1** Social identity
>
> Social identity encompasses participant roles, positions, relationships, reputations, and other dimensions of social personae, which are conventionally linked to epistemic and affective stances.
>
> Ochs (1996: 424)

The sociocultural activities constituting the public world of a white male born into a working-class family in a rural area in northeastern United States, for example, will present different opportunities for group identification and language use from those constituting the community of a white male born into an affluent family residing in the same geographical region. Likewise, the kinds of identity enactments afforded to middle-class women in one region of the world, for example, China, will be quite different from those available to women of a similar socioeconomic class in other geographical regions of the world such as Italy or Russia (Cameron, 2005).

The historically grounded, socially constituted knowledge, skills, beliefs and attitudes comprising our various social identities – predisposing us to act, think and feel in particular ways and to perceive the involvement of others in certain ways – constitute what social theorist Pierre Bourdieu calls our **habitus** (Bourdieu, 1977). We approach our activities with the perceptions and evaluations we have come to associate with both our ascribed and appropriated social identities and those of our interlocutors, and we use them to make sense of each other's involvement in our encounters. That is to say, when we come together in a communicative event we perceive ourselves and others in the manner in which we have been socialised. We carry expectations, built up over time through socialisation into our own social groups, about what we can and cannot do as members of our various groups. We hold similar expectations about what others are likely to do and not do as members of their particular groups. The linguistic resources we use to communicate, and our interpretations of those used by others, are shaped by these mutually held perceptions. In short, who we are, who we think others are, and who others think we are, mediate in important ways our individual uses and evaluations of our linguistic actions in any communicative encounter.

2.2.1   Contextual relevancy of social identity

Even though we each have multiple, intersecting social identities, it is not the case that all of our identities are always relevant. As with the meanings of our linguistic resources, their relevance is dynamic and responsive to contextual conditions. In other words, while we approach our communicative encounters as constellations of various identities, the particular identity or set of identities that becomes significant depends on the activity itself, our goals, and the identities of the other participants. Let us assume, for example, that we are travelling abroad as tourists. In our interactions with others from different geographical regions it is likely that our national identity will be more relevant than, say, our gender or social class. Thus, we are likely to interact with each other as, for example, Americans, Spaniards, Australians or Italians. On the other hand, if we were to interact with these same individuals in schooling events such as parent–teacher conferences, we are likely to find that certain social roles take on more relevance than our nationalities, and we will interact with each other as parents, teachers or school administrators. Likewise, in workplace events, we are likely to orient to each other's professional identity, and interact as, for example, employers, colleagues or clients, rather than as parents and teachers, or Americans and Canadians.

How we enact any particular identity is also responsive to contextual conditions. Philipsen's (1992) study of the ways in which a group of men enacted their identities as 'men' in a town he called Teamsterville is a compelling illustration of the fluid, contextual nature of identity. According to Philipsen, when the relationships between the men of Teamsterville were symmetrical in terms of age, ethnicity or occupational status, the men considered it highly appropriate to engage in a good deal of talk with each other. However, when they considered the relationship to be asymmetrical, that is, when the event included men of different ages, ethnic groups or occupations, little talk was expected. To do otherwise was considered inappropriate.

It is important to remember that our perceptions and evaluations of our own and each other's identities are tied to the groups and communities of which we are members. Expectations for what we, in our role as parent, can say to a child, for example, are shaped by what our social groups consider acceptable and appropriate parental actions. Some groups, for example, do not consider it appropriate for a parent to tell a child how to do something. Instead, the child is expected to observe and then take action (Heath, 1983). Other groups consider it important to discuss the task with the child before the child is allowed to attempt it (Harkness *et al.*, 1992). Our linguistic resources then can perform an action in a communicative event only to the extent to which their expected meanings are shared among the participants. Given the diversity of group memberships we hold, we can expect our linguistic actions and the values attached to them to be equally varied.

2.3   Agency, identity and language use

While our social identities and roles are to a great extent shaped by the groups and communities to which we belong, we as individual agents also play a role in shaping them. However, unlike the more traditional 'linguistics applied' view, which views **agency** as an inherent motivation of individuals, a sociocultural perspective views it as the 'socioculturally mediated capacity to act' (Ahearn, 2001: 112), and thus locates it in the discursive spaces between individual users and the conditions of the moment. In our use of language we represent a particular identity at the same time that we construct it. The degree of individual effort we can exert in shaping our identities, however, is not always equal. Rather, it is 'an aspect of the action' (Altieri, 1994: 4) negotiable in and arising from specific social and cultural circumstances constituting local contexts of action.

Quote 2.2   Individual identity from a sociocultural perspective

[Individual identity is] the situated outcome of a rhetorical and interpretive process in which interactants make situationally motivated selections from socially constituted repertoires of identificational and affiliational resources and craft these semiotic resources into identity claims for presentation to others.

Bauman (2000: 1)

From this perspective, individual identity is always in production, an outcome of agentive moves rather than a given. When we enter a communicative event, we do so as individuals with particular constellations of historically laden social identities. While these social identities influence our linguistic actions, they do not determine them. Rather, they predispose us to participate in our activities and perceive the involvement of others in certain ways. At any communicative moment there exists the possibility of taking up a unique stance towards our own identity and those of others, and of using language in unexpected ways towards unexpected goals.

As with the meanings of our linguistic actions, however, how linguistically pliable our identities are depends to a large extent on the historical and sociopolitical forces embodied in them. Thus, while we have some choice in the ways we choose to create ourselves, our every action takes place within a social context, and thus can never be understood apart from it. Therefore individual agency is neither inherent in nor separate from individual action. Rather 'it exists through routinized action that includes the material (and physical) conditions as well as the social actors' experience in using their bodies while moving through a familiar space' (Duranti, 1997: 45).

> **Quote 2.3** The relationship between individual identity and language use
>
> Identity is constantly interactively constructed on a microlevel, where an individual's identity is claimed, contested and re-constructed in interaction and in relation to the other participants.
>
> Norris (2007: 657)

2.3.1   Giddens's theory of structuration

While current conceptualisations of agency and language use in applied linguistics draw from several sources, one of the more significant is Anthony Giddens's (1984) **theory of structuration**. According to Giddens, individual agency is a semiotic activity, a social construction, 'something that has to be routinely created and sustained in the reflexive activities of the individual' (Giddens, 1991: 52). In our locally occasioned social actions, we, as individual agents, shape and at the same time are given shape by what Giddens refers to as **social structures** – conventionalised, established ways of doing things. In our actions we draw on these structures and in so doing recreate them and ourselves as social actors. Our social structures do not, indeed cannot, exist outside action but rather can only exist in their continued reproduction across time and space. Their repeated use in recurring social practices, in turn, leads to the development of larger social systems, 'patterns of relations in groupings of all kinds, from small, intimate groups, to social networks, to large organizations' (*ibid.*). The mutually constituted act of 'going on' in the contexts of our everyday experiences – the process of creating and being created by our social structures – is what Giddens refers to as the process of structuration.

While Giddens is not particularly concerned with identity and language use *per se*, his ideas are useful in that, by locating individual action in the mutually constituted, continual production of our everyday lives – the dialogue (Bakhtin, 1986) between structure and action – Giddens's social theory provides us with a framework for understanding the inextricable link between human agency and social institutions.

Quote 2.4   Theory of structuration

The basic domain of study of the social sciences, according to the theory of structuration, is neither the experience of the individual actor, nor the existence of any form of social totality, but social practices ordered across space and time. Human social activities, like some self-reproducing items in nature, are recursive. That is to say, they are not brought into being by social actors but continually recreated by them via the very means whereby they express themselves *as* actors. In and through their activities agents reproduce the conditions that make these activities possible.

Giddens (1984: 2; emphasis in the original)

2.3.2   Bourdieu's notion of habitus

Also influential to current understandings is the notion of **habitus**, as popularised by social theorist Pierre Bourdieu. According to Bourdieu (1977, 2000), habitus is a set of bodily dispositions acquired through extended engagement in our everyday activities that dispose us to act in certain ways. We bring them with us to our social experiences, and are inclined to make sense of our experiences, and coordinate our actions with others in particular ways. It is through our lived experiences as individual actors that our habitus is continually being reconstituted.

Quote 2.5   Definition of habitus

Habitus as a system of dispositions to be and to do is a potentiality, a desire to be which, in a certain way, seeks to create the conditions most favourable to what it is. In the absence of any major upheaval (a change of position, for example), the conditions of its formation are also the conditions of its realisation.

Bourdieu (2000: 150)

For both Giddens and Bourdieu, individual identity is not a precondition of social action but rather arises from it. Moreover, in the recursive process of identity production, individuals are constituted 'neither free agents nor completely socially determined products' (Ahearn, 2000: 120). How free or constrained we are by our habitus depends on 'the historically and socially situated conditions of its production' (Bourdieu, 1977: 95). The empirical concern is then to identify the actions that individual actors take in their lived experiences that lead, on the one hand, to the reproduction of their larger social worlds and, on the other, to their transformation.

Quote 2.6 On the mutually constituted relationship between individual agency and habitus

The notion of habitus restores to the agent a generating, unifying, constructing, classifying power, while recalling that this capacity to construct social reality, itself socially constructed, is not that of a transcendental subject but of a socialised body, investing in its practice socially constructed organising principles that are acquired in the course of a situated and dated social experience.

Bourdieu (2000: 136–137)

2.4   Research on language use and identity

2.4.1   Interactional sociolinguistics

One approach to the study of language use and identity that has had great impact on much research in applied linguistics is **interactional socio-linguistics** (IS), an approach that, to a large extent, is based on the work of linguistic anthropologist John Gumperz (1981, 1982a, 1982b). At the heart of IS is the notion of **contextualisation cues**. Gumperz (1999: 461) defines these cues as

> any verbal sign which when processed in co-occurrence with symbolic gram-matical and lexical signs serves to construct the contextual ground for situated interpretations, and thereby affects how constituent messages are understood.

The cues encompass various forms of speech production including the lexical, syntactic, pragmatic and paralinguistic. They also include turn-taking patterns, and even the language code itself. The cues provide individual interlocutors with recognisable markers for signalling and interpreting **contextual presuppositions**. Such signals, in turn, allow for the mutual adjustment of perspectives as the communicative event unfolds.

> **Quote 2.7**   The function of contextualisation cues
>
> How do contextualization cues work communicatively? They serve to highlight, foreground or make salient certain phonological or lexical strings *vis-à-vis* other similar units, that is, they function relationally and cannot be assigned context-independent, stable, core lexical meanings. Foregrounding processes, moreover, do not rest on any one single cue. Rather, assessments depend on cooccurrence judgments that simultaneously evaluate a variety of different cues. When interpreted with reference to lexical and grammatical knowledge, structural position within a clause and sequential location within a stretch of discourse, foregrounding becomes an input to implicatures, yielding situated interpretations. Situated interpretations are intrinsically context-bound and cannot be analyzed apart from the verbal sequences in which they are embedded.
>
> Gumperz (1992: 232)

This approach to the study of language use assumes that individuals enter into communicative activities with others as **cooperative agents**, that is, as individuals interested in working towards a common end. The specific analytic focus is on the particular cues these individuals use to index or signal an aspect of the situational context in which the sign is being used. Any misuse or misinterpretation of cues is assumed to be due to a lack of shared knowledge of cue meanings.

Early studies investigated intercultural and interethnic communicative events, with the aim of uncovering differences in use of cues to signal and interpret meaning and revealing the subtle but significant communicative outcomes resulting from these differences. Gumperz (1982b), for example, examined the misunderstanding resulting from the particular use of cues by a Filipino English-speaking doctor while being interrogated by FBI agents. While the cues the doctor used were familiar to Filipino English speakers, they were not familiar to the American English-speaking FBI agents. Thus, Gumperz argued, the use of the cues by the doctor led to the agents' misreading of his motives. Similarly, in their study of counselling sessions at two community advice centres in the UK, Gumperz and Roberts (1991) found that differences in cue use between British and Punjabi participants in intercultural counselling sessions led to misunderstandings and ultimately negative evaluations of the Punjabi participants. As a final example, Erickson and Shultz (1982) looked at how differences in the rhythmic organisation of discourse, including, for example, the timing of turns, between counsellors and individual students in advising interviews affected the counsellors' evaluation of the students' abilities.

As noted earlier, a basic assumption of much of this early research is that participants are mutually interested in the successful accomplishment of the interaction and that their success is basically a matter of shared understandings on the use of cues. Thus, any miscommunication occurring in interactions is explainable in terms of differences in this knowledge. Several critiques, however, point to the overly simplistic view on communication embedded in this assumption.

Kandiah (1991), for example, noted that such a view could not account fully for those cases of miscommunication between participants who share knowledge of the use and interpretation of cues. Nor could it account for those interactions occurring between participants who do not share cue knowledge but do not break down. He argued that something other than shared knowledge of cues must account for these kinds of communicative interactions. To make his case, Kandiah examined a job interview from the film *Crosstalk*, developed by Gumperz and his colleagues (1979) to illustrate difficulties in cross-cultural communication. In the film, communication difficulties arising between an English interviewer and the interviewee, an Indian immigrant to England, were attributed to differences in the individuals' communicative styles. One difference, for example, was found in the individuals' use of prosodic cues used to draw attention to particular bits of information in their presentation of the information. Kandiah argued that attributing the difficulties to a lack of shared knowledge ignores several crucial factors such as the length of time and experience the interviewee had had in the country before the interview and thus is inadequate for explaining the miscommunication. Instead, there are other possible explanations not accounted for in an analysis of cue use, such as each participant's degree of willingness to accommodate to the other. For example, individuals can knowingly use different cues or misunderstand those used by others to *create* a lack of shared knowledge and thereby distance themselves from each other. Kandiah further contended that research on intercultural communication needed to do more than simply mention these matters; it is, he stated, 'necessary to draw out with care and sophistication the highly complex issues they involve and to examine their close and integral interaction with the communicative behavior under investigation' (Kandiah, 1991: 371). Kandiah concluded that by focusing only on differences in cue use to explain troubles in interaction, interactional sociolinguistics runs the risk of

> divert[ing] attention away from the real, underlying issues that often render communicative exchanges at these points of contact unsuccessful in a fundamental sense to surface issues . . . the diversion of attention from the real issues has the unwelcome effect of legitimizing the behavior that is so destructive of real communicative interaction.
>
> (*ibid.*: 372)

Shea's (1994) study is a compelling example of how lack of interactional cooperation rather than lack of shared knowledge can lead to communication difficulties. Shea examined the interactions occurring in two advising sessions in which a non-native English-speaking student requested a letter of recommendation from two native English-speaking academic advisers. With one, his request was successful; with the other it was not. Shea argued that the different outcomes resulted not from a difference in shared knowledge of contextualisation cue use between the advisers and the student, but rather from the advisers' use of different structuring strategies. In the successful session, the adviser attempted to move past communicative difficulties with the student to construct a shared understanding of what the student was requesting by using affiliating strategies like amplification, requests for clarification and agreement markers. In the unsuccessful interaction, the adviser treated the different cues as obstacles to achieving understanding, using distancing strategies such as interruptions, and exclusions to control the interaction and thereby position the student as 'a disfluent, inappropriate outsider' (Shea, 1994: 25). The different strategies used by the advisers, Shea argued, are rooted not in communicative styles, but in ideological orientations towards the non-native speaker of English. Roberts and her colleagues (Roberts *et al.*, 1992; Roberts and Sarangi, 1999; Roberts and Sayers, 1998) have made similar arguments about ideological influences on judgements about cue use in intercultural interactions.

A related criticism has to do with the view of culture embodied in many of the earlier studies in IS. It is argued that by focusing only on cultural cue use, the studies treat individuals as cultural dupes who reside in well-defined cultural worlds separated by immutable, clear boundaries, and within which they are compelled to act in particular ways. Sarangi (1994: 414) notes the analytic burden of such a view:

> If we define, prior to analysis, an intercultural context in terms of cultural attributes of the participants, then it is very likely that any miscommunication which takes place in the discourse is identified and subsequently explained on the basis of 'cultural differences'.

Locating communication difficulties in cultural norms then ascribes a deterministic role to culture, and thus renders invisible the role of individual agency in shaping social action.

Alongside this deterministic view of culture is the assumption of culture as a one-dimensional, stable, homogeneous and consensual entity, with easily identifiable markers, and whose members share equally in the knowledge of and ability to use its norms. Such a view, it is argued, renders invisible the varied lived experiences of individuals *within* groups. We can only see in our analyses how culture is reflected in communicative encounters. What we cannot see is how it can also be a 'site of social struggle or producer of social relations' (Pratt, 1987: 56).

These criticisms notwithstanding, most agree that IS approaches to the study of language use have made significant contributions to a sociocultural perspective on human action. The concept of contextualisation cues, for example, draws our attention to detailed ways in which language use is tied to individual identities and provides a window into the microprocesses by which such cues are used in the accomplishment of communicative events. Relatedly, in focusing on the moment-to-moment unfolding of interaction, this approach draws our attention to the reflexive nature of context. Context is not a prior condition of interaction, but it is something that is 'both *brought along* and *brought about* in a situated encounter' (Sarangi and Roberts, 1999: 30; emphasis in the original).

2.4.2 Co-construction of identity

Drawing on the strengths of interactional sociolinguistics and incorporating insights from such social theorists as Bourdieu (1977, 1980, 2000), Giddens (1984, 1991) and others (e.g. Butler, 2006; de Certeau, 1984; Foucault, 1972; Weedon, 1999), current research on language, culture and identity is concerned with the ways in which individuals use language to **co-construct** their everyday worlds and, in particular, their own social roles and identities and those of others. The studies assume that identity is multiple and varied, individual representations of which embody particular social histories that are built up through and continually recreated in one's everyday experiences (Bucholtz and Hall, 2005). Moreover, it is acknowledged that individuals belong to varied groups and so take on a variety of identities defined by their memberships in these groups. These identities, however, are not fixed but rather are 'multifaceted in complex and contradictory ways; tied to social practice and interaction as flexible and contextually contingent resources; and tied to processes of differentiation from other identified groups' (Miller, 2000: 72). These studies often draw on a variety of data sources such as field notes, interviews, written documents and observations in the analysis in addition to taped versions of naturally occurring talk to uncover more macro patterns, including institutional and other ideologies, exerting influence on the processes of identity construction.

One particularly productive area of focus has been on identity construction of second language learners. One early influential study is that by Norton (Norton, 2000; Pierce, 1995) on immigrant women learning English in Canada. Using data sources such as personal diaries and interviews, Norton illustrates how these women's identities were differentially constructed in their interactions with others in and out of the classroom. She argues that these different constructions had a significant influence on the women's interest in language learning, making some more willing than others to invest the time and effort needed to learn English.

Another study (Roberts and Sarangi, 1995) takes a more micro-analytic perspective, examining how learner identities are differentially constructed in the interactional strategies employed by teachers in their interactions with the learners. As one example, Roberts and Sarangi examined a teacher's use of 'hyper-questioning' in her interactions with students she perceived to be problematic. Hyper-questioning is repeated questioning within a turn, leaving no opportunity for student response, and an intense rate of questioning across turns. They showed how the teacher's repeated use of this interactional strategy served to create increasingly disengaged learners. Such strategies, they argued, 'appear to disrupt learning not in any creative way but by contribution to the formation of social conditions which are a barrier to learning (p. 373). Similar findings emerged from the study by McKay and Wong (1996), in which they examined the identity construction of four Mandarin-speaking adolescents in the contexts of their schools. Their specific focus was on documenting the many ways in which the learners attempted to negotiate the shaping of their identities as English language learners and users, and the consequences of their attempts relative to the development of their academic skills in English. They concluded that

> learners' historically specific needs, desires, and negotiations are not simply distractions from the proper task of language learning or accidental deviations from a 'pure' or 'ideal' language learning situation. Rather, they must be regarded as constituting the very fabric of students' lives and as determining their investment in learning the target language.
>
> (McKay and Wong, 1996: 603)

In a more recent study, Nguyen and Kellogg (2005) investigated the postings of a group of adult L2 learners of English to an electronic bulletin board and found that the course topics influenced the kinds of identities the learners constructed in their postings and ultimately, the kinds of social relationships they developed among themselves. Those learners whose post-ings highlighted their personal, negative feelings and experiences on the assigned topics were found to participate less frequently in the online dis-cussions, and this limited not only their language learning opportunities but also their opportunities to develop social relationships with their peers.

In terms of teacher–student relationships, a study by Richards (2006) shows how even slight changes to interactions between teachers and students can afford opportunities for classroom members to construct other identities and role relationships in addition to institutional identities as teachers and students. One example provided by Richards shows how a discussion about the meaning of an English idiom provided multiple opportunities for a teacher and her group of Japanese learners of English to create informal, interpersonal relationships among themselves that differed quite substantially from the standard teacher–student relationship.

Also garnering a great deal of research attention is the examination of professional, social and personal identity construction in other institutional settings such as the workplace. In such settings, individuals have been shown to construct and manage a number of different aspects of their professional and social roles and role relationships. As one example, Holmes (2005) examined workplace narratives and, specifically, the linguistic and interactional resources used by individuals to negotiate aspects of their professional and personal identities in the stories they told each other.

Other studies have been concerned with the interactional construction of professional competence or expertise in health care and other institutional settings. Candlin (2002), for example, compared interactions between two nurses, one trained and one untrained, and a patient and found that the more expert nurse used specific strategies such as topic expansion to gather enough pertinent information from the patient so that health advice could be given. The untrained nurse, in contrast, exerted more control over the topic and thus limited opportunities to gather useful information. Also taking place in a health care setting, a study by Sarangi and Clarke (2002) examined the complex interactional strategies used by a counsellor in a genetic counselling session to negotiate the delicate balance between meeting the client's desire for a definitive risk assessment in an area defined by uncertainty while maintaining the counsellor's authority as expert adviser and, at the same time, her nondirective stance towards the advice-giving. Together, these and other studies exemplify in compelling ways the dynamic, contingent and co-constructed character of a range of identities including culture and ethnicity (e.g. Bucholtz, 2004; Day, 1998; Kiesling, 2005), educational identities (e.g. Dagenais *et al.*, 2006; Higgins, 2009), gender (e.g. Huffaker and Calvert, 2005; Ford, 2008), geographical identity (e.g. Johnstone, 1999, 2007; Waugh, 2010), non-native-speaking status (e.g. Wong, 2000a, 2000b; Park, 2007), professional roles and role relationships (e.g. Campbell and Roberts, 2007; Clarke, 2008; Cotter and Marschall, 2006), interpersonal associations such as friendship (e.g. Goodwin, 2006; Kyratzis, 2004), and other more locally contingent identities such as bystanders and law-breakers (e.g. Smith, 2010; Woolard, 2007).

A related, and growing, focus of attention in research on language use and identity is on the creative formation of hybrid social identities through **speech stylisation** and **language crossing**. This emerging focus is due in part to the rise in global migration, which has brought individuals and groups from different homelands into sustained contact with each other. As defined by Rampton (2009: 149), stylisation involves 'reflexive communicative action in which speakers produce specially marked and often exaggerated representations of languages, dialects, and styles that lie outside their own habitual repertoire. . . . Crossing . . . involves a stronger sense of social or ethnic boundary transgression'.

Rampton's (2005) study is a compelling example of these phenomena. His central concern was with the ways in which youths from mixed-race peer groups in Britain used language to construct hybrid identities. The groups were ethnically mixed, and included not only Anglos but also youths from Caribbean, Indian and Pakistani descent. Using observations and interviews in addition to audio-tapes as his primary sources of data,

Rampton found that the youngsters often used the languages associated with each other's ethnic and racial identities in creative, unexpected ways. For example, Afro-Caribbean youths often made use of Punjabi in their interactions with others. Rampton calls such uses 'crossing' and found that they occurred most often when individuals wanted to mark their stances towards particular social relationships. Asian adolescents, for example, often used stylised Asian English with teachers in their schools to feign a minimal level of English language competence and thus playfully resist teacher attempts to involve them in class activities. The youths also 'crossed' when playing games with their peers, or when they interacted with members of the opposite sex.

Chun (2001) revealed similar language stylisations and crossings in her analysis of Korean American discourse. Specifically, she found that in a discussion among young adult Korean Americans, one frequently incorporated lexical elements of African American English (AAE) into his otherwise mainstream American English speech. Chun argues that through his use of AAE, and his interlocutors' appreciative responses, the young men projected a male identity for themselves that challenged the dominant view of Korean American men as 'passive, feminine, and desirous of whiteness' (p. 61). Findings from these and other such studies (e.g. Auer, 2007; Rajadurai, 2007; Stroud and Wee, 2007; Tetreault, 2009), make visible the multiple, permeable, hybrid and contextualised nature of identity, and thereby 'subvert essentialist preconceptions of linguistic ownership' (Bucholtz and Hall, 2005: 588). The pedagogical significance of the various strands of research highlighted in this chapter is discussed in Section II.

2.5 Summary

As we have discussed in this chapter, a sociocultural perspective on identity and language use is based on several key premises. One of the more significant premises replaces the traditional understanding of language users as unitary, unique and internally motivated individuals with a view of language users as social actors whose identities are multiple, varied and emergent from their everyday lived experiences. Through involvement in their socioculturally significant activities, individuals take on or inhabit particular social identities, and use their understandings of their social roles and relationships to others to mediate their involvement and the involvement of others in their practices. These identities are not stable or held constant across contexts, but rather are emergent, locally situated and at the same time historically constituted, and thus are 'precarious, contradictory and in process, constantly being reconstituted in discourse each time we think or speak' (Weedon, 1997: 32).

In the contexts of our experience we use language not as solitary, isolated individuals giving voice to personal intentions. Rather, we 'take up a position in a social field in which all positions are moving and defined relative to one another' (Hanks, 1996: 201). Social action becomes a site of dialogue, in some cases of consensus, in others of struggle where, in choosing among the various linguistic resources available (and not so available) to us in our roles, we attempt to mould them for our own purposes, and thereby become authors of those moments.

Finally, this view recognises that culture does not exist apart from language or apart from us, as language users. It sees culture, instead, as reflexive, made and remade in our language games, our lived experiences, and 'exist[ing] through routinized action that includes the material (and physical) conditions as well as the social actors' experience in using their bodies while moving through a familiar space' (Duranti, 1997: 45). On this view, no use of language, no individual language user, is considered to be 'culture-free'. Rather, in our every communicative encounter we are always at the same time carriers and agents of culture.

Quote 2.8   On the dialogic relationship between language, culture and identity

In this view as well, while language is a socio-historical product, language is also an instrument for forming and transforming social order. Interlocutors actively use language as a semiotic tool (Vygotsky, 1978) to either reproduce social forms and meanings or produce novel ones. In reproducing historically accomplished structures, interlocutors may use conventional forms in conventional ways to constitute the local social situation. For example, they may use a conventional form in a conventional way to call into play a particular gender identity. In other cases, interlocutors may bring novel forms to this end or use existing forms in innovative ways. In both cases, interlocutors wield language to (re)constitute their interlocutory environment. Every social interaction in this sense has the potential for both cultural persistence and change, and past and future are manifest in the interactional present.

Ochs (1996: 416)

Such a view of language, culture and identity leads to concerns with articulating 'the relationship between the structures of society and culture on the one hand and the nature of human action on the other' (Ortner, 1989: 11); a central focus of research becomes the identification of ways we as individuals use the cues available to us in our communicative encounters in the (re)constitution of our social identities and those of others.

Further reading

Block, D. (2007) *Second Language Identities*, London: Continuum. Drawing on a wide range of social theory, the author provides a comprehensive, insightful overview of research on second language identities in three learning contexts: adult migration, foreign-language classrooms and study-abroad programmes.

Bührig, K. and Thije, J. (2006) *Beyond Misunderstanding: Linguistic Analyses of Intercultural Communication*, Amsterdam: John Benjamins. The twelve chapters in this volume examine intercultural communication in a variety of settings and from a variety of theoretical frameworks to demonstrate how individuals draw on a range of linguistic resources to construct mutual understandings in their interactions.

De Fina, A., Schiffrin, D. and Bamberg, M. (eds) (2006) *Discourse and Identity*, Cambridge: Cambridge University Press. The studies in this volume explore the dynamic relationship between identity and social context. Using a variety of methods to investigate numerous settings including the workplace, medical interviews and education, across different communities, the studies demonstrate in revealing ways how our social practices help to shape our identities.

Hall, C., Slembrouck, S. and Sarangi, S. (2006) *Language Practice in Social Work: Categorisation and Accountability in Child Welfare*, London: Routledge. This book examines the language practices of social workers, their clients and other professionals to uncover ways in which the doing of social work is managed. It includes the study of such key practices as interviews, case conferences and home visits. Its purpose is to increase the profession's awareness of how language is used to create and sustain professional contexts of interaction, identities and relationships so that they may better serve their clients.

Maybin, J. (2006) *Children's Voices: Talk, Knowledge and Identity*, London: Palgrave Macmillan. Drawing on ethnographic data from inside and outside of the classroom, the author examines in great detail the various strategies used by young children, ages 10–12, to construct their knowledge and identities in their encounters with each other.

Language and culture learning

This chapter:

- describes current thinking and research on language and culture learning;
- discusses the implications of these insights and findings for an integrated theory of teaching and learning;
- offers a list of additional readings on the topics covered in this chapter.

3.1   Introduction

Language and culture learning has long been considered an important area of study in applied linguistics. However, as our understandings of the notions of language and culture have changed, so have the concerns on which such study is based. Research relying on understandings embodied in a more traditional 'linguistics applied' approach has rested on rationalist assumptions of learning. These assumptions consider language acquisition to be a process by which the human mind, with its innate, coherent and abstract systems, imposes order on incoming linguistic and non-linguistic data.

Studies of language learning from a 'linguistics applied' approach have ranged from attempts to uncover the universal properties of an innate language capacity to concerns with the roles played by particular cognitive processes and various external factors in the developmental sequence by which particular aspects of language and culture systems are acquired. Of concern, too, has been the examination of various forms of pedagogical interventions to determine the most effective way to facilitate learners' assimilation of new systemic knowledge into known knowledge structures.

Current understandings stand in marked contrast to the more traditional view in that language and culture learning is considered to be a fundamentally

collaborative process whereby socially formed knowledge and skills are transformed into individual abilities. This view draws from theoretical insights
and findings from investigations of learning drawn from areas outside what
has traditionally been considered the main theoretical territory of applied
linguistics. A primary source is psychologist Lev Vygotsky's (1978, 1981,
1986) sociocultural theory of development first proposed over sixty years
ago, and the more recent formulations by scholars such as A. A. Leontiev
(1981), the son of A. N. Leontiev who was a contemporary of Vygotsky,
and cultural psychologists Michael Cole (1996) and James Wertsch (1991,
1998). Also contributing to current views is recent research on language
development in the fields of linguistic anthropology, developmental psychology and functional and cognitive linguistics. In this chapter we look more
closely at some of the more significant assumptions and empirical findings
providing direction to current studies of language and culture learning in
applied linguistics.

3.2   A sociocultural perspective on language and culture learning

A major premise of a sociocultural perspective on language and culture
learning locates the source of learning in the pursuit of action in our
social worlds. As discussed in Chapter 1, our worlds are constituted by a
varied mix of goal-directed regularly occurring, intellectual and practical
activities comprising various linguistic and other symbolic resources for
their accomplishment. We acquire the knowledge and skills needed to
be full participating members in these activities through the assisted guidance of more capable members. With time and experience in our activities
with the more experienced members, we learn to recognise what is taking
place and to anticipate the typical uses and consequences of the uses of the
activities' resources. In addition to learning how to take action with our
words, we also develop a shared base of knowledge about the world, including frameworks of expectations for what counts as knowledge and for what
we can and cannot do as individuals and as group members in using the
resources to build upon our understandings of this knowledge. Likewise, we
develop an understanding of the sociocultural importance of the activity,
its values and goals, and the roles we, and the other participants, are appropriated into playing.

This process of **appropriation**, according to Vygotsky (1978), takes
place in the **zone of proximal development** (ZPD). The ZPD is 'the distance between the actual development level as determined by independent
problem solving and the level of potential development as determined

through problem solving under adult guidance or in collaboration with more capable peers' (*ibid.*: 86). The specific means of assistance provided by the more capable members in the ZPD can take many forms and includes **scaffolding**, in which the more capable members share responsibility with the less capable members in the doing of an act, gradually letting them assume greater responsibility; **modelling**, where the more experienced members provide models or examples of the expected behaviours for the novices to notice, observe and imitate; and **training**, in which the more expert members coach or directly instruct the learners in the realisation of expected actions. Also considered significant to the process are the varied ways in which we, as learners, individually positions ourselves in relation to the different modes of assistance and to the role and relationships made available to us.

With such socially mediated assistance, our performances are raised to a level they could not have achieved on their own, and in the process of learning we transform the specific linguistic symbols and other means for realising these activities that were once conjointly enacted into individual knowledge and abilities. We also acquire the communicative intentions and specific perspectives on the world that are embedded in them. In this way, habits of language use become the tools by which we make sense of, and participate in, our communicative worlds. It is our eventual internalisation or self-regulation of the specific means for realising our activities, including the particular worldviews embodied in them, which characterises psychological growth.

On this view the essence of mind does not exist separately from the varied worlds it inhabits. More precisely, the communicative contexts in which we spend our time and the means we use to realise our activities and the relationships we form with others, do not simply enhance the development of mental processes that already exist. Rather, they fundamentally shape and transform them. As noted by Vygotsky (1981) and others (A. N. Leontiev, 1981; A. A. Leontiev, 1981), the inherited biological characteristics of language and our innate abilities to learn – including the cognitive means to perceive, categorise, take a perspective and make patterns and analogies – constitute only the necessary preconditions for the ability to learn language. In the process of interacting with others, our innate capacities dynamically merge with and are ultimately shaped by the sociocultural, constituted by the myriad communicative activities made available to us as social actors in our sociocultural worlds. Also helping to shape our inner capabilities are the actions we take and respond to as we learn to make sense of and take part in our activities. The linguistic signs arising from this process 'are living evidence of a continuing social process' into which we are born and thus 'are at once [our] socialization and individuation' (R. Williams, 1977: 37).

> **Quote 3.1** The social nature of development
>
> Any function in the child's cultural development appears twice, or on two planes. First it appears on the social plane, and then on the psychological plane. First it appears between people as an interpsychological category, and then within the child as an intrapsychological category ... Social relations or relations among people genetically underlie all higher functions and their relationships.
>
> Vygotsky (1981: 163)

3.2.1 Mediational means

A key concept to understanding learning from a sociocultural perspective is the notion of **mediational means**. Considered 'the "carriers" of sociocultural patterns and knowledge' (Wertsch, 1994: 204), these are the cultural tools and resources with which more expert members assist less competent participants in noticing, ordering, representing and remembering their involvement in their communicative activities. The means can be visual or physical in addition to verbal. They can also include computational resources such as computers and calculators, graphic resources such as diagrams, maps and drawings, and writing systems. We use calendars, for example, to help us to remember when events will take place and to organise our commitments; we use maps to help us to get from one place to another; and we use diagrams and drawings to help us to visualise spatial and other kinds of arrangements.

> **Concept 3.1 Mediated action and mediational means**
>
> From a sociocultural perspective, almost all human action is **mediated action** whereby we use linguistic and other cultural tools and resources – **mediational means** – to move through, respond to and make sense of our worlds. Understanding the links between human action and development entails understanding the nature of these means. Drawing on his own work and the work of James Wertsch (1994), Ron Scollon (2001: 120–121) describes the fundamental features of mediated means:
>
> 1 dialectical: there is a dialectic between the material (external) and psychological (internal) aspects of the means;
>
> 2 historical: meditational means embed both a social and an individual history;
>
> 3 partial: meditational means constrain, enable and transform action;

4 connective: meditational means connect multiple purposes and multiple participants;

5 classificatory and representational: meditational means constitute classes of objects that are suited to particular classes of actions, and more generally, classes of practices.

In the ways we use them to carry on our lives, these meaning-making resources give shape to the environments or settings within which development occurs and, more specifically, to the paths that individual development takes via the specific actions we take as participants. In other words, the means themselves and the ways in which we use them in the pursuit of action with others in our activities do not simply enhance our individual development. Indeed, they give it its fundamental form. Thus, it is, as Vygotsky argues, that we 'grow into the intellectual world of those around us' (1978: 88).

> **Quote 3.2** The role of mediational means in development
>
> The greatest characteristic feature of child development is that this development is achieved under particular conditions of interactions with the environment, where the ideal and final form (ideal in the sense that it acts as a model for that which should be achieved at the end of the developmental period; and final in the sense that it represents what the child is supposed to attain at the end of its development) is not only already present and from the very start in contact with the child, but actually interacts and exerts a real influence on the primary form, on the first steps of the child's development. Something which is only supposed to take shape at the very end of development, somehow influences the very first steps in this development.
>
> Vygotsky (1994: 344)

On this view of development, language is a primary vehicle for creating human mind. It is at one and the same time the means by which our history is generalised and handed down to us, a significant condition for our individual appropriation of our experiences, the means by which we pursue our goals in our experiences, and its form of existence in our consciousness (A. N. Leontiev, 1981).

As noted earlier, the linguistic means we use to engage in our communicative contexts often vary, sometimes widely, across groups. Likewise, the uses to which we put similar-appearing means can also vary. Given the fundamentally social nature of learning, our participation in different activities, different uses of means in similar activities, or even different opportunities and experiences with using similar resources, give shape to equally different developmental paths.

In defining learning as a process of sociocultural transformation, this view makes it impossible to consider it outside its specific contexts, that is, to consider the psychological conditions of learning apart from its social conditions. As Scribner (1997: 268) suggests, 'neither mind as such nor behavior as such can be taken as the principal category of analysis. . . . The starting point and primary object of analysis is the actual process of interaction in which humans engage the world and each other'. So, if individual learning begins in one's goal-directed socioculturally significant and interpersonally realised activities, the key to understanding learning is to study the processes by which individual language use is linked to its external worlds. Such study must begin with an analysis of the cultural, historical and institutional language-based contexts in which individuals live their everyday lives and, more specifically, the mediational means or cultural tools that individuals use to take action in these contexts. As important is analysis of the linguistic and other developmental consequences that result from individuals' varied uses of these tools as they engage with others in their socioculturally significant settings (Wertsch, 1994, 1998).

3.3 Language socialisation

Research on language development among children in several different cultural communities, undertaken by linguistic anthropologist Elinor Ochs (1988) and her colleague Bambi Schieffelin (1990), lends empirical support to these theoretical insights on the intrinsic link between communicative activities and language and culture development. In their investigations of Western Samoan and Kaluli communicative activities Ochs and Schieffelin reveal the connections between community beliefs about language use, the language activities in which children are regularly engaged, and the specific kinds of linguistic resources children eventually acquire.

In her investigations of Western Samoan caregivers' communicative practices, for example, Ochs found evidence linking these practices to larger community beliefs about language use on the one hand, and to children's acquisition of language on the other. In her analysis of one particular communicative activity regularly engaged in by caregivers and children, for example, she found that when some clarification of the children's utterances was needed, caregivers were reluctant to expand or guess their meaning. Instead, they preferred to use what Ochs calls minimal grasp strategies such as using statements of non-understanding (e.g. 'what?' and 'huh?'), issuing directives (e.g. 'Say it again'), and making quizzical facial expressions. Such actions, Ochs argued, reflect a cultural dispreference or unwillingness to speculate on the mental states of others. These same strategies that were prevalent in caregiver interactions with children were found in peer interactions as well, evidencing, Ochs argued, the children's developing proficiency in using such strategies.

These findings led Ochs to conclude that in their activities with caregivers children were not only being socialised into particular ways of using and interpreting linguistic means for clarifying speech. They were at the same time being socialised into local epistemologies on the appropriateness and value of such means for self- and other-expression. A comparison of findings on caregiver–child interactions from Samoan, Kaluli and white middle-class American communities (Ochs and Schieffelin, 1982) offers further evidence on the subtle but significant ways that language is used to socialise children into meaningful, appropriate and effective uses of language and at the same time into culturally specific ways of thinking and knowing.

This and other research on the language practices of communities (for example, see studies by Eisenberg, 1986; Heath, 1983; Peters and Boggs, 1986; Phillips, 1983) has led to the development of an integrated approach to the study of language use and acquisition called **language socialisation**. A key premise of this approach considers language and cultural development to be interconnected processes. It is through experts' regular, extended use of language and other semiotic means by which novices and newcomers become able at using and knowing the language and culture specific to their social groups. It is not only *what* is **encoded** *in language forms*, but more crucially, *how* meaning is constructed *in social action* that shapes development.

At the heart of the language socialisation approach is the notion of **indexicality**. This is the process by which situational meanings (e.g. social identity, resource meaning, affective and epistemic stances) are assigned to forms (e.g. intonation patterns, speech acts, turn-taking patterns). For example, for many groups, the use of high pitch, exclamations and extended laughter index high affect or emotional involvement. Meanings of forms arise from their past uses in particular contexts by particular individuals in certain roles with certain goals, and from their relation to co-occurring forms at the time of their uses. Their uses at particular times in particular contexts **index** or invoke those meanings that are conventionally associated with them. The process of invoking meaning is what Ochs refers to as **linguistic indexing**, and the cues used in the process are called **linguistic indexes** or **indexicals**.

These cues 'either alone or in sets, either directly or indirectly, and either retrospectively, prospectively or currently, establish contexts and as such are powerful socializing structures' (Ochs, 1988: 227). The concept of indexicals as used in language socialisation research is very close to Gumperz's notion of contextualisation cues as used in research taking an interactional sociolinguistics approach to the study of language use and identity (discussed in Chapter 2).

> **Quote 3.3** The link between language and culture learning
>
> The acquisition of language and the acquisition of social and cultural competence are not developmentally independent processes, nor is one process a developmental prerequisite of the other. Rather the two processes are intertwined from the moment a human being enters society (at birth, in the womb, or at whatever point local philosophy defines as 'entering society'). Each process facilitates the others as children and other novices come to a perspective on social life in part through signs and come to understand signs in part through social experience.
>
> Ochs (1996: 407)

According to Ochs (1988, 1996), knowledge of these cues is the basis for both linguistic and cultural competence. Understanding language forms necessarily involves understanding their conventional social meanings, that is, their indexical potentials. Likewise, understanding social order involves knowing how such order is linguistically instantiated, and more precisely, knowing which forms to use to point to and make relevant particular aspects of one's sociocultural worlds. A key challenge of research on language socialisation is to identify how language activities 'encode and socialize information about society and culture' (Ochs, 1996: 409).

Early studies gave their attention to the socialisation of children by their caregivers into the sociocultural practices of their homes (for examples of such studies see Brown, 1998; Clancy, 1999; Watson-Gegeo and Gegeo, 1986). While much of this early research focused on the socialisation of children and adolescents, as Ochs and Schieffelin (2008) make clear, the process is not limited to early childhood but rather is a lifespan experience. It occurs

> whenever there is an asymmetry in knowledge and power and characterizes our human interactions throughout adulthood as we become socialized into novel activities, identities and objects relevant to work, family, recreation civic, religious, and other environments in increasingly globalized communities.
>
> (Ochs and Shieffelin, 2008: 11)

More recent studies reflect this view as their attention has been extended to a greater diversity of settings, including schools, workplaces and other institutions (for examples of such studies, see Field, 2001; Li, 2000; Swan *et al.*, 2002). Still other studies have examined settings distinguished by the presence of two or more languages and cultures and the connections between socialisation practices or lack thereof across the different domains (see, for example, Baquedano-Lopez, 2001; Bayley and Schecter, 2003; Zentella, 1997). The different areas of language socialisation research and their relevance to the teaching of language and culture are discussed in greater detail in Section II.

3.4   Learning how to mean

Much current research on child language development further corroborates this sociocultural perspective on language and culture learning. One early influential study was undertaken by the linguist Michael Halliday (1975). Using language data gathered from his own child during the period covering the child's growth from 9 to 18 months, Halliday demonstrated the intrinsic links between language learning and social context. He showed how adults, by interpreting the child's utterances in ways that made sense to them in their interactions with the child, influenced what the child eventually learned. In their interpretations, the adults afforded particular socially based meanings to the child's language. Eventually, his meanings – what the child ultimately took on as his own – became those meanings encoded in the adults' language. Halliday concluded that children learn language by 'learning how to behave in situations, not by learning rules about what to say' (Halliday *et al.*, 1965: 179).

Like Vygotsky (1978, 1986), Ochs (1988, 1996) and others, Halliday understands the act of learning language and the act of learning culture to be mutually constitutive. Halliday considers language to be the quintessential cultural tool, an embodiment of the social system of meanings that enables its users to coordinate activities with others and, at the same time, learn the knowledge and practices, beliefs and values of their culture. In other words, as the child participates in communicative events of her daily life, she 'builds up a potential for exchanging the meanings that are engendered by the system' (Halliday, 1975: 121). Likewise, like Vygotsky, Halliday sees learning as an integration of both social and cognitive processes. He states (*ibid.*: 140):

> In learning a language the child's task is to construct the system of meanings that represents his own model of social reality. This process takes place inside his own head; it is a cognitive process. But it takes place in contexts of social interaction, and there is no way it can take place except in these contexts. As well as being a cognitive process, the learning of the mother tongue is also an interactive process. . . . The social context is therefore not so much an external condition of the learning of meanings as a generator of the meanings that are learnt.

Halliday's research on child language development forms the basis for his theory of systemic functional linguistics (discussed in Chapter 1). Implications of this theory for the teaching of language and culture are discussed in Section II.

> **Quote 3.4** On language learning
>
> In the development of the child as a social being, language has the central role. Language is the main channel through which the patterns of living are transmitted to him, through which he learns to act as a member of a 'society' – in and through the various social groups, the family, the neighbourhood, and so on – and to adopt its 'culture', its modes of thought and action, its beliefs and its values. This does not happen by instruction, at least not in the pre-school years; nobody teaches him the principles on which social groups are organized, or their systems of beliefs, nor would he understand it if they tried. It happens indirectly, through the accumulated experience of a number of small events, insignificant in themselves, in which his behaviour is guided and controlled, and in the course of which he contracts and develops personal relationships of all kinds. All this takes place through the medium of language.
>
> Halliday (1978: 9)

3.5   Social activity and language development

Additional research on language development from the fields of developmental psychology and functional and cognitive linguistics including the work of, for example, Boyland (2001); Bybee (2002); Hopper (1998); Bybee and Hopper (2001), Ninio and Snow (1996), and Tomasello (2001, 2003, 2006) further substantiates the social nature of language learning. Findings from the work of these and other scholars demonstrate the links between the development of language and the participation of children or newcomers in their socioculturally important communicative activities with other more competent participants. More specifically, it has been shown that less experienced individuals acquire both the forms and meanings of their linguistic resources from repeated experiences in regularly occurring communicative activities with more experienced others.

Essential to the construction and organisation of individual language knowledge are the distribution and frequency with which sequences of actions and their specific linguistic components are encountered in these communicative activities. The more frequent and reliable the uses of particular patterns and structures are in the unfolding actions of the activities, the more likely they will be stored and remembered. Also key are sociopragmatic actions used by more expert participants that make salient these patterns and structures and their form–function relationships, which assist novices and newcomers in noticing, experiencing, representing and remembering them. These can include non-verbal cues such as gazing and gesturing, and verbal cues such as cue repetition and tone and pitch changes. Less experienced individuals are also provided with verbal instructions that direct them to perceive or notice these cues and make connections between them and their contexts.

These actions alone do not give shape to individual knowledge, as individuals are active explorers of the structures and patterns of their activities. From the beginning, they use their cognitive capacities to figure out the goals of their interlocutors' actions, and to reproduce the actions used by their interlocutors to reach those goals (Tomasello, 2000). Likewise, they actively select and attend to particular structures and patterns of actions, hypothesise about the meanings and motivations of their and others' actions and continually try out their hunches to see if their intended goals were met in their interactions. This recurring process of testing, using and testing again, is basic to human behaviour (Levinson 2006a, 2006b). Over time, and with help from more expert participants, less experienced participants learn to recognise the activity taking place and the goals embedded within it, and to anticipate turns and sequences of actions along with the linguistic and other resources used to interpret and construct actions.

Eventually, their initial actions approximate the conventional forms used by the more expert participants, and thus serve as building blocks upon which their subsequent communicative development is based. As individuals assume more responsibility in using language to accomplish their activities, they develop shared collections of language knowledge, comprised of 'largely prefabricated particulars' (Hopper, 1998: 164) that are 'variable and probabilistic' (Bybee and Hopper 2001: 219), available for use in appropriate contexts and activities. In addition to conventional syntactic and lexical units, such knowledge includes various kinds of routine formulas, fixed and semi-fixed expressions, and formulaic language and idioms. These shared, dynamic grammars are the cognitive tools by which individuals make sense of and participate in their social worlds. Because different communicative activities comprise different arrangements of linguistic resources, different conditions for communicative development are created. In turn, these different conditions, the varied means of assistance in recognising and using the linguistic cues, and the individual responses to them give rise to distinct developmental outcomes.

Quote 3.5 The role of regularly occurring activities in the development of language

To acquire language the child must live in a world that has structured social activities she can understand. . . . For children, this often involves the recurrence of the same general activity on a regular or routine basis so that they can come to discern how the activity works and how the various social roles in it function. And of course if we are interested in language acquisition it must be the case that the adult uses a novel linguistic symbol in a way that the child can comprehend as relevant to that shared activity. In general, if a child were born into a world in which the same event never recurred, the same object never appeared twice, and adults never used the same language in the same context, it is difficult to see how that child – whatever her cognitive capabilities – could acquire a natural language.

Tomasello (1999: 109)

The analysis of mother–child interaction by Yont *et al.* (2003) illustrates the contextually contingent nature of the process. They compared the speech of mothers and their 12-month-old children in toy play contexts to mothers' speech in book reading contexts and found differences in the kinds of communicative actions performed by the mothers and the level of sophistication of expression by the children. More specifically, in the toy play interactions, it was found that mothers tended to direct and negotiate the children's attention and mark actions and events. In contrast, during the reading interactions, mothers most often described and compared objects in the book to the children's experiences with similar real objects. The effects of these differences were evidenced in the children's talk in that their communicative actions in each context mirrored those performed by the mothers. In the toy play contexts the children directed the mother's attention while in the reading contexts they jointly attended to objects and pictures by labelling and pointing. Furthermore, these different actions revealed differences in the language the children used in that the mean length of children's utterances and their production of word types were greater during free play interactions than during book reading interactions.

While much research has been concerned with first language development, a growing number of studies provide equally compelling data on the relationship between communicative activities and the development of additional languages. An early study by Snow and her colleagues (1991), for example, found that school-aged children's abilities to produce formal definitions in both English and French were tied to their involvement in activities in which the lexical, syntactic and discourse structures typical of such definitions were frequently and regularly used. They concluded that the development of linguistic skills in an additional language, if not first acquired in the first language, is strongly related to children's engagement in activities employing those skills in the target language rather than to their access to decontextualised, linguistic structures associated with the target language.

A more recent study by Bongartz and Schneider (2003) of two brothers, ages 5 and 7, learning German as a second language found similar connections between social context and language development. As one example, they found that the children engaged differently in negotiations with each other and others about what they wanted to do together, including deciding where, when and with whom they were going to play. The different opportunities, in turn, afforded them different motivations for language use and ultimately resulted in their development of different inventories of linguistic resources in German. An increasing number of studies of adult second language acquisition (e.g. Ellis and Ferreira-Junior, 2009; Eskildsen, 2009; Larsen-Freeman, 2006; Year and Gordon, 2009) further corroborate the inextricable links between social experiences with language and language acquisition.

To recap, current research on language development reveals it to be a consequence of extended involvement in regularly occurring communicative activities in which less experienced participants and their more capable interlocutors 'have various pragmatic goals towards the world and towards one another' (Tomasello, 2001: 136). Contextual conditions playing a fundamental role in the process include the frequency with which particular features appear in the linguistic environment, the clarity of their form–function relationships, and the newcomers' regular engagement in the activity. In addition, language development depends on individuals' ability to understand the purposeful, communicative intentions of their more experienced interlocutors in constructing their shared worlds in particular communicative circumstances. The linguistic resources used in the various courses of actions taken with them are linked to language development in that they structure both the form and content of what is learned.

3.6 Social activity and cognitive development

Alongside this research on the social constitution of language development are recent advances in developmental psycholinguistics examining the relation between language and cognition. A number of recent cross-linguistic studies, for example, have demonstrated differences in young children's spatial representations in populations from different language groups. These differences are not, as universal claims about cognition development would have it, age-related. Rather, findings show that young children's descriptions of spatial arrangements are more similar to descriptions by adult speakers of their particular language group than they are to descriptions by children of the same age group but in different language groups.

Bowerman (1996) and Bowerman and Choi (2001) provide examples of these cross-group differences in their studies on spatial semantic representation across various language groups. One example they provide concerns the differences in the way that spatial configurations are construed in English and Korean. According to the authors, English makes a distinction between putting a figure into contact with a supporting, external ground object [on] and putting a figure into some kind of container [in]. In contrast, Korean makes a spatial distinction that cuts across the *in–on* distinction, and for which no morpheme exists in English. The Korean verb *kkita* describes the fitting together of two objects with complementary, interlocking shapes. The verb is used to describe a figure interlocking with an external flat ground, such as fitting a finger into a ring ([on] is typically used in English to describe such a relationship, to wit, put the ring *on* the finger). *Kkita* is also used to describe an arrangement where the figure is placed tightly within the ground, such as slipping a video cassette into its container ([in] is typically used in English to describe such a relationship, as in, put the cassette *in* the box). As a final example, *kkita* is used to describe a spatial configuration in which the figure is placed in and through the ground object, such as placing a button through a buttonhole (a relationship for which neither [in] nor [on] is used in English. Instead, the verb 'to button' is typically used, as in 'button the [article]').

In their examinations of spontaneous speech of English- and Korean-speaking children between the ages of 1 and 3, the authors found that, rather than relying on some universal set of basic spatial concepts, these children, from as early as the one-word stage of language development, categorised their spatial events according to their language-specific means for doing so. That is, each group's encoding of spatial configurations reflected the major semantic distinctions and grouping principles of their respective languages. These findings, they argue, demonstrate 'a pervasive interaction between nonlinguistic conceptual development and the semantic categories of the input language' (Bowerman and Choi, 2001: 477).

Accumulating evidence from additional studies (see, for example, the work of Bowerman and Levinson, 2001; Brown and Levinson, 2010; Levinson, 2003; Slobin, 1997, 2003; Slobin *et al.*, 2009), further document the essential role of language-specific development in the construction and organisation of non-linguistic concepts such as space, time and object classification. In the process of acquiring a language, the individual's attention is directed to those aspects of objects and events that are regularly encoded in the grammar and lexicon of that language. These habits of language use result in the formation of culture-specific habits of thinking and speaking about the world (Slobin, 2003).

As we noted in Chapter 1, this process is encapsulated in the concept. As Slobin (1996: 91) notes, 'the language or languages that we learn in childhood are not neutral coding systems of an objective reality. Rather, each one is a subjective orientation to the world of human experience'.

Learning a language, then, entails learning particular ways to construe one's experiences. Learning languages in addition to one's first language entails learning alternative ways of understanding and constructing one's experiences (Ellis and Cadierno, 2009). In conceiving of language not as mere expression of cognitive development, but as shaper and change agent of cognition, the expanding body of research on cognition and language use provides further convincing evidence in support of Vygotsky's (1978, 1981) and others' theoretical insights linking language use to the development of mind.

Quote 3.6 On the significance of linguistic symbols in perceptual development

Linguistic symbols are especially important symbolic artifacts for developing children because they embody the ways that previous generations of human beings in a social group have found it useful to categorize and construe the world for purposes of interpersonal communication. For example, in different communicative situations one and the same object may be construed as a dog, an animal, a pet, or a pest; one and the same event may be construed as running, moving, fleeing, or surviving; one and the same place may be construed as the coast, the shore, the beach, or the sand – all depending on the communicative goals of the speaker. As the child masters the linguistic symbols of her culture she thereby acquires the ability to adopt multiple perspectives simultaneously on one and the same perceptual situation. As perspectively based cognitive representations, then, linguistic symbols are based . . . on the ways in which individuals choose to construe things out of a number of other ways they might have construed them, as embodied in the other available linguistic symbols that they might have chosen, but did not.

Tomasello (1999: 8–9)

3.7   Contexts of learning

3.7.1   Language classrooms as fundamental sites of learning

Historically, language teaching has always been considered one of the field's more significant concerns. In fact, one of the earliest official uses of the term *applied linguistics* dates back to the late 1940s when the University of Michigan offered a course on the topic, with the central focus on the teaching of foreign languages. Equally indicative of the field's concern with language teaching is the collection of seminal writings found in *The Edinburgh Course in Applied Linguistics* (Allen and Corder, 1973) all of which are exclusively devoted to language pedagogy. However, irrespective of the field's deep-seated scholarly interests in language pedagogy, until recently, they have been treated as distinct from scholarly interests in learning. In fact, some applied linguists continue to regard teaching as an independent phenomenon that may or may not travel over to learning (cf. Freeman, 2006; R. Ellis, 1997). Given the assumptions about language and learning embedded in the more traditional 'linguistics applied' approach, these doubts about the relevance of learning to teaching are understandable.

Current insights and research findings on language learning have broadened and in many ways transformed our understanding of its inextricable link to language teaching. As we discussed in this chapter, there is extensive evidence that connects language development to our extended participation and active apprenticeship in sociocultural events and activities considered significant to our everyday worlds. Extending this understanding to important contexts such as schools makes clear the significance of classrooms and, more specifically, the meditational means by which teachers and learners together constitute their instructional environments, in shaping the substance of learners' knowledge.

A fairly large body of work examining school-based learning from this sociocultural perspective provides compelling evidence on the intrinsic links between teaching and learning. This research is reviewed in Chapter 5, but for our purposes here it is useful to point out that, among other findings, it has been demonstrated that recurring classroom activities, with their fairly conventionalised semiotic resources for sense-making, set up structures of expectations within which their communicative values can be learned. Through their extended participation in these activities with other more experienced participants, such as their teachers, learners develop particular habits of participation. These habits are consequential in that they socialise students into particular understandings of the roles and relationships considered important to their lives as students. Likewise, they are socialised into particular formulations of what counts as the official curriculum and of themselves as students of that subject matter. Students draw upon these patterns and norms to participate in subsequent classroom activities and thus the patterns and norms are consequential in terms of shaping not only what students ultimately learn, but also, more broadly, their participation in future educational events and the roles and group memberships that they hold within these events.

One illustrative example of the links between students' participation in their classroom instructional activities and their development as language learners and users is Smagorinsky and Fly's (1993) investigation of large and small literature discussion groups in two high school English language arts classrooms. In a comparison of the norms and patterns of the discussions as realised by both large and small groups in each classroom, they found that the students' small group linguistic actions reflected the values and processes that were evident in their teacher's actions in the large group discussions. In one classroom, both teacher-directed large group discussions and student-directed small group discussions were characterised by brief unelaborated interactions that did not draw on external knowledge sources. In contrast, in the other classroom, both large and small group discussions were characterised by lengthy, detailed interactions that drew on a variety of external sources. Smagorinsky and Fly argued that the different ways in which literature discussions were accomplished in the two classrooms led to the creation of two distinct communities of learners with different interpretive frameworks and communicative means for engaging in discussions on literature. They concluded that differences in instructional discourse patterns across classrooms, in terms of the kinds of learning opportunities teachers make available to their students in their interactions with them, help to shape individual developmental outcomes in distinct and consequential ways. Such findings on classroom discourse and learning help us to understand that, rather than being peripheral to learning, teaching is at its centre.

3.7.2   Learning beyond the traditional classroom

While classrooms are indeed important sites of learning, they are not the only places where language learning occurs. The workplace, and health care and other non-formal community-based institutions such as recreational organisations, day care centres, and churches, are equally significant settings (e.g. Norton, 2000; Sefton-Green 2006). In these sites, individuals come into extended contact with others, develop significant social relationships with them, and in their interactions exert influence on each other's cultural and language abilities.

Identifying the complex webs of activities and relationship that develop in these contexts of activity and following the paths down which individual participation in the activities lead in terms of language and culture learning can help us to understand more fully the intrinsic links between the communicative environments in which individuals spend their time and their developmental consequences. More generally, they can help us to construct a theory of learning – a psychological theory of communicative action (A. A. Leontiev, 1981) – that explains the fundamental relationship between social activity and learning in ways that more mainstream theories of language learning do not, and indeed, cannot.

> **Quote 3.7** On a sociocultural theory of learning
>
> A comprehensive language-based theory of learning not only explains how language is learned and how cultural knowledge is learned through language. It should also show how this knowledge arises out of collaborative practical and intellectual activities and, in turn, mediates the actions and operations by means of which these activities are carried out, in the light of the conditions and exigencies that obtain in particular situations. Finally, such a theory should explain how changes, both individual development and social and cultural change, occurs through the individual's linguistically mediated internalization and subsequent externalization of the goals and processes of action and inter-action in the course of these activities.
>
> Wells (1999: 48)

3.7.3   The effects of globalisation on sites of learning

As we move more fully into the twenty-first century, **globalisation** has become an increasingly major force in transforming our learning experiences in classrooms and other institutional settings. One outcome of significance is the growing number of **transnational communities** in regions around the world. These are communities whose members move between two or more countries for political, social or economic reasons. The moves may be temporary, exemplified by families who travel to English-speaking countries to afford their children the opportunity to learn English and develop academic credentials needed to compete in a global market (Song, 2010). Other moves are more permanent, such as those undertaken by refugees and asylum seekers or by those who have developed strong inter-personal bonds with another via marriage or other official arrangement. Still other moves occur on a recurring basis, with individuals retaining some type of residency in two or more countries and engaging in regular travel to and from their communities.

These changes in community life have given rise to several significant challenges in designing and maintaining sites of learning that are relevant to learners. For example, the professional, social, economic, political and other issues that learners deal with in having to accommodate to, negotiate with and maintain connections with communities across national boundaries are often brought into the traditional classroom, changing the discursive activities, their meditational means and opportunities for using them afforded to learners. The diversity of contemporary life outside of classrooms is trans-forming classrooms into 'complex communicative space[s] criss-crossed with the traces of other communicative encounters and discourses both institutional and everyday' (Baynham, 2006: 25).

Another challenge is creating sites of learning that address the needs of vocationally oriented learners who seek professional credentials or whose credentials may not meet the requirements of the ever-changing labour markets in their new communities (e.g. Duff *et al.*, 2000). The challenge with perhaps the greatest potential to impact our understandings of language and culture learning is the almost daily inclusion of new digital technologies into our social worlds. The varied constellations of the global and the local afforded by these media have not only increased but, more significantly, transformed the myriad possibilities we have at our disposal to socialise, conduct business and learn with others (e.g. Lam, 2009; Lam and Rosario-Ramos, 2009). These possibilities are already transforming in fundamental ways, how and what we learn about languages and cultures. Pedagogical responses to these challenges are discussed in Section II.

Table 3.1   Traditional and sociocultural perspectives on language, culture and learning

	'Linguistics Applied' perspective	*Sociocultural perspective*
Language	Internally coherent structural systems, knowledge of which precedes use	Tools and resources for social action, structural and functional regularities of which result from use
Culture	Logical systems of representational knowledge	Sociwal systems of communicatively realised practices
Learning	Internal activation of the language acquisition device for the assimilation of new knowledge structures into existing systems	Process of being socialised into the communicative and other social activities of sociocultural importance to the group(s) or community(ies) one aspires to be a member of
Individual	Self-reliant, autonomous, internally coherent and stable across contexts	Historically constructed, complex nexus of socially contingent identities
Purpose of research on language and culture learning	To uncover the universal properties of the innate language capacity and the role of cognitive processes in the assimilation of new language systems and cultural knowledge	To examine the developmental consequences of appropriation into particular communicative activities in terms of an individual's developing repertoire of means for taking action

3.8 Summary

To recap, unlike the more traditional 'linguistics applied' approach, which views language learning as an innate process of linguistic system-building, a sociocultural perspective views it as the jointly constructed process of transforming socially formed knowledge and skills into individual abilities. It is, as Gee and Green (1998: 147) explain, a socioculturally constructed process of 'changing patterns of participation in specific social practices within communities of practice'. On this view, language learning is the 'fundamental facilitator of . . . the very foundations for human cultural abilities' (Levinson, 2003: 307) in that what we learn, including conceptual understandings of and higher-level skills for engaging in our social worlds, is shaped by our history of lived experiences in our communicative environments, and in particular the relationships we develop with other participants, the available meditational means, and the particular opportunities provided to and created by us to use them.

For a more complete understanding of the socioculturally mediated nature of language learning, we need expanded investigations of the varied sites where learning occurs, and which address, minimally, the following:

- the identification and characterisation of the constellations of communicative activities, including the means for their accomplishment;
- specifications of how learners' appropriation into the resources of the activities both reflect and create particular kinds of social identities; and
- examination of the skills, abilities, conceptual understandings and other habits of actions resulting from the varied paths down which the processes of appropriation lead.

Further reading

Lantolf, J. and Thorne, S. (2006) *Sociocultural Theory and the Genesis of Second Language Development*, Oxford: Oxford University Press. The book provides an extensive treatment of second and foreign language learning through the lens of Vygotsky's theory of development. Topics include mediation, internalisation, activity theory and the zone of proximal development. Also provided are two pedagogical applications of sociocultural theory to instructed second and foreign language learning.

Norris, S. and Jones, R. (eds) (2005) *Discourse in Action: Introducing Mediated Discourse Analysis*, London: Routledge. Sharing a view that all human action is mediated through cultural tools, the chapters in this volume examine social actions accomplished by individuals' use of spoken and written language and the consequences of these actions in various sociocultural contexts. Chapters are written by scholars from around the world who work in fields such as discourse analysis, linguistic anthropology, sociolinguistics and communication.

Robinson, P. and Ellis, N.C. (eds) (2008) *Handbook of Cognitive Linguistics and Second Language Acquisition*, London: Routledge. The chapters in this volume offer a comprehensive discussion on cognitive linguistics and its significance for the study of second and foreign language learning and teaching. Chapters in the first two sections discuss various theoretical and empirical elements of cognitive linguistics. Chapters in the third section link cognitive linguistics to SLA, offer a research agenda for the field and draw implications for language teaching.

Tomasello, M. (2003) *Constructing a Language: A Usage-Based Theory of Language Acquisition*, Cambridge, MA: Harvard University Press. Tomasello provides a rich, detailed and eminently readable overview of a usage-based theory on language development that draws on current theoretical insights and empirical findings from cognitive linguistics and developmental psychology.

Van Lier, L. (2004) *The Ecology and Semiotics of Language Learning*, Boston: Kluwer Academic Publishers. The book presents an ecological perspective on language and language learning. It includes comprehensive theoretical discussions on language, semiotics, and emergence. It also includes a discussion on the implications of such a view for classroom teaching.

Section

II Teaching language and culture

The sociocultural worlds of learners

This chapter:

- provides an overview of current research investigating learners' sociocultural worlds;
- describes several pedagogical innovations arising from this research;
- offers a list of additional readings on the topics covered in this chapter.

4.1   Introduction

Language and culture teaching has always been considered an important component of applied linguistics. More traditional approaches to teaching, however, rarely took into account learners' linguistic and cultural worlds outside the classroom. Rather, it was assumed that learners entered the classroom as empty vessels to be filled with information about the world. The information itself was thought to consist of immutable, discrete elements that existed independently of individuals' worlds. The process of knowledge acquisition, as noted previously, was assumed to be an internally driven one in which the elements were pieced together, unit by unit, in the building of autonomous systems of rules.

Since learning was viewed as primarily a cognitive process, realised by internal mechanisms that all normally developing individuals possessed, learners' experiences in their sociocultural worlds were not considered significant to the process. When they *were* given consideration, they were usually treated as independent variables needing to be controlled in order to get a clear, unimpeded view of the internal process and outcomes of language learning.

The view of language as internally coherent systems and learning as an internally driven, universal process of assimilation resulted in a conceptualisation of learner *differences* as individual *deficiencies*. That is to say, differences in levels of academic achievement were often attributed to differences in individual learners' linguistic and cognitive capabilities. Those who did not succeed were considered deficient or lacking in requisite cognitive and linguistic skills. Where learners' home contexts were considered, lack of academic success was often attributed to the learner's upbringing in settings considered to be linguistically and culturally deprived. In making apparent the inextricable links between individuals' sociocultural worlds and learning, a sociocultural perspective embodies a fundamental change from the more traditional perspective. We now know that, rather than being peripheral to learning, the sociocultural worlds into which learners are appropriated play a fundamental role in shaping their language and cognitive abilities and, more generally, their cultural beliefs about the language and their identities as language users.

These understandings of the significance of individuals' linguistic and cultural worlds, coupled with a growing awareness of the inadequacy of the deficiency view on learning for explaining the academic difficulties of learners who are not generally considered to be linguistically or culturally mainstream, have given direction to two strands of research in applied linguistics. While taking slightly different tacks, each strand has as its goal to understand and ultimately enhance connections between the linguistic and cultural worlds of learners' homes and communities and the linguistic and cultural worlds of their schools. The purpose of this chapter is to overview the directions this research has taken, discuss the insights on the teaching of language and culture arising from the research findings, and present some current pedagogical practices and programmes that have been developed from these insights.

4.2   Language socialisation practices: Home and school connections

One direction of research concerned with learners' sociocultural worlds and their connections to mainstream institutional settings draws primarily from linguistic anthropology and, in particular, the research on **language socialisation practices** (discussed in Chapter 3). A primary aim of this research has been to compare the particular sociocultural practices into which learners are socialised in their homes and communities with the practices they encounter in schools. The studies by Shirley Brice Heath (1983) and Susan Phillips (1983) are arguably two of the more influential investigations in this area. Each provides comparative descriptive analyses of the language socialisation activities and practices, and larger sociocultural beliefs and values found in home communities of learners who are not considered to be standard English speakers with those found in their mainstream schooling institutions.

Heath's study was a longitudinal, comparative investigation of the socialisation practices of two rural, working-class communities – Trackton, a black community, and Roadville, a white community – and one urban, middle-class community comprising both black and white families. Her analysis revealed that the two rural communities differed from each other in fairly significant ways in terms of how the children were raised to use language and to see themselves as language users. For example, Heath discovered that the children in each community were socialised into different understandings of the activity of 'storytelling' and into using different linguistic resources for accomplishing the activity. The Trackton children were encouraged to exaggerate and to fantasise when telling their stories, whereas children from Roadville were expected to stick to the facts, providing details where necessary, but never straying from what the adults considered to be 'the truth'.

Not only did the socialisation practices of these two rural communities differ from each other, but they also differed from the instructional practices found in schools which, Heath revealed, more closely mirrored the socialisation practices of the urban, middle-class community. These differences, she argued, resulted in different learning outcomes in school. Children from the rural communities whose practices differed from their schools' practices had more difficulty succeeding academically than did their urban counterparts, whose home practices more closely resembled the practices of school. This was so, Heath argued, because the contexts of schooling were a natural extension of the home contexts of the middle-class children. Consequently, the children were able to use what they had learned at home as a foundation for their learning in schools, whereas those from the rural communities could not.

In her comparative study on the socialisation practices of the Warm Springs Indian home and school communities, Susan Phillips (1983) reported similar findings. Like Heath, she argued that the differences in language socialisation practices found in the Warm Spring Indian children's home and school contexts made it more difficult for the children to do as well as their Anglo counterparts in schools, whose home practices more closely reflected the school's practices.

This concern with understanding the links between learners' *language* practices in and out of school has been taken up by those interested in the comparative study of **literacy practices**. Like research on language practices, the studies here aimed to understand more fully the social, cultural and historical links between the ways that learners are socialised into the activities of reading and writing in their home contexts and to use this knowledge to inform school-based instructional practices (Barton, 1991). For example, Fishman's (1991) investigation of the literacy practices of one Amish community residing in the state of Pennsylvania in the United States revealed a fairly significant variation in their practices in and out of school. Similar findings revealing differences between home and school literacy practices were reported in the studies by, to name but a few, McCarty and Watahomigie (1998), who investigated the literacy practices of American Indian and Alaskan native communities; Dien (1998), who investigated the literacy practices of Vietnamese American communities; and Martin-Jones and Bhatt (1998), who investigated the literacy practices of immigrant Gujarati-speaking groups living in Britain.

These studies on the language and literacy practices of different communities and groups have added greatly to our understandings of the links between learners' sociocultural worlds *outside* the classroom and their worlds *inside* the classroom. We know, for example, that home language and literacy practices, particularly those of non-mainstream groups and communities, often differ from those found in schools. We also know that learners whose worlds differ do not perform as well as those learners whose worlds are more similar. The reason for the differences in performances, however, is not because some home practices are inherently inferior. In other words, it is not anything intrinsic to the language and literacy practices found in students' homes that hinders students' abilities to do well in school. Rather, it is more a matter of compatibility. Learners whose home language and literacy activities reflect the dominant practices of schools are likely to have more opportunities for success since they only need to build on and extend what they have learned at home. On the other hand, learners whose home practices differ from those of their school are likely to have more difficulty since they will need to add additional repertoires of practices to those they already know. In these cases, institutional perspective also plays a role. In institutions where learners' home language and literacy practices are perceived as resources to be drawn on, difficulties are often assuaged. In contrast, in institutions where learners' practices are perceived as obstacles to be overcome, difficulties are likely to be exacerbated.

Currently, connections between home and school practices are turning out to be even more complex. Impacted by the large-scale migration taking place in regions around the world, contemporary communities are becoming progressively more diverse, comprising families of mixed unions, with members who are bilingual and multilingual and who have ties to multiple cultural groups. Findings from studies examining these communities reveal that home practices in the communities are equally varied, distinguished by the use of two or more languages or language varieties and by access to a range of media in addition to print (see, for example, the studies by Harris, 2003; Lam, 2004; Moore, 1999; Zentella, 1997).

4.3   Language variation

In addition to studies of home and school socialisation practices, research on language variation has helped to shape pedagogical concerns with the teaching of language and culture. The focus of much of this research has been on describing the regular features of languages and dialects of particular groups and communities for the general purpose of informing discussions on linguistic and cultural diversity. By revealing the systematic regularities of language varieties, such studies aim to counter the view on language variation as a deficient or incomplete version of the standard variety. This has been considered especially significant for schooling and workplace contexts, since it is often the case that teachers, administrators, employers and other institutional authorities who are unfamiliar with the linguistic varieties of non-mainstream students and workers consider these individuals to be linguistically and culturally deprived.

Early research on variation sought to illustrate the patterned phonological, syntactic and lexical features typical of different varieties of English found in the United States. Linguistic descriptions have been done, for example, of American varieties of English such as African American English (Labov, 1972), Appalachian and Ozark Englishes (Wolfram and Christian, 1976; Christian et al., 1988), and Puerto Rican English (Wolfram, 1974). More recent studies have examined varieties of English found in regions around the world, including, for example, Great Britain (e.g. Montgomery, 2006), India (Sailaja, 2009), Singapore (e.g. Zhiming and Huaging, 2006) and South Africa (e.g. Hartmann and Zerbian, 2009).

Studies on variation have also extended their reach to languages other than English (e.g. Dong and Blommaert, 2009; Miller and Schmitt, 2010; Violin-Wigent, 2009) and to the investigation of variation in pragmatic units such as speech acts (e.g. Félix-Brasdefer, 2009) and markers of politeness (e.g. Chakorn, 2006), to name a few. The substantial evidence on the regularities of language varieties found around the world documented in these and other studies reveals that instead of reflecting some deficient version of an idealised notion of language, these varieties, and more specifically their linguistic resources, are legitimate, meaningful tools by which members of linguistically diverse groups and communities participate in their sociocultural worlds. These findings, and those from studies on home and school language and literacy practices, have led to the development of three pedagogical innovations for teaching language and culture that use the richness of learners' sociocultural worlds *outside* the classroom to inform the worlds created *inside* the classroom. These approaches are described in the sections that follow.

4.4   Redesigning curriculum and instruction

Taking a broad-based approach to redesigning school programmes, two pedagogical innovations to the teaching of language and culture call attention to the importance of sociocultural compatibility between the students' home lives and their school lives for promoting academic success. Although their emphases are slightly different, both approaches are based on the following two premises. First, they recognise that classroom-based curricula and instruction have historically drawn on the activities, knowledge, skills, beliefs and values of certain mainstream sociocultural groups which, as the research on home and school links has shown, do not usually include those of non-mainstream groups such as language minority students. Although the practices of these groups are different, however, it does not make them any less valuable as sources of learning.

A second premise recognises that effective learning begins with making learning culturally relevant and meaningful to learners. To do this depends not so much on changing the learners so that they become interested in the more mainstream ways of knowing. Rather, in recognising learners' experiences as important sources of knowledge, these approaches call for using the sociocultural worlds that students bring with them to school to create culturally relevant and meaningful curricula and instructional practices in the classroom.

4.4.1   Culturally responsive educational programmes

One early educational response to studies documenting differences between home and school practices was to develop instructional programmes specific to particular culture groups whose levels of academic achievement were below average and whose sociocultural activities, norms of participation and other patterns and beliefs, were found to differ fairly significantly from mainstream, school-based norms and patterns. One of the first such culture-specific programmes in the United States was the Kamehameha Early Education Program (KEEP).

KEEP was first developed in 1972 to improve the academic achievement of low-income, elementary school-aged Native Hawaiian children. Early studies (e.g. Gallimore *et al.*, 1974; Au, 1980; Au and Mason, 1983) demonstrated incompatibility between the school and home environments of Native Hawaiian children. It was found, for example, that when at home, children often sought help from peers and siblings rather than from adults. It was also found that the children's home culture promoted joint turntaking during conversation rather than the one-person-at-a-time pattern typically found in school contexts.

KEEP drew on this research to develop instructional practices and classroom management techniques that were more compatible with the Native Hawaiian children's home activities. Key features of the instructional programme included organising opportunities not around teacher-directed, large group activities, but rather around small, cooperative learning groups and peer-based learning centres in which 'the students have a fair degree of responsibility for their own learning, much like the Hawaiian children have in their own homes' (Villegas, 1991: 14). It also entailed incorporating the students' preferred means of interaction into the classroom. For example, students were allowed to engage in the joint construction of stories, taking turns as they wished, instead of depending on the teacher for allocation of turns. Villegas (1991: 14) notes:

> By design, the allocation of turns at speaking during the lessons resembles the rules for participation in the *talk story*, a recurrent speech event in Hawaiian culture. Specifically, students are allowed to build joint responses during story time, either among themselves or together with the teacher. This strategy of collective turntaking parallels the joint narration of a story by two or more individuals, which is typical of the talk story.

Recognising KEEP's success in enhancing Hawaiian children's academic performance, other socioculturally congruous elementary school programmes in the United States have been developed. For example, Rough Rock Community Elementary School, located on the Navajo reservation in Arizona, a state of the United States, was initially begun as a collaboration between the KEEP team and the Rough Rock elementary school team to investigate whether the classroom conditions that were successful in KEEP would be equally successful in a school for Navajo children (McCarty, 1989; Begay *et al.*, 1995).

This collaboration led to the finding that while some factors were indeed equally successful in fostering learning, other practices worked better for the Navajo children, as they were more congruent with the Navajo home culture. For example, because of the traditional separation of children by gender in Navajo homes, children at Rough Rock were found to prefer to work alone on tasks or in same-sex groups rather than participating in mixed teams (Begay *et al.*, 1995). Similar to KEEP, it was found that changing instructional practices so that they affirmed and built on the Navajo children's home socialisation practices was successful in raising the children's levels of academic achievement. Similar findings on the value of socioculturally congruent home and school practices are emerging in other culture-specific school programmes (e.g. Hilberg *et al.*, 2000).

Efforts such as these have coalesced into a model of pedagogy which has been termed **culturally responsive teaching** (CRT). CRT is a collection of best teaching practices in contexts of diversity that 'responds to the sociocultural context and seeks to integrate the cultural content of the learner in shaping an effective learning environment' (Pang, 2005: 336). The model requires, minimally, teachers who are knowledgeable about the linguistic and cultural characteristics of the cultural groups to which their students belong. Such knowledge transcends recognition and appreciation of differences to include substantive information about the contributions of the various groups that can be integrated into curricula across disciplines. It also calls for teachers who can build curricular bridges between home and school practices and who have high expectations and can draw on a range of strategies that affirm the multiplicity of perspectives students bring with them to their schooling communities and, at the same time, ensure academic success for all learners (Kubota, 2004).

Quote 4.1 Theoretical underpinnings of culturally responsive teaching

CRT affirms students' cultures, viewing them as transformative and emancipatory strengths (rather than deficits); incorporates students' cultures in the teaching process, thus empowering them to take ownership of their learning; and leads to increased future participation in societal activities. . . . CRT acknowledges that student achievement is influenced by home and community cultures by ways in which these attributes play out in learners' educational, sociopolitical, and historical contexts. In short, CRT is based on the premise that culture profoundly influences the ways in which children learn.

Santamaria (2009: 226–227)

While much literature on culturally responsive teaching is addressed primarily to K-6 levels of education, it is making headway into secondary and adult programmes as well. For example, Mehan (2008) provides an overview of a culturally responsive programme called Advancement via Individual Development (AVID), which prepares students of lower class families for entrance into college and university by channelling their interests and abilities into academically successful knowledge and skills. Likewise, Ivanič and Satchwell (2007) discuss a culturally responsive project they developed that is aimed to 'recognise, respect and harness students' existing literacy practices as resources to enhance their success' (p. 103) in their college courses. Drawing on the concept of code-meshing (Canagarajah, 2006), which describes the polylinguistic practices of multilinguals living in hybrid communities, Michael-Luna and Canagarajah (2007) discuss several possibilities for using the polylinguistic practices to transform academic discourses from primary schools to university contexts.

4.4.2   Funds of knowledge

Another innovation emerging from pedagogical concerns with connecting to learners' worlds outside the classroom is the **funds of knowledge** approach to curricular development and design. The concept of funds of knowledge refers to the historically developed, significant sociocultural practices, skills, abilities, beliefs and bodies of knowledge that embody the households of learners in the immediate school community. First developed by Luis Moll (1992), and expanded by others (e.g. González *et al.*, 1995), this approach combines Vygotsky's insights on learning (as discussed in Chapter 3) with ethnographic methods for conducting research on learners' sociocultural worlds outside the classroom. The purpose of such research is to use the findings on learners' worlds to transform school curricula.

Similar to the culture-specific programmes mentioned above, this particular approach seeks to redesign curricula and instruction so that they are more culturally meaningful to students. It differs slightly in that it focuses on involving classroom teachers in redesigning instructional programmes. It rests on the premise that if educational innovations are to have any chance of long-term success, teachers must be actively engaged in the transformation process itself, from conducting research on the sociocultural worlds of their students outside school to creating and implementing new curricula and instructional activities.

Example 4.1   Funds of Knowledge Teachers' Project

The Funds of Knowledge Teachers' Project is a teacher-research project designed by González and her colleagues. Its purpose was to draw upon the knowledge and other resources found in local households to develop, transform and enrich classroom curriculum and instructional activities. It comprised the following three activities:

1 *Community investigations.* This entailed ethnographic studies of the origin, use and distribution of funds of knowledge among households in a predominantly Mexican working-class community of Tucson, Arizona. Before engaging in the community study, teachers were trained in the use of ethnographic methods for collecting data, with a central focus on the ethnographic interview. It also entailed training teachers in methods for conducting thematic analyses of the data.

2 *After-school teacher study groups.* These groups, comprising teacher-researchers and university-based researchers, met on a regular basis to discuss research findings and to plan and design innovative curricula and instructional activities using the content and methods of home learning, gleaned from the household funds of knowledge study, to inform the content and methods of school learning.

3 *Classroom investigations*. This component entailed teacher-researchers engaging in studies of existing methods of instruction in their own classrooms. They then used these findings to compare the ways the children learned at home and in the community with the opportunities provided at school. Based on these comparisons, the teachers made curricular and instructional changes, using the activities designed in the study groups.

Source: Based on González *et al.*, 1995

The funds of knowledge approach begins with the engagement of teachers in the ethnographic study of the origin, use and distribution of the communicative activities and events, and ways of thinking about, believing in and valuing these activities that are significant to their students' home and community lives. Collecting data usually involves extended visits to learners' communities and homes and interviews with important family and community members for the purpose of identifying and documenting existing knowledge, skills, behaviour and beliefs. Once the data have been collected and analysed, teachers compare existing curricula and instructional methods with content and methods of home learning, and use findings from their comparative analyses to devise new academic materials and instructional activities that build on what language minority learners know and can do outside school.

Most funds of knowledge projects have been conducted by teachers from public schools, primarily at the elementary level, in the United States (González and Amanti, 1992; Moll *et al.*, 1992). In the study by Moll and colleagues, for example, teachers visited their Mexican American students' homes to collect evidence of the funds of knowledge manifested in their homes. The teachers used their new understandings to create curriculum units on topics and activities considered to be significant to those households. In one case, it was found that when returning from their regular trips to Mexico, one family often brought back products to sell, such as candy. Building on this family's specific fund of knowledge, the teacher developed an integrated instructional unit based on various aspects of the nutritional content of candy. The class then made an inquiry-based comparison of US and Mexican candy and sugar-processing operations. Members of the family became participants and 'resident experts', visiting the class to share their knowledge and experience.

According to González *et al.* (1993: 1), participation in the project engendered 'pivotal and transformative shifts in teachers and in relations between households and schools and between parents and teachers'. For example, their research efforts helped teachers to redefine their understanding of the notion of culture by moving them away from a traditional perspective of culture as an accumulation of disembodied facts on foods, clothes, history and holidays or, as González *et al.* noted, 'as a static and uniform grab bag of tamales, *quinceañeras*, and *cinco de mayo* celebrations'

(p. 10). Instead, the teachers came to understand culture as a vital, dynamic process, which 'emphasized the lived contexts and practices of the students and their families' (*ibid.*).

Quote 4.2 **The effect of participation in a funds of knowledge project on teachers**

Each teacher, as she came to know the households personally and emotionally, came away changed in some way. Some were struck by the sheer survival of the household against seemingly overwhelming odds. Others were astonished at the sacrifices the households made in order to gain a better education for their children. They all found parents who were engineers, teachers, and small business owners in Mexico, who pulled up stakes and now work in jobs far below their capabilities in order to obtain a better life and education for their children. They found immigrant families with 15 people in a household, with all adult males and females working in order to pay for rent and everyday necessities. As Raquel Gonzáles notes, 'I came away from the household visits changed in the way that I viewed the children. I became aware of the whole child, who had a life outside the classroom, and that I had to be sensitive to that. I feel that I was somewhat sensitive before the visits, but it doesn't compare to my outlook following the visits'.

González *et al.* (1993: 11–12)

The approach also helped teachers to understand the value of their non-mainstream students' home lives. As pointed out earlier in the chapter, non-mainstream students' homes were traditionally viewed as places lacking in cultural knowledge and experiences and from which children needed to be rescued if they were to have any chance of academic success. The teachers' research experiences helped them to see things differently and, consequently, they came away with an understanding of their learners' homes as rich reservoirs of knowledge and experience. This recognition in turn helped the teachers to see their students as rich sources of linguistic and cultural knowledge and experiences, which ultimately resulted in the increase of their expectations of the learners' capabilities.

More recently, educational contexts in other parts of the world have begun to incorporate this approach into their practices. For example, drawing on the funds of knowledge framework, Martin-Jones (2003) documented how bilingual classroom assistants in three primary classrooms in England integrated language and literacy practices from the children's homes and communities into their instructional routines in the classrooms. Smythe and Toohey (2009) describe a project they call a 'community scan' (p. 37) in which various kinds of information were collected from a Canadian Punjabi Sikh community in order to understand the kinds of language and literacy activities in which the children from these communities regularly participated.

Marshall and Toohey (2010) recorded the efforts of teachers to incorporate these funds of knowledge into a Canadian elementary school. Additional studies (see, for example, Davis *et al.*, 2005; Stein, 2004) have documented various ways in which teachers have successfully incorporated students' marginalised multilingual and multimodal literacies into school lessons and curricula.

4.4.3 Language awareness curriculum

A third response to concerns with the sociocultural worlds that learners bring with them to the classroom is the development of **language awareness curriculum**. The scope of this response differs from the other two in that it is far more modest in its aims. Unlike the other two, which seek to transform entire programmes, this response seeks to add a curricular component to currently existing programmes. Its purpose is to raise individuals' awareness of the social nature of language, and thereby sensitise them to an understanding of language use as 'a uniquely social and human activity reflecting an array of choices to be made, not isolated or decontextualized rules to be *obeyed*' (Andrews, 1998: xxii; emphasis in the original). Svalberg (2009) suggests that a distinguishing feature of language awareness curricula is learners' engagement with language. Such engagement is considered 'a cognitive, and/or affective, and/or social state and a process in which the learner is the agent and language is the object' (*ibid.*: 247). Language engagement helps learners to understand the communicative capabilities not only of their own varieties but of others as well. It also helps them to realise the social, historical and political conditions within which and by which language standards are defined and maintained.

One example of a language awareness curricular component is **dialect education**, developed by Wolfram *et al.* (1999) specifically for adolescent and young adult learners. Its purpose is to help students to understand how languages are structured and used. One way they do this is by promoting the involvement of learners in their own studies of language variation in their communities. Example 4.2 outlines the general steps for engaging in dialect study.

Example 4.2 Steps for engaging in dialect study

1 Identify a possible dialect feature for study.
2 Collect data.
  a Listen to casual talk in the speech community to determine that the structure is widely used.
  b Write down actual examples from casual talk.
  c Identify corresponding form(s) in other dialects.

3 Analyse data.

  a Develop hypotheses about the linguistic context in which the form occurs. Hunt for patterns in the data, considering:

    i Linguistic forms preceding and following the features.

    ii Various forms the feature can assume.

    iii Etcetera.

  b Check the hypotheses against more data.

  c Accept hypotheses, reject or refine.

  d Repeat the two previous steps, looking for both differences and similarities with other dialects and testing stereotyped explanations.

  e Stop when no new information appears.

Source: Wolfram *et al.* (1999: 43)

In addition to conducting their own studies on community language use, students undertaking dialect education are provided with lessons that serve to raise their awareness of different linguistic features. Example 4.3 contains a sample lesson plan developed by Wolfram, Adger and Christian.

Example 4.3 **Sample lesson from a curriculum on dialect and language variation**

Southern vowel pronunciation

In some Southern dialects of English, words like *pin* and *pen* are pronounced the same. Usually, both words are pronounced as *pin*. This pattern of pronunciation is also found in other words. List A has words where the *i* and *e* are pronounced the same in these dialects.

List A: *i* and *e* pronounced the same

1 *tin* and *ten*

2 *kin* and *Ken*

3 *Lin* and *Len*

4 *windy* and *Wendy*

5 *sinned* and *send*

Although *i* and *e* in List A are pronounced the same, there are other words where *i* and *e* are pronounced differently. List B has word pairs where the vowels are pronounced differently.

List B: *i* and *e* pronounced differently

1 *lit* and *let*

2 *pick* and *peck*

3 *pig* and *peg*

4 *rip* and *rep*

5 *litter* and *letter*

Is there a pattern that can explain why the words in List A are pronounced the same and why the words in List B are pronounced differently? To answer this question, you have to look at the sounds that are next to the vowels. Look at the sounds that come after the vowel. What sound is found next to the vowel in all of the examples given in List A?

Source: Wolfram *et al.* (1999: 194)

Improvement and expansion of the availability of digital technologies has had a positive impact on the development of language awareness curricula by affording access to large repositories of language data. Increased access to data and appropriate software with which to analyse the data have made possible the incorporation of corpus-based approaches to the study of language use into classroom instruction. In general, the goal of these approaches is to raise learners' awareness of how language is used in real-world contexts. Because of the large banks of data these approaches make available, the teacher's role is changed from that of language expert to the role of facilitator of students' independent exploration and analysis of authentic language data. Example 4.4, taken from Krieger (2003), provides an example of how even a small corpus can be used for instructional purposes. The goal of Krieger's lesson is for students to discover the three general patterns of usage and their frequency for the word 'any'. He based his lesson on a study by Mindt (1997), which concluded that 50 per cent of the use of the word 'any' occurs in affirmative statements, 40 per cent occurs in negative statements, and only 10 per cent occurs in interrogatives.

Example 4.4 Sample lesson using a corpus

A closer look at 'any'

Part 1
Read through the following lines taken from a concordance of the word *any*.

* This is going to be a test like **any** other test, like, for example

* working with you. If there are **any** questions about how we're going to

* and I didn't receive **any** materials for the November meeting
* and it probably won't make **any** difference. I mean, that's the next
* You can do it **any** way you want.
* Do you want to ask **any** questions? make any comments?
* I don't have **any** problem with that. I'm just saying
* if they make **any** changes, they would be minor changes.
* I think we ought to use **any** kind of calculator. I think that way
* I see it and it doesn't make **any** sense to me, but I can take that

Source: Corpus of Spoken Professional American English

What conclusions can you draw about the use of *any*?

Part 2
What are the three main uses of *any* in order of frequency?

Any 1:

Any 2:

Any 3:

Schools are not the only institutions dealing with linguistic and cultural diversity brought on by worldwide migration. Both the personnel and the clients being served in professions such as health care, law and business have become increasingly multilingual and multicultural. Curricular responses to the increasingly diverse workforce include the development of profession-specific language awareness materials (e.g. Tipton, 2005) and the development of intercultural awareness programmes. The purpose of such programmes is to raise professionals' understandings of the cultural meanings embodied in their and their clients' language and enhance their analytic abilities to detect and sort out potential sites of miscommunication (see, for example, Pauwels, 1994; Roberts *et al.*, 1992; and Roberts, 1998).

4.5 Summary

As we have seen in this chapter, research on learners' linguistic and cultural worlds has helped to make visible their vitality and richness as sources of significant experiences, knowledge, skills and beliefs. It has also made visible the significant role they play in shaping learners' developmental paths. These understandings, in turn, have helped to transform pedagogical concerns with the teaching of language and culture. The different worlds that non-mainstream learners bring with them to the classroom are no longer viewed as sources of linguistic and cultural deprivation, or explained away as individual deficiencies. Rather, they are viewed as important linguistic and cultural resources on which to build. Consequently, rather than trying to change learners so that they fit more squarely into traditional schooling practices, current pedagogical practices seek to change schools so that they more adequately reflect and build on the linguistic and cultural diversity of learners' worlds.

The efforts described in this chapter have enjoyed success in transforming educational programmes and enhancing the academic performances of linguistically and culturally diverse learners. However, to continue doing so, future research and education concerns must face several challenges. The first has to do with the conceptualisation of learners' home and community practices. As we discussed in Chapter 2, and above, that communities continue to grow in diversity and complexity, makes visible the need to move away from treating learners' worlds as consensual and homogeneous, participation in which is shared equally among members of a particular group or community. In addition to the efforts described in this chapter, additional research is needed to help us to understand more fully the linguistic, social, historical and political dynamics of contemporary communities and the challenges they pose for educational contexts (Collins, 2007).

A related challenge concerns issues of representation. Educational approaches like culturally responsive teaching and the funds of knowledge are based on the assumption that communities in which schools are nested consist of one homogeneous culture group. Such a view, however, does not reflect current demographics showing that many communities actually comprise many groups, with many languages and many cultures. These groups, in turn, include individuals who have multiple identities and multiple group memberships, which may overlap and conflict, and from which arise diverse sets of linguistic and cultural knowledge and abilities. Equally challenging are the burgeoning transnational learning communities, brought about by improvements in electronic technologies. The range of diversity in classrooms is no longer limited by geographic boundaries, as students in settings around the world can become members of virtual classrooms. As Leander *et al.* (2010) argue, classrooms can no longer be viewed as self-contained units but rather must be viewed as one locale 'positioned in a *nexus of relations*' (p. 337, emphasis in the original) with other locales both near and distant. A challenge facing researchers and teachers is to understand how these communities are afforded access to learning resources within 'the simultaneity of multiple locales, and the contact zones between them' (*ibid.*).

With the continued rise of linguistically and culturally diverse communities around the world, the spaces, social networks, communication technologies and purposes for learning will continue to expand and change, making it impossible to envision a universally effective educational solution for addressing the academic and other needs of learners. Instead, as Hall (2008: 9) noted, going forward, a hallmark of effective educational programmes will be 'their ability to remain provisional, always in the state-of-becoming, with their practices and policies tied to the specific historical, social, and political conditions that arise from and in turn help shape the diversity of experiences in ours and our learners' everyday lives'.

Further reading

Adams, L. and Kirova, A. (eds) (2008) *Global Migration and Education: Schools, Children, and Families*, Mahwah, NJ: Lawrence Erlbaum. This collection of 19 chapters addresses the many challenges confronting immigrant children, their families and their schools. Representing 14 countries, the chapters are organised around five themes and all offer recommendations for educational policy and pedagogy.

Andrews, L. (2006) *Language Exploration and Awareness: A Resource Book for Teachers*, 3rd edn, London: Routledge. The book provides an introduction to the English language. It includes discussions of the history of the language, regional and social dialects, and social and pragmatic conventions of language use. It also offers awareness-raising activities for teachers to use in their classrooms with their students.

Gonzalez, N., Moll, L. and Amanti, C. (eds) (2005) *Funds of Knowledge: Theorizing Practices in Households, Communities, and Classrooms*, Mahwah, NJ: Lawrence Erlbaum. This volume is comprised of 16 chapters that describe the theory behind the Funds of Knowledge approach to pedagogy and explore its application to the innovative design of curriculum and instruction. Also discussed are new directions for undertaking research that links students' communities outside of school to their classroom communities.

Miller, J., Kostogriz, A. and Gearon, M. (eds) (2009) *Culturally and Linguistically Diverse Classrooms*, Clevedon: Multilingual Matters. Scholars from around the world offer insights on the challenges of teaching in culturally and linguistically diverse classrooms. Addressed to second and foreign language teachers, the 15 chapters are organised into three sections focusing on pedagogical issues, language policy and the curriculum, and research possibilities.

Sinclair, J. (ed.) (2004) *How to Use Corpora in Language Teaching*, Amsterdam: John Benjamins. The text is a collection of papers that offer insights on the practicalities of using corpora in language classrooms. The chapters are organised into five themes: the corpus and the teacher, corpora resources, computing resources, research using corpora, and future directions for research and pedagogy.

Language and culture of the classroom

This chapter:

- provides an overview of research concerned with the communicative environments of schools and classrooms;
- describes some pedagogical innovations that focus on creating particular kinds of communities in the classroom;
- offers a list of additional readings on the topics covered in this chapter.

5.1 Introduction

In addition to enhanced understanding of the significance of individuals' linguistic and cultural worlds outside the classroom to what and how they learn in classrooms, a sociocultural perspective on language and culture considers classrooms to be sociocultural communities in their own right. Thus, it draws attention to the important role that the languages and cultures *of* classrooms play in shaping both the processes and outcomes of language and culture learning. In their classrooms, teachers and students together create communities based on shared goals, shared resources and shared patterns and norms for participating as legitimate members of the communities. In their interactions with each other, teachers and students assume particular identities and roles, and together they develop understandings of what constitutes not only the substance of what is to be learned, but also the very process of learning itself. These understandings, in turn, give fundamental shape to learners' development as language learners and users. Given the jointly constructed nature of learning, the differences in learning opportunities that teachers make available to their students in their classroom practices, and differences in these practices across classrooms lead to the development of different communities of language learners, and within those communities, individual learners with different developmental trajectories.

An understanding of classrooms as sociocultural communities important in their own right and as significant sites of language and culture learning has informed several strands of research in applied linguistics. This chapter details the directions that research concerned with communities in classrooms has taken. For the most part, the review will be limited to two kinds of classrooms: language classrooms, be they first, second or foreign, and mainstream classrooms comprising linguistically and culturally diverse learners. A sociocultural understanding of classrooms also forms the foundation of at least two approaches concerned with the teaching of language and culture. Details on these approaches are also provided in this chapter.

5.2 Schools and classrooms as sociocultural communities

One strand of current research concerned with the language and culture *of* classrooms looks at the language and literacy contexts of schools and classrooms. Drawing on Hymes's ethnography of communication approach (cf. Chapters 1 and 8), and using ethnographic methods such as participant-observation and audio and video recordings, early studies sought answers to questions such as: What do classroom communities look like? What are their typical language and literacy events and activities? What are the conventional norms and patterns of participation? Who are the participants and what roles do they play?

Examples of early ethnographies of classrooms include those by Saville-Troike and Kleifgen (1986) and Saville-Troike (1987), which investigated the various activities and their conventional patterns and norms of participation comprising elementary classrooms in the United States that included linguistically and culturally diverse students, and that by Duff (1995), which examined the different patterns of language use found in content-based English immersion classrooms in Hungary. Additional studies drew more explicitly on the language socialisation paradigm, focusing their attention on classroom socialisation practices and their consequences for learner development. For example, studies by Willett (1995) and Toohey (1998) examined the practices found in mainstream elementary classrooms that included ESL learners and found that the children's involvement in their different routines with the teachers led their teachers to have different perceptions of their learners' language abilities and prospects as good language learners. These perceptions, in turn, led to further differentiation in the kinds of learning opportunities the teachers made available to the learners, which influenced the children's subsequent language and academic development.

Other studies have drawn on critical perspectives (e.g. Bakhtin, 1981, 1986; Bourdieu, 1977; Giddens, 1984; Weedon, 1997, 1999) and expanded their scope to include examination of the connections between teachers' and learners' lives in the classroom and the larger social, political, economic and historical conditions giving them shape. Canagarajah's 1993 study is an early example of such research. Taking a first-year ESOL university classroom of which he was the teacher as his unit of analysis, Canagarajah investigated his students' investment in learning English. Findings revealed that while they were resistant to the Americanised cultural discourses found in their textbooks, for the most part, the learners were strongly motivated to learn English for socioeconomic advancement in their communities. He concluded that full understanding of what happens inside a classroom must also be based on an understanding of the sociopolitical forces with which students must contend outside the school.

Reflecting the changing demographics of classrooms brought on by the large-scale migration in communities around the world, the scope of ethnographic research on language classrooms has been extended to include those of heritage language schools. Also known as complementary schools and community language schools, the purpose of such schools is to expose learners to a language and culture to which they have some birthright but with which they do not have sustained contact in their mainstream schools or in the communities in which they reside. Findings on the classroom communities of these schools reveal the contingent, sometimes contested, process by which students are socialised into their cultural and linguistic legacies. He (2004), for example, revealed the various ways the teacher in a Chinese heritage classroom in the United States attempted to position her American students as Chinese and the varied ways that students aligned to or resisted this positioning. In contrast, a study by Creese et al. (2006) of two Gujarati complementary schools in the United Kingdom showed how the schools promoted a more expansive space for the construction of student identities, affording some students the opportunity to position themselves as multicultural and multilingual, rather than to be bound to one language or culture.

Additional studies have shown other ways in which learners are not 'passive, ready, and uniform recipients of socialization' (He, 2003: 128). Studies by Hall (2004) and Canagarajah (2004), for example, reveal how students responded to what they perceived to be marginalising forces of the official instructional practices by creating 'safe houses' (Canagarajah, 2004: 12) in the classroom, speaking softly to neighbouring seatmates, catching up on work for other classes, daydreaming, and in other ways living quietly in the interstices of the instructional practices. Talmy's study (2008) of first-year high school ESL classes revealed more active student resistance to official classroom practices. Despite the fact that the student population in these classes included local students who had experience with US schooling contexts and practices, the curriculum was structured for 'recently-arrived cultural and linguistic "Others", or more precisely, for the iconic, stereotypical "ESL Student", or "FOB" ("fresh off the boat")' (*ibid.*: 626). This mismatch between the ESL student identity embodied in the official institutional structures and the students' self-identifications led to the students' development of a repertoire of classroom practices that worked to subvert the identity ascribed to them by their school. Furthermore, Talmy's data reveal that not only did other students appropriate the oppositional practices of these students but, even more significantly, the teachers developed a repertoire of practices that increasingly accommodated the students' resistance. By making visible the varied trajectories of development in these classrooms, Talmy's findings belie assumptions that socialisation always proceeds '"straightforwardly" or "inevitably"', particularly along lines of hierarchical status, institutional role, or age' (*ibid.*: 639).

5.3   The role of classroom discourse

From a sociocultural perspective, the interaction between teacher and students takes on particular significance in terms of how learning is accomplished. Through their interactions with their teachers, students are socialised into particular understandings of what counts as the official curriculum and of themselves as learners of that subject matter. The patterns of interaction also help define the norms by which individual student achievement is assessed. Students draw upon these patterns and norms to participate in subsequent classroom activities and thus they are consequential in terms of not only what students ultimately learn, but also, more broadly, their participation in future educational events and the roles and group memberships that they hold within these events.

5.3.1   The dominant pattern of interaction in classrooms

Early research on classroom interaction was focused on capturing the typical patterns of interaction. One of the earliest descriptions is provided in a study by Sinclair and Coulthard (1975). Drawing on Halliday's functional theory of language (cf. Chapters 1 and 3), Sinclair and Coulthard were interested in describing the form–function relationship of typical classroom utterances, and the larger patterned sequences of activity into which the utterances fell. They described what they found to be the basic pattern of teacher–student interaction, the **IRF**. Specialised for instruction, the pattern consists of a three-part sequence of action in which the teacher asks a question or in some way directs the learner to do something (I), the learner responds (R) and the teacher takes some kind of follow-up action (F).

A great deal of research on classroom interaction has revealed the dominance of one variation of this pattern, the **IRE**. In this pattern, often referred to as the recitation script, the first action takes the form of a known-answer question or directive (I), issued by the teacher, which serves to elicit information from the students in order to ascertain whether they know the material. The second action is the student response (R), which serves to display students' understanding of what they are expected to do and know. The third action, teacher evaluation (E), serves to assess and, when necessary, remediate that which is deemed inaccurate or insufficient in the student response. In fact, research has shown consistently that the IRE is the default interactional pattern in western schooling, from kindergarten to the higher levels of education and across all curricular areas. In the IRE, the teacher plays the role of expert, whose primary instructional task is to elicit information from the students in order to ascertain whether they know the material. He or she also serves as the sole gatekeeper to learning opportunities. It is the teacher who decides who will participate, when students can take a turn, how much they can contribute, and whether their contributions are worthy and appropriate.

Micro-analytic studies informed by conversation analytic methods have provided even more architectural detail on the teacher contributions to the IRE. For example, Hellermann (2005) found that a specialised question template is a frequently used resource by teachers to elicit information from students. The template differs from the canonical wh-question format in that it locates the question word at the end of the utterance, creating a fill-in-the-blank template for students to complete. Example 5.1 illustrates this pattern. As we can see in the first elicitation, rather than using the canonical question form, 'In which of these three regions did most of them live?' the teacher begins the turn as an assertion and inserts the question word toward the end, stating 'most of them lived in which of the three regions?' The same fill-in-the-blank format is used in the second elicitation.

Example 5.1 Fill-in-the-blank format of teacher elicitations

1st elicitation	T: →	most of them lived in which of the three regions.
	students:	middle
	T:	the middle.
2nd elicitation	T: →	with the exception of ↑ what major group,

Source: Hellermann (2005: 118)

Another study by Hellermann (2003) in which he examined the third action of the sequence, the teacher evaluation, revealed that, in addition to explicit markers such as 'yes', 'good' and so on, indicators of positive assessments included teacher repetitions of student responses. The repetitions were uttered with falling pitch contour and a mid level pitch that, while matching the intonational pattern of the student response, lasted slightly longer. Indicators of an incomplete or negatively assessed student response included repetitions ending with a slightly rising pitch contour. Additional studies (e.g. Lee, 2007; Waring, 2008) provide even more detail on the cues used in this third action to respond to and act on student responses.

In addition to describing the patterns of interaction characteristic of classrooms, research has sought to draw connections between the patterns and academic, including language, development. In an early study, Cazden (1988) revealed how the use of the IRE pattern more often facilitated teacher control of the interaction rather than student learning of the content of the lesson. Similarly, in his study of classroom discourse, Barnes (1992) found that the frequent use of the IRE sequence did not allow for complex ways of communicating between the teacher and students. Gutierrez (1994) came to the same conclusion in her study of 'journal sharing' in language arts classrooms. Her analysis revealed that in classrooms in which the activity was based on a strict use of the IRE, the teacher did most of the talking by commenting or elaborating on the journal entries of individual students. Student participation, on the other hand, was limited to providing brief responses to the teacher's questions. Gutierrez concluded that prolonged participation in this script gave students few opportunities to develop the skills they needed to construct extended oral and written texts.

A more recent study by Hall (2004) revealed its pervasiveness in a high school Spanish-as-a-foreign-language classroom. She argued that persistent use of the IRE pattern limited students' involvement to listing and labelling in the target language, and gave them no opportunity to participate in more intellectually and communicatively complex language events. Example 5.2 contains an example of the typical pattern of interaction found in the classroom in Hall's study. Lin (1999a, 1999b, 2000) reported similar findings in her investigations of junior form English language classrooms in Hong Kong. In her analysis of the discourse of these classrooms, Lin found that, with one exception, the recitation script was the common pattern, and it was linked to limited student participation. Moreover, she found that the recitation script most often occurred in classrooms consisting primarily of students from socio-economically disadvantaged backgrounds. Lin argued that by keeping to a strict IRE pattern of interaction, the teachers in her study ran the risk of pushing their students 'further away from any possibility of developing an interest in English as a language and culture that they can appropriate for their own communicative and sociocultural purposes' (2000: 75).

Example 5.2   Recitation script

1 T: Tú tienes sueño señor? la verdad
         (*I'm not sleepy are you sleepy sir the truth*)
2   (.)
3 T: Sí
         (*yes*)
4 S2:   ()
5 T: Tengo sueño.
         (*I'm sleepy*)
6 S2:   Sí tengo sueño.
         (*I'm sleepy*)
7 T: Sí tengo sueño. Sí tengo sueño.
         (*yes I'm sleepy yes I'm sleepy*)

Key: (.) = 1 second of silence; () = unclear talk; (*English translation*)

Source: Hall (2004: 78)

While many studies on classroom interaction have argued that prolonged participation in the recitation script provides limited learning opportunities, few have actually documented in detail links between participation in the IRE and academic development. Studies by Nystrand and his colleagues (1997, 2003) are notable exceptions. In their investigation of over 200 eighth and ninth grade classrooms, the researchers found that the overwhelming majority of teachers in these classrooms used the recitation script almost exclusively and that its use was negatively correlated with learning. Students whose learning was accomplished almost exclusively through the IRE were less able to recall and understand the topical content than students who were involved in more topically related, self-initiated discussions. Moreover, similar to Lin's findings noted above, the researchers found that the use of the IRE was more prevalent in lower-track classes. The dominant use of the IRE in these classrooms led, they argued, to the construction of significant inequalities in student opportunities to develop intellectually and com-municatively complex knowledge and skills.

5.3.2   Changes in the third-turn that enhance learning opportunities

In an attempt to understand more fully the links between particular patterns of classroom discourse and learning, Wells (1993, 1996) conducted an extensive analysis of the interactions of classrooms where extended student participation was common. He was surprised by his initial analysis of transcriptions of the interactions, which revealed what appeared to be a sizeable number of IRE sequences. Closer inspection, however, uncovered a subtle but significant difference from the more typical IRE pattern. More specifically, it was found that the teachers in the classrooms often initiated questions to students, but instead of closing down the sequence with a narrow evaluation of their responses in the third part of the three-part sequence, they more often followed up by asking students to elaborate or clarify, and in other ways treated students' responses as valuable contributions to the ongoing discussion.

Wells concluded that it was not the use of the full teacher-directed IRE pattern that constrained students' learning opportunities; rather, it was the teacher's evaluation (E) of the student response in the third part of the sequence that was limiting. Where the teacher followed up (F) on students' responses by asking them to expand their thinking, justify or clarify their opinions, or make connections to their own and other's experiences, student participation was increased and their opportunities for learning were enhanced. Based on these findings, Wells argued for a consideration of the IRF pattern as potentially beneficial to learner development.

These differences between the IRE and IRF patterns of interaction were confirmed in a comprehensive six-year study by Nassaji and Wells (2000) involving nine elementary and middle school classrooms and in the studies by Nystrand and his colleagues noted above. In their studies, Nystrand and his colleagues found that the discourse of classrooms with high student achievement was characterised by authentic teacher questions rather than known-answer questions, uptake of student contributions and high-level evaluations. According to the researchers, the intellectual value of authentic questions is that they indicate to students that the teacher is interested in what they think and know and invites them to contribute their own ideas to the ongoing interaction. Uptake incorporates student contributions into the ongoing interaction and thereby establishes 'intertextual links among speakers . . . [and] promote[s] coherence within the discourse' (*ibid.*: 15). High-level evaluations validate student contributions in such a way that they affect the subsequent course of the discussion. Example 5.3 provides an illustration of such an evaluation. Long-term use of these interactional strategies was shown to create an inclusive, intellectually rich classroom community that valued participation and learning, and ultimately enhanced students' academic performances. Even more significantly, the researchers found that their prolonged use 'suppressed potentially negative effects of macro variables such as track, SES, race, and ethnicity' (Nystrand, 2006: 403).

Example 5.3 High-level teacher evaluation

Teacher: Anybody else have a definition of a dictator?
Student: Someone who usurps the rights of others.
Teacher: That's exactly right. How did you learn that? [Certification + follow-up]

Source: Nystrand *et al.* (2003: 16)

The potential value of the IRF for supporting and promoting student interaction has been confirmed in studies of second and foreign language classrooms. For example, in her study of a high school Spanish-as-a-foreign language classroom, Hall (1998) found that when the teacher asked students to expand and elaborate on each other's contributions, more participation occurred. When the teacher limited her responses to a short evaluation of the students' responses, participation was constrained and learning opportunities were limited. Likewise, in his examination of the interaction of nine English language classrooms in Brazil, Consolo (2000) found that in classrooms characterised by ample student participation, teachers more often followed up on student responses in ways that validated student contributions and helped to create topical connections among them. As a final example, in their study of an elementary ESOL classroom, Boyd and Rubin (2002) confirmed findings on the value of teacher contributions that built on student utterances and pushed students to elaborate on their own and their peers' contributions. For the ESOL students in this classroom, these actions were especially helpful in scaffolding their contributions. Taken together, findings from these studies show that regardless of the medium or content matter of the classroom, teacher actions that expand student responses, invite elaboration from others, and in other ways treat students' contributions as valuable and legitimate foster active student participation in communicatively and intellectually rich interactions and more generally, help to create a vibrant academic community.

5.3.3   Social dimensions of classroom discourse

Recent interest in uncovering additional aspects of classroom interaction that facilitate a highly engaged classroom community has documented the value of cultivating **relational identities** (Boxer and Cortés-Conde, 2000), that is, interpersonal rapport among classroom members, to enhance members' investment in the classroom community. In their examination of two university-level ESL classrooms, Boxer and Cortés-Conde found that in the classroom where both the teacher and students reported having developed positive interpersonal relationships and feelings of solidarity, the instructional activities frequently promoted collaboratively produced inter-actions among the teacher and students which were marked by regular use of affective markers such as 'really?' and laughter. Similarly, in her examin-ation of the discourse in a college preparatory course for ESL adult learners in the United States, Nguyen (2007) found that both the teacher and students regularly used multiple verbal and nonverbal resources such as facial expres-sions, formulaic expressions, and speech tempo to display and maintain rapport with each other while orienting to the instructional task-at-hand. Although she did not connect these interpersonal features directly to student learning outcomes, Nguyen concluded that they helped to sustain 'a friendly, productive classroom atmosphere in which the teacher and students effectively carried out their tasks while building a positive relationship' (*ibid.*: 298).

Other studies (e.g. Boyd and Maloof, 2000; Richards, 2006) have shown that within instructional talk, teachers' self-disclosures engender similar types of contributions from students, and together, contribute to the building of social relationships among the class members. As Nguyen (2007: 299) notes, 'the language classroom is the place where people come together not only to talk *about* language . . . but also to *use* language to create and maintain their own social environment'. Increasing the scope of discourse opportunities available in the IRF to include such social practices helps to sustain a mutually engaged, learning environment (Breen, 2001).

Another feature of classroom interaction found to help build and sustain a highly engaged community is language play. Some studies have focused on the teacher's role in promoting such play within the IRF. For example, Sullivan (2000) documented how collaborative repartee occurring between a teacher and his students as they completed an instructional task served two functions: It called attention to the language of focus in the task at the same time that it fostered a sense of affiliation among the class members. Other studies have focused on students' creativity in using playful language in such a way to open up interactional spaces for themselves and at the same time strengthen the sense of community among the members of the class-room (e.g. Cekaite and Aronsson, 2004; Cekaite, 2009; Pomerantz and Bell, 2007). Together, the findings reveal how language play affords teachers and students opportunities to enhance solidarity and prosocial affiliations with each other, and at the same time, affords learners access to a broader range of communicative practices comprised of complex and varied linguistic forms (cf. Cook, 2000).

To be sure, creating and sustaining such intellectually and socially enriching classroom communities through classroom interaction is not 'a smooth and seamless process' (He, 2003: 128). Duff's (2002) examination of a Canadian high school social studies class containing linguistically and culturally diverse learners exemplifies the challenges of engaging students from different cultural backgrounds in class discussions. In her analyses, Duff showed how strategies used by the teacher to create rapport and facili-tate the participation of these students such as asking them about practices associated with their home culture had the opposite effect, and actually served to reduce their participation. Based on interviews she conducted with the students, Duff found that their limited participation resulted in part from their reluctance to publicly identify with traditions or practices of their home culture that marked them as culturally different.

In sum, studies on the discourse of a range of classrooms have revealed the ubiquity of one pattern of interaction, the IRE. Moreover, they have revealed that pervasive use of the pattern creates fairly deprived learning environments with limited opportunity for participation calling for socially, communicatively or cognitively complex actions. Additional research has shown that with subtle changes to this pattern, specifically in terms of the kinds of questions teachers ask and the follow-up to student responses, significantly different learning communities can be created. Additional studies have demonstrated the value in cultivating social relationships and engaging in playful linguistic practices for enhancing learning opportunities in classroom communities.

Findings from these and other ethnographic studies have added much to our understanding of classrooms as legitimate sociocultural communities of learners with institutionally sanctioned affordances that privilege some activities and events at the expense of others and the consequential role of classroom interaction in affording the creation of different kinds of communities. In particular, we understand more fully the varied roles that teachers and students play in their communities, and the subtle yet significant influences that teachers' and students' understandings of their roles have on the learning environments they create. Likewise, we have gained an understanding of how the social, economic, historical and political conditions of larger social communities give shape to the types of learning communities that evolve in these classrooms and, more particularly, the identities that teachers and learners assume or are ascribed and, on a larger scale, the values and ideologies associated with these identities, and how both teachers and students position themselves in relation to these various identities and ideologies and the communicative means they use to do so.

5.4   Redesigning curriculum and instruction

The view of classrooms as significant sociocultural communities in their own right, coupled with an understanding of the intrinsic relationship between teaching, as instantiated in classroom discourse, and learning, has led to the design of two pedagogical approaches concerned with creating effectual learning conditions in the classroom. One approach is broad-based in that it focuses on reconceptualising classrooms as communities of learners. The second is more restricted in that it focuses on incorporating cooperative learning practices into the traditional classroom. While they are slightly different in scope, they share a view of the importance of using language and other cultural resources to create supportive and effective learning communities.

5.4.1   Communities of learners

One response to concerns with classroom environments has been to conceptualise classrooms as **communities of learners**. In such communities, teaching and learning are considered to be inseparable parts of a socially situated, collaborative and mutually beneficial process in which learners, through their participation in their classroom activities, assume new understandings, take on new skills, and ultimately develop new sociocultural identities. Because language is considered to be a primary tool for socialising learners into these communities, classroom interaction is seen as fundamental to the process. In their interactions with each other, teachers and students work together to address issues, concerns and problems important to their community. The role of the teachers is to provide ample support to learners to ensure their success in appropriating the communicative and cultural knowledge, skills and values that have been deemed important to participation in their classroom communities and ultimately, to their larger social communities outside the classroom.

Communities of practice

The concept of a community of learners draws in part from the anthropological work on **communities of practice** (CoPs) (e.g. Chaiklin and Lave, 1993; Lave and Wenger, 1991; Rogoff *et al.*, 1996; Wenger, 1998). CoPs are social activity units consisting of individuals who share a common identity and come together for shared purposes organised around, for example, academic, professional or community goals. Drawing on Vygotsky's theoretical insights on the fundamentally social nature of learning (see Chapter 3), this work situates learning within the CoPs to which we belong or aspire to belong. Through mutual, sustained engagement with more experienced members using various meditational means, newcomers or novices to these communities appropriate the particular behaviours, beliefs, values and ways of orienting to the world and to each other as bona fide members of these groups. The means by which newcomers are apprenticed into their communities depend on the traditions of learning embodied in them (Gee, 2008; Rogoff *et al.*, 2007).

> **Quote 5.1**   Definition of communities of practice
>
> Communities of practice are 'Groups of people who share a concern, a set of problems, or a passion about a topic, and who deepen their knowledge and expertise in this area by interacting on an ongoing basis.
>
> Wenger *et al.* (2002: 7)

Much of the scholarship on CoPs has its roots in early ethnographic studies of community-based apprenticeship programmes in different cultural communities. These studies focused on the social processes by which inexperienced individuals were apprenticed into particular professional trades. Using findings from these studies, Lave and Wenger (1991) proposed an apprenticeship model of learning in CoPs, which they call **legitimate peripheral participation**. According to Lave and Wenger, newcomers to a CoP begin on its periphery. Their interest in wanting to become full participating members and their acceptance by the more experienced members as potential, full participating members give them legitimacy for being there. As they become more active and engage with more experienced members in working towards a common set of goals, the newcomers or novices move from the periphery of the community to its centre, eventually assuming roles as experts.

Concept 5.1   **Legitimate peripheral participation**

Legitimate peripheral participation captures the socially situated, relational nature of learning, in which learners are viewed as novice members who are given increased access to opportunities for developing expertise in those activities in which they aspire to develop competence. As they move from limited – *peripheral* – participation to full participation, they appropriate the knowledge, skills, abilities and attitudes towards their role in the activity evidenced by those who are considered to be expert.

While the concept of CoP has been useful in theorising the fundamental social quality of learning, some scholars have found the concept to be limiting, arguing that it assumes no distinction between different types of participants other than newcomers and old-timers. Moreover, it is argued, the concept presupposes that movement is unidirectional, proceeding from the periphery to the core, and that opportunities for movement are the same for all newcomers, 'uniformly benign, undifferentiated, and apolitical' (Duff, 2007a: 316). Also critiqued is the general lack of attention to the specific ways in which language and other semiotic means are used to negotiate meaning in a CoP (cf. Tusting, 2005) and to the multiple memberships individuals bring to a CoP (cf. Candlin and Candlin, 2007).

Gee (2004, 2007) proposed the notion of **affinity spaces** as an alternative concept. According to Gee, members of affinity spaces share 'interests, endeavours, goals or practices' (2004: 85). Gee proposed the concept to counteract the idealism embodied in the notion of community, since affinity spaces can be 'good, evil, or anything in between' (2007: 206). Lave and Wenger (1991) acknowledged that, as initially proposed, the concept was underdeveloped and indeed, earlier research may have downplayed the dynamic nature of CoPs (cf. Talmy, 2008). The current trend, however, reflected in the studies reviewed above, is to make visible how in CoPs 'agent, activity, and the world mutually constitute one another' (Lave and Wenger, 1991: 33) and how power and other ideological differentials, instantiated in the communicative resources by which meaning is negotiated, can lead to varied, complex, and sometimes contested, trajectories of participation in CoPs.

Concept 5.2   **Features of affinity spaces**

1 Common endeavour, not race, class, gender, or disability, is primary.
2 Newbies and masers and everyone else share common space.
3 Some portals are strong generators.
4 Content organisation is transformed by interactional organisation.
5 Both intensive and extensive knowledge are encouraged.
6 Both individual and distributed knowledge are encouraged.
7 Dispersed knowledge is encouraged.
8 Tacit knowledge is encouraged and honoured.
9 There are many different forms and routes to participation.
10 There are lots of different routes to status.
11 Leadership is porous and leaders are resources.

Gee (2004: 85–86)

Setting aside discussions on the usefulness of the term community, the view of learning embodied in the CoP framework has been a valuable lens with which to conceptualise what happens in contexts of learning. In a community of learners, learning is considered to be a mutually constituted transformation of skills and knowledge and, at a more fundamental level, a mutually constituted experience of identity transformation. In these communities, teachers and students come together as mentors and apprentices, with the shared goal of moving the learners from limited, novice participation to full, expert participation (Rogoff *et al.*, 1996). This occurs as the learners gradually increase their involvement, and gain access to a wide range of activities and roles in their classroom experiences. In the process, teachers and students serve as resources for each other, each taking 'varying roles according to their understanding of the activity at hand and differing (and shifting) responsibilities in the system' (*ibid.*: 397).

Key design principles in creating a community of learners

Characterised by 'dynamic participation structures and the strategic use of a wide range of meditational tools, including hybrid language practices'

(Gutierrez, 2002: 318) that foster 'productive disciplinary engagement' (Engle and Conant, 2002: 400), a community of learners embodies the following principles:

- *Language is a primary tool for learning.* Language is not only the primary means of communication; it is also the principal tool for thinking. As noted by Halliday, 'language is the essential condition of knowing, the process by which experience *becomes* knowledge' (1993: 94; emphasis in the original). Learners are given opportunities to use language in a range of intellectually challenging communicative activities such as interpreting, offering opinions, predicting, reasoning and evaluating.

- *Through joint activity learners are socialised into their community's practices.* Through interaction among members of a community of learners individuals are able to achieve the social and communicative goals of the larger community.

- *Learning requires taking on successively more complex roles and identities.* In the context of language learning, or any kind of learning, learners assume successively more complex roles and participation opportunities and in so doing, acquire the skills and knowledge needed to participate in a wide variety of communicative activities.

- *Learners share responsibility for learning.* Authority and control over the processes and content of what is to be learned do not rest with the teacher. Instead, they are shared with learners, thus enabling the learners to enhance their investment in the activities of the community.

- *The teacher plays an essential role.* Teachers' actions as coach, mentor, instructor and supporter in the activities they undertake with learners serve to assist learners in appropriating the knowledge, skills and meanings needed for full participation in their classroom activities. Teacher actions also function to help learners to stand back from and become fully aware of the knowledge and skills they are developing so that they may act responsibly and creatively in achieving their goals.

- *The affective is integrated with the cognitive.* In addition to building meaningful and challenging academic learning environments, teachers and learners work to develop strong interpersonal connections, and feelings of solidarity and affiliation among the members of their classroom communities.

- *Knowledge and skill building are intrinsically tied to a community's instructional activities.* Classroom activities are structured around specific patterns of social interaction where members, in collaboration with each other, have opportunities to observe, reflect on, and practice the means and modes by which socially accepted and valued communicative events and activities are accomplished.

Classrooms as communities of inquiry

The concept of **communities of inquiry** draws on the larger conceptual framework of *communities of learners*. In such communities, inquiry is viewed not as a particular instructional method, undertaken occasionally for particular kinds of projects. It is, instead, the fundamental principle around which curriculum and instruction are organised. A key premise of inquiry-based learning communities holds that learning takes place in the process of exploring with others answers to questions that arise from shared experiences. The central functions of teaching are to facilitate the organisation of collaborative activities for the exploration of answers to the questions and to guide students' participation in them. Related terms for this approach include **dialogic inquiry** (e.g. Wells, 1999) and **dialogic teaching** (e.g. Alexander, 2008).

Quote 5.2 **On dialogic inquiry**

A vision of education derived from sociocultural theory . . . proposes a dialogic conceptualization of learning-and-teaching in which knowledge is *co-constructed* by teacher and students together as they engage in *joint activities*, which are negotiated rather than imposed . . . the primary object of education is growth in understanding . . . through the appropriation and exploitation of the culture's resources as tools for engaging in inquiries which are of both individual and social signification, and which have implications for action beyond the classroom.

Wells (1999: 227, emphasis in the original)

Concept 5.3   **Key features of communities of inquiry**

- The curriculum is organised around questions for investigation that are purposeful, practical and relevant to the members of the community; the goal is not to find the right answers but instead to seek appropriate resolutions to questions.

- Learning is collaborative, dialogic and co-constructed; teachers and learners together engage in learning activities.

- The interaction occurring between teachers and students and among students is the primary means for co-constructing knowledge; in the process, teachers and students build on each others' ideas and link them into reasoned strands of thinking focused on addressing the questions.

- Classroom interactions are inclusive, fair, respectful, challenging and supportive.

In addition to its transforming traditional pedagogy in K–12 schooling contexts, the communities of inquiry framework for online and blended learning contexts in higher education has been developed by a research team in Canada (see Garrison *et al.*, 2010, for an historical account of its development and current applications). It has also been used to reconceptualise pedagogy in university-level courses (Archer, 2010) and in professional development programmes for teachers (e.g. Curry, 2008; Melville and Bartley, 2010).

5.4.2 Cooperative learning practices

A second pedagogical approach concerned with the language and culture of the classroom is **cooperative learning**. Cooperative learning refers to various methods and activities for organising classroom instruction. Unlike an approach based on the community of learners concept, which involves a full transformation of education programmes, this approach is better viewed as a particular instructional strategy for fostering cooperation among learners to accomplish shared goals in supportive learning environments.

Originally based on Allport's (1954) contact theory of intergroup relations, cooperative learning was first developed as a means of helping students from different social and cultural backgrounds to develop interpersonal relationships in schools. According to Allport's theory, the kinds of contacts that occur between individuals from different social groups shape the kinds of social relationships they develop. The more the purpose of the contact is cooperative, built on common goals and officially supported by the larger institution that is bringing the individuals together, the more likely that the individuals will view each other positively and work towards building mutually beneficial relationships.

Early research on cooperative learning methods in classrooms (e.g. Weigel *et al.*, 1975; Sharan, 1980, 1984) revealed the value of such methods for enhancing the building of relationships between socially and culturally diverse learners. More recent research (e.g. Gillies, 2008; Webb and Mastergeorge, 2003) has revealed its effectiveness for enhancing academic performance, fostering self-esteem and increasing motivation for learning in addition to promoting the development of prosocial interpersonal relationships among learners from different linguistic, cultural, ethnic and socioeconomic backgrounds. According to a recent review of research on cooperative learning (Johnson and Johnson, 2009), because of its great successes in promoting academic and social development, it has become one of the dominant instructional practices around the world, utilised in schools, universities and adult training programmes in every subject area.

Components of cooperative learning practices

The primary aim of cooperative learning practices is to develop learning opportunities that are based on cooperation and mutual respect. According to Johnson and his colleagues (Johnson and Johnson, 1997, 2002, 2009; Johnson *et al.*, 2008) their essential components include the following:

- *Small, heterogeneous teams.* Groups are usually composed of four or five members who represent different social identities in terms of ability level, gender, social class, and linguistic and cultural backgrounds. The value of heterogeneous grouping is based on the premise that each individual brings different abilities and perspectives to a task, and that these differences constitute a valuable resource for learning.

- *Positive interdependence.* Positive interdependence involves designing instructional tasks so that each group member's efforts are required for group success and each group member has a unique contribution to make to the joint effort. There are three ways to structure positive interdependence: *interdependent goals*, where students share a group goal of producing a project, or learning the assigned material; *interdependent reward*, where each group member receives the same reward when the group achieves its goals; and *interdependent resources*, where each group member has only a portion of the resources but it must be combined with the other members' resources to complete the task and enable the group to achieve its goals.

- *Individual and group accountability.* Learners are held accountable at two levels in their cooperative tasks. The group as a whole is accountable for achieving the task's goals. In addition, each individual member of the group is accountable for contributing his or her share of the work.

- *Facilitative interaction.* Students are encouraged to share resources and to support each other's efforts in accomplishing the group's goals. Such supportive behaviours include explaining to each other how to solve problems, exchanging needed resources, providing effective assistance, and building on each other's contributions.

- *Interpersonal and small group skills.* In addition to needing skills to assist each other in completing task work, learners need strong interpersonal and social skills, which include skills for conflict management, consensual decision-making and trust-building. It is assumed here that, like task-based skills, these skills are essential to learning and need to be taught to learners.

Successful incorporation of cooperative learning activities into classrooms entails the following steps (Johnson and Johnson, 2009):

- Deciding on the objectives of the activity, the size of the groups, and materials needed to complete the activity;

- Setting out clear expectations for students, including the criteria for success and expected social skills;
- Systematically monitoring the group as it works to complete the activity, intervening when necessary to assist students;
- Evaluating students' performances and helping them to reflect on their effectiveness as a group.

It is worth reiterating that many of the premises on which cooperative learning practices are based are similar to those underlying the concept of community of learners. Where they vary is in terms of scope. Literature on cooperative learning methods (reviewed above) often discuss them as particular types of group-based activities, among other kinds that can be incorporated into classrooms without making major changes to the curriculum.

Example 5.4 Two methods of cooperative learning

A   Student Team Learning (STL)
Originally developed by Robert Slavin (1980, 1989/1990, 1995) at Johns Hopkins University, *Student Team Learning* emphasises individual account-ability, team goals and team success. It works most effectively when learning objectives are well-defined. Two forms of SLT adaptable to most ages and levels are:

1 *STAD: Student teams-achievement divisions.* Students are assigned to teams of four or five, mixed by ability, ethnicity and gender. The teacher presents a lesson and the teams work together to ensure that all members have mastered the material. Students are tested individually on the lesson. Teams are awarded points based on how well each member meets or exceeds his or her own past performances.

2 *Teams–Games–Tournaments (TCT).* Similar to STAD but instead of quizzes and tests, students play academic games with members of other teams to contribute points to the team score. Cross-team players are at the same ability levels (low achievers compete with low achievers, and so on) to ensure that each has an equal opportunity for success. Team-mates can help each other to prepare for the games.

B   Jigsaw
Originally designed by Elliot Aronson and his colleagues (Aronson and Yates, 1983; Aronson and Patnoe, 1997), this technique emphasises group cooper-ation and individual accountability. The technique is based on the premise that giving each student of the group an essential role in the activity encourages active engagement with the task, facilitates interaction among all students in

the class, and leads them to value each other as contributors to the achieve-ment of their common goal. Steps for implementing a jigsaw activity are as follows:

- Assign students to small groups of five or six members. Ideally, the groups should be mixed in terms of gender, ethnicity, and ability.
- Divide the academic material into five or six segments (depending on the number of students in each group) and assign each member of each team a section of the material to read. These are the jigsaw groups.
- Form 'expert groups' comprised of members from the different jigsaw teams who have studied the same sections. Give them time to discuss the information and rehearse the presentations they will make to their jigsaw groups.
- Once students feel prepared, bring them together with their jigsaw team and have each member take turns presenting their segment of material to their team-mates. Encourage the team-mates to ask questions of clarification where appropriate.
- Test the students on the material.

5.5 Summary

As we have discussed in this chapter, a concern of research on teaching and learning in applied linguistics has been with investigating the worlds of classrooms as authentic communities, comprised of particular communi-cative activities and events that socialise learners into culturally specific ways of knowing, thinking and valuing their communities, themselves, and each other as participants in those communities. In addition to making visible the worlds within classrooms, some studies have made visible the influences that the larger social, historical and political forces outside the classrooms exert on what takes place within them, including the kinds of identities participants assume and the activities and resources that are made available to them for appropriation.

Other studies have looked more closely within classroom communities to uncover the particular means by which individuals become socialised into their worlds *through* language. Findings have shown the consequential role that teachers play in structuring and managing the particular kinds of worlds into which learners are socialised. In the learning environments that they design, teachers make relevant to the learners what they are to learn and how they are to learn it. They also make relevant their own assumptions about the value of what they are learning, and of the routes learners take in the process.

Pedagogical approaches that take a sociocultural view of classrooms and learning have sought to create particular kinds of learning communities in the classroom. These are characterised by an atmosphere of cooperation, shared trust and mutual respect, built on shared goals, and realised through jointly constructed activities. Language is viewed as especially significant in these communities since the way in which language is used in the classroom creates both the shape and content of the language that learners learn. To state another way, language is not just a means by which information is conveyed. It is also, and more significantly, the quintessential sociocognitive tool by which learners move through, respond to, and make sense of their worlds.

While the approaches described in this chapter vary in scope, they have had increasing success in transforming classrooms. Cooperative learning methods, for example, have been shown to be effective in various kinds of classrooms, including those with linguistically and culturally diverse learners. The concepts of communities of learners and communities of enquiry are making an impact as well on the transformation of classroom environments.

Where do we go from here? Given the intrinsic link between teaching and learning, we still know very little of the various shapes that communities of learners take in social contexts outside of the classroom such as the workplace and other professional institutions, and in virtual, electronically mediated, transregional and transnational sites. To understand these worlds more fully, we need investigations identifying the specific social, historical and political contexts within which the various communities of learners are nested, and the communicative events, activities and ever-emerging multimodal technologies of communication giving shape to these learning communities.

Also needed are additional investigations that examine the varied paths of learning created by members' participation in their communities, the different ways that individual learners position themselves relative to the activities and the processes by which they are being socialised into them, and the varied consequences – in terms of identity and ideological development in addition to communicative development – that arise from these actions. Finally, there is the need to connect findings from these studies to efforts to address the challenges that are revealed. As we move forward, a significant hallmark of effective research on both formal and informal sites of learning will be for researchers to work in close collaboration with educators, parents, policy makers, professional organisations and other stakeholders to nurture effectual communities of learners that are indigenous to their particular social contexts and in ways that are considered to be appropriate to their specific social, cultural, communicative, professional and other needs.

Further reading

Gillies, R. M. (2007) *Cooperative Learning: Integrating Theory and Practice*, Thousand Oaks, CA: Sage. This text provides a detailed overview of the usefulness of cooperative learning activities and strategies for teachers to promote student involvement and learning in small groups. Included are exercises that demonstrate how teachers can create cooperative learning activities for learners across various levels and of diverse abilities.

Hall, J. K., Vitanova, G. and Marchenkova, L. (eds) (2005) *Dialogue with Bakhtin on Second and Foreign Language Learning: New Perspectives*, Mahwah, NJ: Lawrence Erlbaum. Written by scholars from around the world, the 11 chapters in this volume draw on some of Bakhtin's more significant concepts, such as *dialogue, heteroglossia, voice,* and *addressivity* to examine real-world contexts of language learning. The chapters are arranged in two parts. Chapters in the first section report on investigations into specific contexts of language learning and teaching. Chapters in the second part discuss the broader implications for theory and practice in second and foreign language learning.

Hughes, J., Jewson, J. and Unwin, L. (eds) (2007) *Communities of Practice: Critical Perspectives*, London: Routledge. The chapters in this edited volume provide a critical introduction to the theoretical tenets of the concept of communities of practice and use the concept to examine the relation between learning and identity among, for example, male and female workers, professionals and managers, and low-skilled and high-skilled workers in a diverse range of managerial and professional contexts.

Mercer, N. and Littleton, K. (2007) *Dialogue and the Development of Children's Thinking: A Sociocultural Approach*, London: Routledge. Drawing on sociocultural theory, the text explores the importance of teacher–student dialogue to students' intellectual development. The authors draw on findings from their research to show how teachers and students collectively construct knowledge and how such actions give shape to the learners' academic progress.

Rex, L. A. and Schiller, L. (2009) *Using Discourse Analysis to Improve Classroom Interaction*, New York: Routledge. The authors offer a primer on using the tools of discourse analysis to understand the fundamental components of classroom interaction. Readers are guided through exercises that help them to increase their awareness of the role that interaction plays in learning, with the ultimate goal of improving their teaching.

Language and culture as curricular content

This chapter:

- examines how language and culture are treated as curricular content in classrooms based on a sociocultural perspective;
- describes some pedagogical approaches that incorporate current understandings of language and culture into their curricular and instructional designs;
- offers a list of additional readings on the topics covered in this chapter.

6.1   Introduction

Several popular practices for teaching language and culture in applied linguistics have evolved from traditional perspectives on language and learning. These include the Natural Approach (Krashen and Terrell, 1983), developed in the early 1980s as an extension of Chomsky's linguistic theory of language, and cognitive approaches such as focus-on-form instruction (e.g. Doughty and Williams, 1998) and TBLT (task-based language teaching) (e.g. Ellis, 2003; Samuda and Bygate, 2008).

While these approaches differ in terms of, for example, the role that interaction is thought to play in language learning and the degree and kind of instructional intervention they call for, they are similar in that they all give primacy to linguistic structures in forming the curricular content of language classrooms. Moreover, they agree that even though the process of acquiring linguistic structures is influenced primarily by learners' internal grammar, there is a role for instruction. Specifically, they agree that instruction should create opportunities in the classroom that facilitate learners' abilities to make use of general cognitive processing capacities to speed up the rate at which learners gain control of the linguistic forms in an otherwise naturally occurring, internally driven process.

Understandings of language and culture embodied in a sociocultural perspective are quite different from those embodied in more traditional perspectives and these differences have given rise to different conceptual-isations of curricular content in language classrooms. The purpose of this chapter is to present an overview of how language and culture as content are dealt with from a sociocultural perspective, to discuss concerns with defining norms and standards for learning raised by this perspective, and to consider pedagogical approaches that incorporate current understandings of language, culture and learning into their curricular and instructional designs.

6.2   Defining knowledge of language and culture

6.2.1   Communicative competence

An early attempt in applied linguistics to define the content of language classrooms from a sociocultural perspective for the purposes of curriculum design is Canale and Swain's framework of **communicative competence**, proposed in 1980. The concept of communicative competence was first made popular by Dell Hymes (cf. Chapter 1) in the mid-1960s as an alternative to the concept of linguistic competence, as first proposed by Chomsky (1965, 1966). According to Chomsky's theory of language, individuals are born with a universal grammar, a mental blueprint for processing and generating language. Presumed to be a fixed property of mind, the capacity for language is defined as sets of principles and conditions from which the grammatical rules for language systems are derived. Chomsky proposed the concept of linguistic competence to capture those sets of principles, conditions and rules for generating the structural components of a language, which any 'speaker of a language knows implicitly' (1966: 9).

For Hymes, who considered social function to be the source of linguistic form, Chomsky's definition of language knowledge was inadequate in that it could not account for the knowledge and skills that individuals must have to understand and produce utterances appropriate to the particular cultural contexts in which they occur. Drawing on rich ethnographic data on lan-guage use from a variety of social groups, Hymes called for a significantly different understanding of competence that included the knowledge and ability to use linguistic resources in communicative contexts constitutive of the different groups and communities of which individuals are members.

He coined the term 'communicative competence' to refer to these cap-acities and defined it in terms of four dimensions. The first, **systemic**

potential, involves knowledge and use of language that is formally possible. The second dimension is **appropriateness**, which is knowledge of and ability to use language that is 'adequate, happy, successful in relation to a context' (Widdowson, 2007: 210). The third dimension, **probability**, refers to knowledge and use of language that actually occurs. So, in addition to knowledge of what can be possible grammatically, communicative competence entails knowing what is likely to occur. The last dimension, **feasibility**, refers to the extent to which something is practical. An utterance that has several relative clauses may be grammatical but not very feasible. Of particular importance is the fact that, for Hymes, the development of communicative competence was defined in terms of accessibility rather than considered to be an innate trait.

Quote 6.1 On the link between knowledge and ability in communicative competence

Knowledge also is to be understood as subtending all four parameters of communication just noted. There is knowledge of each. Ability for use also may relate to all four parameters. Certainly, it may be the case that individuals differ with regard to ability to use knowledge of each: to interpret, differentiate, etc. The specification of ability for use as part of competence allows for the role of non-cognitive factors, such as motivations, as partly determining competence.

Hymes (1972b: 282–283)

Canale and Swain (1980) were among the first in applied linguistics to use Hymes's notion of communicative competence to design a framework for second and foreign language curriculum and evaluation. Their initial model of communicative competence contained three components: **grammatical**, which included knowledge of lexical items and rules of morphology, syntax, semantics and phonology; **sociolinguistic**, which included knowledge of the rules of language use; and **strategic**, which included knowledge of strategies to compensate for breakdowns in communication.

Acknowledging that their initial model was more concerned with oral language use, Canale (1982) added a fourth component, **discourse competence**, which dealt with the knowledge needed to participate in literacy activities. According to Canale and Swain, choices for what to include in a curriculum for language classrooms were to be based on an analysis of the specific features of each of the four components comprising those communicative activities in which learners of additional languages were interested in becoming competent.

While others in the field (e.g. Bachman, 1990; Bachman and Palmer, 1996) have presented similar constructs, they have been used mainly for the design of language tests. Up until the mid-1990s, the Canale and Swain model remained the principal framework in discussions on curricula for language classrooms. In 1995, Celce-Murcia, Dornyei and Thurrell proposed four changes to the model: they added **sociocultural competence** as a fifth component; they changed sociolinguistic competence to **sociocultural competence** to include the cultural knowledge to use and interpret language use appropriately; they changed grammatical competence to **linguistic competence** to encompass the sound system and the lexicon in addition to morphology and syntax; and they explained the interrelatedness of the concept's five components.

6.2.2   Interactional competence

As sociocultural perspectives became more firmly planted in the field, limitations of the concept of communicative competence were becoming visible. Critics (e.g. Young, 2000; Lüdi, 2006; McNamara and Roever, 2006) noted, for example, that despite their sociocultural origins, the components were often treated as static, innate properties of individuals, thereby rendering invisible their social foundations. They also noted that when framing oral activities, discussions of the components were focused on competence for speaking and not on competence for interaction. In a prescient essay Kramsch (1986) critiqued the proficiency guidelines of the American Council on the Teaching of Foreign Languages (ACTFL), a US-based organisation dedicated to foreign language teaching and learning, claiming that they emphasised accuracy over other skills and thus took an 'oversimplified view on human interactions' (p. 367). She ended by proposing the concept of **interactional competence** to capture the skills and knowledge needed for successful interaction.

By the 1990s elaborations and investigations of the concept were on the rise (e.g. Hall, 1993b, 1995, 1999; Young, 2000). The incorporation of conversation analysis and its methods by applied linguists into their studies of communicative activities (cf. Chapter 1) helped to elaborate and further refine the concept of interactional competence and it has since informed much research on the competences involved in formal and informal contexts of learning. Nguyen (2004, 2006), for example, investigated changes in the interactional competences of two pharmacy students over the course of their participation in a pharmacy internship. Similarly, Rine (2009) used the concept to investigate changes in the interactional competences of an international teaching assistant through his participation in a professional development course. It has also informed pedagogy in formal school contexts (e.g. Wong, 2002; Wong and Waring, 2010) and professional development in settings such as the health care and business fields (e.g. Heritage and Maynard, 2006; Nielsen, 2009).

> **Quote 6.2** Definition of interactional competence
>
> Interactional competence includes 'knowledge of culture-specific communicative events or activity types and their typical goals and trajectories of actions by which the goals are realized. Also included is knowledge of the prosodic, linguistic, interactional and other verbal and nonverbal tools conventionally used to infer meanings of turns and actions, to construct them so that they are interpreted by others in ways that they are intended to be, and to anticipate and produce larger action sequence configurations.
>
> Hall (2009: 3)

6.2.3   Communicative competence revisited

In light of the burgeoning research on interactional competence and further advancements in research on language development (cf. Chapter 3), in 2007, Celce-Murcia revised the 1995 model of communicative competence. The current version is depicted in Figure 6.1. It includes six interrelated

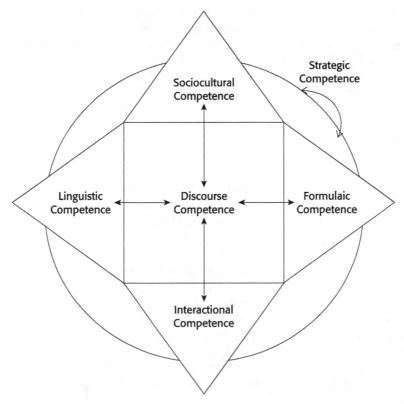

Figure 6.1   *Model of communicative competence* (Celce-Murcia, 2007: 45)

dimensions of communicative competence: sociocultural, discourse, linguistic, formulaic, interactional and strategic.

Retained in this model are sociocultural competence, discourse competence and linguistic competence. Added as a counterbalance to linguistic competence is the fourth component, **formulaic competence**. Defined as 'prefabricated chunks of language that speakers use heavily in everyday interactions' (Celce-Murcia, 2007: 47), this component includes knowledge of fixed phrases and various types of collocations, idioms and lexical frames. Examples in English include fixed phrases such as 'of course' and 'all of a sudden'; collocations such as 'spend money' (verb-noun) and 'forever young' (adverb-adjective), and lexical frames such as 'see you (tomorrow, later, etc.).

Another added component is **interactional competence**. It consists of three related components: actional competence, which is knowledge of how to perform speech acts and speech act sets; conversational competence, which includes how to open and close conversations, how to establish and change topics, and so on; and non-verbal/paralinguistic competence, which includes knowledge of kinesics, proxemics, haptics and non-linguistic resources such as pausing, silence and so on. Weaving through these five components is strategic competence, which was in the earlier model, but here is expanded to include two types of strategies: learning strategies and communication strategies. Learning strategies comprise the cognitive, meta-cognitive and memory-related behaviours that individuals use to enhance their own learning. Communication strategies include the knowledge and skills to resolve communicative difficulties and enhance communicative effectiveness.

The notion of communicative competence helps us to see that language use involves not just knowledge of and ability to use language forms. It also involves knowledge and ability to use language in ways that are, to use Hymes's terms, socially appropriate, feasible and contextually called for. The many attempts to conceptualise the various socially constituted dimensions of our communicative resources with this concept in mind have helped in the design of curricula for language classrooms by providing blueprints for identifying the substance of the communicative plans that more experienced participants use to guide their participation in activities and events. As such, they have provided some basis for making principled decisions about the curricular content of language classrooms.

6.2.4 Intercultural communicative competence

Alongside attempts to create an adequate framework for conceptualising the knowledge, skills and abilities that are tied to our communicative actions is the work on **intercultural communicative competence** (ICC). Made popular by Byram (1997) and his colleagues (Byram and Zarate, 1997; Byram and Fleming, 1998), this concept was developed as an expansion of communicative competence in response to what Byram argued was the need to consider the competence that learners of additional languages develop to be qualitatively different from the competence that members develop as native speakers of social groups and communities. Learners of other languages, he argued, should be treated not as aspiring native speakers but as developing intercultural communicators.

To capture the knowledge and skills that users of more than one language develop, Byram (1997, 2008) proposed the concept of intercultural communicative competence. He defined it as the knowledge, skills, and attitudes necessary to participate in activities where the target language is the primary communicative code and in situations where it is the common code for those with different preferred languages. Specific components of ICC include the following, grouped into five dimensions:

- *Savoir-être*: general attitudinal dispositions. These include a curiosity with and openness to difference, a readiness to suspend disbelief and judgement with respect to others' meanings, beliefs and behaviours, and a willingness to understand and be sensitive to the perspectives of others;

- *Savoirs*: knowledge of relevant sociocultural groups and their significant communicative practices and products;

- *Savoir-comprendre*: skills of identification, interpretation and analysis of patterns, perspectives and potential sources of miscommunication and incompatibilities. Also included are skills for negotiating agreement in places of conflict and acceptance of differences and incompatibilities;

- *Savoir-apprendre*: skills to communicate with others in conventional or expected ways at the levels of both the individual and group. Also included is the ability to sort through, reflect on and use one's understanding of the differences and similarities across individuals and across groups to form open, flexible communicative plans and perspectives;

- *Savoir s'engager*: skills to evaluate critically from 'a rational and explicit standpoint' (Byram, 1997: 54) one's own perspectives, practices and products and those of other sociocultural groups.

Referring to this last component as **trans-cultural competence**, Lussier (2007) expands its parameters to include 'the integration of new values, the respect of other values and the valorization of otherness which derives from the coexistence of different ethnic groups and cultures evolving in a same society or in distinct societies while advocating the enrichment of identity of each culture in contact' (p. 324).

A pedagogy based on ICC focuses on developing in learners 'the capability to exchange meaning in communication with people across languages and cultures in a way that foregrounds their positioning in the language and culture that they are learning' (Scarino, 2010: 325). Ultimately, it leads to the development of the intercultural citizen, that is, 'a social agent active in a multicultural society, whether "national–state" or international polity' (Byram, 2010: 320).

Quote 6.3 Goals of an intercultural orientation to language teaching

An *intercultural* orientation to teaching languages seeks the transformation of students' identities in the act of learning. This is achieved on the part of students through a constant referencing of the language being learned with their own language(s) and culture(s). In so doing, students decenter from their linguistic and cultural world to consider their own situatedness from the perspective of another. They learn to constantly move between their linguistic and cultural world and that of the users of the target language. In this process, they come to understand culture not only as information about diverse people and their practices but also, and most importantly, as the contextual framework that people use to exchange meaning in communication with others and through which they understand their social world.

Scarino (2010: 324)

Like its companion concept, communicative competence, the concept of intercultural communicative competence affords course designers a principled basis for making decisions about what to include in a curriculum. In fact, its components, and those of communicative competence, are in the Common European Framework of Reference for Languages (CEFR; Council of Europe, 2001). The CEFR is a document that describes the performance and assessment standards for promoting plurilingualism as a goal of foreign and second language programmes across Europe. According to the report, plurilingualism 'emphasizes the fact that an individual person's experience of language in its cultural contexts expands from the language of the home to that of society at large and then to languages of other peoples (whether learnt at school or college, or by direct experience)' (*ibid.*, p. 4).

6.2.5   Learning outcomes: Where are we going?

It is generally agreed that the goal of language learning from a sociocultural perspective is for learners to add alternative knowledge, skills and abilities for understanding and participating in a wide range of intellectual and practical activities to their already established repertoires of sense-making knowledge and abilities. This is to enable learners to broaden their communicative experiences, their worldviews, and their understandings of the active, creative roles they as responsible intercultural citizens play in constructing these worlds.

While the concepts of communicative competence and intercultural communicative competence have provided the field with useful frameworks with which to consider the various dimensions of knowledge, skills and abilities embodied in our sociocultural worlds, they are incomplete in that they leave open the question of whose sociocultural worlds learners are to be exposed to. A view of learning as socialisation into particular sociocultural worlds with sanctioned tools and signs for mediating participation in various communicative activities constitutive of these worlds implies a commitment, howsoever tacit, to some outcome. While the two concepts discussed above afford us a framework for understanding what *could* be involved, they do not address the issue of whose communicative worlds and, more specifically, whose sociocultural tools and whose ways of using the tools learners are to be socialised into. It has been suggested that learners' individual goals for learning languages be balanced with educational goals embodied in the learners' sociocultural worlds (cf. Hall, 2002; Widdowson, 2003, 2007). While on one level this suggestion seems practical, we are still left with having to decide on not only the specific worlds we wish to draw on for curricular content but also the norms by which learning outcomes are to be assessed. For example, let's say we decide that one of the goals of learning another language is to be able to use it in contexts considered significant to users of the target language. Given the variety of groups that speak the languages we typically teach in language classrooms, the cultural, linguistic and other differences that exist across these groups, and across social identities within language groups, we are still left with the question of *whose contexts*. For learners of English, for example, are the contexts those of groups from the United States? From Australia? From India? Likewise, for learners of Spanish, are the contexts we bring to the classroom those of groups from Spain? From Mexico? From the Dominican Republic? Do these contexts consist primarily of adults? Of adolescents? Are they typical of affluent communities? Of middle-class communities? Are these communities linguistically and culturally homogeneous or are they transnational, ethno-culturally and linguistically diverse communities?

Even if we cannot articulate the kinds of sociocultural contexts and their resources we would like to make part of the curricular content in our language classrooms, the textbooks and materials we use in our classrooms often do (cf. Cook, 1999; Wallace, 2006). A close inspection of them reveals that what we are making available to learners in terms of communicative options is at best incomplete. Perhaps, as Widdowson (1998) suggests, rather than attempt to bring unfamiliar worlds to the classroom, we should 'create a [classroom] community with its own cultural reality, with its own conventions of what is feasible and appropriate; conventions which are contrived, but which carry conviction' (p. 331). Putting aside the issue of *what* we decide to include in our curriculum, as research on learning shows

(National Research Council, 1999), such decisions need to be made. For having a clear understanding of what learners are to learn and being able to articulate the goals to learners provides them with a clear sense of where they are going and thus can help them to share in the responsibility for getting there.

Quote 6.4 On curricular considerations for language classrooms

What students need to have acquired at the end of their course, it seems to me, is a knowledge of the language which will provide them with a capability for further learning. This has essentially to be a knowledge of the possible. ... This need not be, indeed cannot be comprehensive: the pedagogic task is to identify what features of the possible have the most potential for subsequent realization. In other words specifying objectives is a matter of investment in what seems likely to yield the best returns. ... To think of objectives in terms of investment, rather than rehearsal, is to recognize that the end of a course of teaching does not by any means constitute the end of learning, but is only a stage in its development. The purpose of the course is to give momentum and direction, to establish vectors, so to speak, for sub-sequent learning, and thus to provide bearings whereby learners can make sense and learn from their own linguistic experience.

Widdowson (2003: 115)

6.3   Redesigning curriculum and instruction

Concerns with the need to define curricular content and learning outcomes notwithstanding, two general approaches to teaching language and culture from a sociocultural perspective have emerged in the field of applied linguistics. While their general goals are similar, they differ slightly in terms of the kinds of instructional environments they seek to create in their classrooms. The first approach, **critical pedagogy**, is more learner-centred in that it uses the worlds of the learners as the primary basis for designing curriculum and instructional activities with the goal to develop in learners the critical skills needed to explore their and others' beliefs and understandings of their worlds. A second approach combines a learner-centred focus with a knowledge-centred focus in that it seeks to design a learning environment that not only helps learners to understand and live within their own worlds, but is also concerned with helping students to acquire the knowledge, skills and abilities they need to expand their communicative horizons, and move into other worlds.

6.3.1   Critical pedagogy

Critical pedagogy (CP) is a general approach to language education that draws on the work of Brazilian educator Paulo Freire (1972, 1973). Freire developed an alternative model of education as a response to what he perceived to be shortcomings in the more traditional model. The more traditional model, he argued, is based on an understanding of learning as a process of transmitting or depositing neutral, value-free and universally applicable information into the empty heads of learners. For their part, learners are thought to be little more than passive and uncritical receptors of the deposited information. Their only role is to store the information for use at a later date. In such a view of pedagogy, Freire argued, social, cultural, political and historical concerns are kept invisible, the *status quo* is maintained, and learners continue to think they are powerless, unable to make a difference in their worlds.

In response to these shortcomings, Freire developed an approach in which the overall aim is to help learners to develop their own voices in response to their local conditions and circumstances, and in so doing, transform their lives in socially meaningful ways. Building on these insights, and keeping within a sociocultural perspective on learning, current formulations of CP consider learning to be a socially situated, collaborative process of transformation whereby teachers and students, together, build a common base of knowledge, frameworks of understanding and a shared system of meanings, values and beliefs for purposes of mutual growth.

While CP draws on similar concepts and ideas as other sociocultural approaches presented in earlier chapters, three features distinguish it from other methods. First, CP does not locate curricular issues and concerns in differences between learners' home and school cultures. Nor does it begin with a predetermined, content-based curriculum. Rather, it locates the focus of learning in a nexus of political, social, and economic conditions defining the communities within which learners live. This concern with learners' lives both in and out of the classroom is translated into a curriculum that is organised around experiences, needs and challenges that learners themselves have identified as central to their lives. Thus, it views teaching and learning as a 'dynamic process of constructing knowledge with learners, not as a set course to transmit a body of "hard" knowledge' (Byram and Feng, 2004: 158).

Also referred to as **participatory pedagogy**, CP aims to create environments in the classroom that assist learners in appropriating the knowledge and skills needed for full participation in their larger social worlds outside the classroom. Classroom activities are structured in such a way as to provide learners with opportunities to explore concerns and issues that are of utmost important to them, to raise their awareness of the social, cultural and political inequities manifested in their experiences, and to work to transform them by articulating their own directions for living. In addition to helping learners to identify their concerns and transform them into curricular content, the role of the teacher is to ensure a safe environment in which learners feel comfortable and validated as they raise questions and consider alternatives.

A second distinguishing feature of CP is its focus on informed action as a central aim of learning. In other words, language learning is not considered to be about just developing a deeper understanding of one's lived experiences. It is also about knowing how to take action to make a difference in one's world. Thus, the tools and resources arising from their class discussions afford learners the means to engage in a 'language of critique' and a 'language of possibility'. In this way, language learning becomes not an end in itself but a tool for critical analysis and transformation of the social conditions limiting learners' full participation in their lives inside and outside school (cf. Kubota, 2004).

A final feature is its emphasis on developing mutual respect and trust, and shared norms for participating in their class discussions and other activities. By forming social bonds with the members of their classroom communities, learners build 'social capital', defined as networks of social relationships that can help foster the development of interpersonal, academic and career opportunities beyond the classroom and learners' own social groups (Alfred, 2010).

Problem-posing approach

One type of CP commonly found in many adult immigrant community-based language programmes is the **problem-posing approach**. This approach uses learners' experiences, and in particular, the problems or complex concerns or challenges they face in their communities outside the classroom as its curricular focus. Its aim is to help to make visible the social, political and cultural underpinnings of their learners' experiences, to raise learners' their awareness of these links, and to help them to acquire the specific communicative skills and knowledge necessary for engaging with the social forces restricting their lives and taking action in ways that they feel will be beneficial.

Learners' experiences are typically brought to the classroom using such media as pictures, comics, short stories, songs, and dramas to generate discussion centered on the problem depicted in the materials. Wallerstein (1983) points out that in order to represent these experiences adequately and meaningfully in the classroom, it is essential that teachers be intimately connected with the lives of their students outside of the classroom and have some shared understandings of these experiences and the realities the students face. It may also mean bringing the classroom to the learners, locating it in safe sites in their communities, rather than expecting learners to come to the classroom (cf. Auerbach, 2000).

To help to generate discussion, the teacher typically asks a series of open-ended questions about the situation depicted in the materials. The aim of the questions is to encourage students to define the real-life problem, share their experiences and elaborate on what they see. The objective is not to generate a particular solution but to explore the complexities of the issue, and to identify actions that respond constructively to the issue. The particular communicative resources that form the content of class lessons evolve from these conversations and identified actions, and thus provide learners with personally meaningful purposes for their development. In integrating learning of communicative skills and knowledge with the particular social activities of reflection and analysis, they become appropriated by learners as new tools for implementing real change in their lives.

Concept 6.1   **Basic components of a problem-posing approach**

This approach consists of the following three components:

1 *Listening*: Through listening to and observing students in and out of class, the teacher defines and codifies student concerns for use in structured language learning and dialogue.

2 *Dialogue*: Using the codified concerns as springboards, the teacher and students engage in dialogue about the concerns or issues, and ways to view and respond to them.

3 *Action*: The discussions move students to use what they have learned to take action outside the classroom.

Wallerstein (1983)

Alternative forms of a problem-posing approach include **participatory action research** (e.g. Cammarota and Romero, 2009) and **critical performative pedagogy** (e.g. Louis, 2005). The first organises curricula around problems arising from students' social contexts including schools, neighbourhoods and workplaces, that in some way constrain their opportunities for self-determination. These problems become the focus of collaborative investigation into the identified problems to gather additional information that is then used by the learners to take action. The second is based on Boal's Theatre of the Oppressed (Boal, 1995) and uses performance as a way for learners to imagine and explore alternative means for transforming the conditions of their lives. In its various instantiations, CP is considered to be at one and the same time, a 'pedagogy of reflection, a pedagogy of dissent, a pedagogy of dialogue, a pedagogy of empowerment, a pedagogy of action and a pedagogy of hope' (McLaren, 1995: 34).

It should be noted that not all learners embrace CP. Some prefer a seemingly more neutral approach, one that stays away from rather than embraces what some might consider to be controversial matters. Advocates point out that the aim of CP is not to lay out a particular agenda or point of view for learners to follow. Rather, it is to provide them with opportunities to engage with critical issues, and to voice their concerns. Thus, if learners are resistant, teachers need to make official space for their resistances, for once students name their resistances they can become objects of collaborative reflection and dialogue (cf. Auerbach, 2000). In other words, the resistances themselves can become the basis for curricular development by affording learners the chance to talk about their needs and learning strategies and, more generally, to analyse social and pedagogical issues that are of great importance to them.

6.3.2   Project-based learning

Project-based learning (PBL) is an approach that is both learner- and knowledge-centred. It organises learning around extended tasks or projects that seek to address a challenging question or problem. In formal language programmes, projects are typically organised around a topic from an academic content area such as history, health, physical science and so on. In community and professional programmes, projects are organised around issues or problems identified as significant to the interested parties. Basic phases of PBL include selecting a topic or theme, deciding on the final product, planning and implementing procedures for completing it, and sharing the outcome, usually to a wider audience than just members of the learning group.

While much of the project work is done by learners, teachers play an important role in facilitating the process of gathering and processing information by providing them with the linguistic and other resources they need to complete project tasks, giving advice when needed, and helping learners to reflect on what they are learning as they complete the project. What distinguishes PBL from other project work is that PBL is the primary organiser of curriculum and instruction; the projects define both the curricular matter and the means by which it is accessed and learned. Project work, on the other hand, is inserted into instruction as one means to present or illustrate curricular topics or concepts.

According to Stoller (2006), students derive several benefits from their participation in PBL, including increased investment in the topic, improved skills for working in small groups, and increased autonomy and willingness to take responsibility for their own learning.

Quote 6.5   On the value of PBL

PBL is important not just as a different and more efficient way to afford language learning opportunities, but in a wider sense as a semiotic-ecological endeavor that focuses on the making and using of signs that are multisensory and multimodal.

van Lier (2006: xiv)

Pragmatic ethnography

A type of project-based learning that has found its way into language programmes concerned with developing intercultural communicative competence is '**pragmatic ethnography**' (Damen, 1987: 63). With theoretical roots in linguistic anthropology, ethnography is a research method used to provide rich, detailed descriptions of the sociocultural patterns and practices of cultural groups (cf. Chapters 1 and 8). Pragmatic ethnography differs from ethnography used as a research method in that it is undertaken for 'personal and practical purposes and not to provide scientific data and theory' (*ibid*.: 63). Conducting a pragmatic ethnography entails having learners gather information on the group of interest through observations of and participation in the group's communicative practices, interviews with members of the group, collection of pertinent documents related to the group and the practices, and so on. The gathered data form the basis for learner reflections and enhanced understandings not only of the cultural practices of the group under study but of the cultural dimensions of their own practices.

> **Quote 6.6** On the pedagogical value of ethnography
>
> Of all forms of scientific knowledge, ethnography is the most open, the most compatible with a democratic way of life, the least likely to produce a world in which experts control knowledge at the expense of those who are studied. The skills of ethnography are enhancements of skills all normal persons employ in everyday life. . . . It [ethnography] mediates between what members of a given community know and do, and accumulates comparative understanding of what members of communities generally have known and done.
>
> Hymes (1981: 57)

While such an approach works well for learners living in the same community as members of the cultural group being studied, with the wide availability of the internet and electronic communication tools that allow for social networking activities such as e-mailing, blogging, and video conferencing, it can also be used effectively in contexts where face-to-face contact is unlikely or impossible. This is illustrated by *Cultura*, a programme started by a team of faculty in the Foreign Languages and Literatures Section of the Massachusetts Institute of Technology (MIT) in the late 1990s (Furstenberg, 2010). In this programme, groups of English language speakers who are studying another language at MIT team up via electronic communication media with a group of target language speakers who are also English language learners for an 'intercultural journey' (*ibid*.: 330). They share a website and, via online discussion forums, they collaboratively analyse and compare perspectives on a variety of digital textual and visual materials from their respective cultures. As Furstenberg notes, the use of electronic technology is essential to the success of the programme in that it makes possible learner engagement with 'a multiplicity of viewpoints and a real insider's view of the other culture that were simply unattainable prior to this' (p. 331).

Concept 6.2   **Key steps in conducting a pragmatic ethnography**

1 Collect data intensively and extensively.

2 Organise data systematically.

3 Be reflexive about the data, regularly questioning how it was produced and your initial assumptions.

4 Be steeped in the data, constantly rereading and searching for further illumination.

5 Be accountable to the data, making sure that all claims are grounded in the data.

6 Look for patterns but keep a look out for contradictory evidence.

7 Go for a story line or central theme that draws your ethnography together.

Roberts *et al.* (2001: 149)

6.3.3   The multiliteracies project

Another innovative approach that is both learner- and knowledge-centred is the **multiliteracies project** (New London Group, 1996, 2000). The project was developed by a group of international scholars in response to what they had identified as two important challenges to education. The first is the increasing cultural and linguistic diversity of communities around the world which, they argue, has changed the nature of schooling. Students are now required to learn

> to negotiate regional, ethnic, or class-based dialects; cultural discourses; the code switching often to be found within a text among different languages, dialects, or registers; different visual and iconic meanings; and variation in the gestural relationships among people, language, and material objects.
> (New London Group, 2000: 14)

The second challenge they identified is the proliferation of means for communicating within and across these communities. Not only have additional communication technologies been created, but communicating through them is 'increasingly multimodal – in which written-linguistic modes of meaning are part and parcel of visual, audio, and spatial patterns of meaning' (Cope and Kalantis, 2000: 5). Pedagogies based on one formal, standard notion of language and on a mono-modal, mono-cultural literacy are inadequate for meeting these challenges. What is required, the New London Group argued, is a pedagogy that seeks to 'recruit . . . the different subjectivities, interests, intentions, commitments and purposes that students bring to learning' (New London Group, 2000: 18), rather than trying to remove or ignore them. Such a pedagogy needs to open doors to new communicative practices and resources that expand students' options for participating in their worlds, and enable them to draw on multiple meaning-making modes to bring their cultural worlds into existence, maintain them and transform them for their own purposes.

To meet these challenges, the New London Group proposed **a pedagogy of multiliteracies**, consisting of four interrelated spheres of learning opportunities. **Situated practice** learning opportunities socialise learners into those communicative activities in which they are expected to become competent. The assumption embodied in situated practice is that mastery of skills and knowledge needed for competent performance is partially dependent on learner involvement in the very activities in which they wish to become competent from the beginning of instruction. **Overt instruction** opportunities provide learners with explicit instruction on the various resources used to make meaning. **Critical framing** opportunities engage learners in the critical analysis of their activities and the resources used in their design so that they can identify the diverse and multiple perspectives embodied in them, and ultimately make informed choices about their participation in their social worlds. The knowledge and skills developed in these learning opportunities form the base of **transformed practice**, where learners are provided with opportunities to take the lead in their own learning. They use their new understandings, knowledge and skills to try out different voices in familiar contexts, to invent new means and, where possible, create new contexts and new goals for self-expression and connecting with others.

The four dimensions of learning opportunities in a multiliteracies pedagogy are not considered to be rigid, hierarchical stages of learning. Rather, they are complexly interrelated, 'elements of each [which] may occur simultaneously, while at different times one or the other will predominate, and all of them are repeatedly revisited at different levels' (New London Group, 2000: 85). Together, the conditions for learning fostered across the four dimensions aim to promote learners' development of a complex range of understandings and perspectives, knowledge and skills, and values and motivations needed for full personal, social and cultural participation in their classroom communities as well as in their larger, social communities.

Underlying the dimensions of learning in a multiliteracies pedagogy is the concept of **design**, which is offered as an alternative to competence. As Kress (2010: 4) notes, competence suggests 'social regulation' whereas design focuses on learners' present actions in terms of their future outcomes.

Design is thus forward-looking, 'a means of projecting an individual's interest into their world with the intent of effect in the future' (*ibid.*: 23).

Quote 6.7 Designs of meaning in a multiliteracies pedagogy

The starting point for the Multiliteracies framework is the notion that knowledge and meaning are historically and socially located and produced, that they are 'designed' artefacts. But more than artefacts, Design is a dynamic process, a process of subjective self-interest and transformation, consisting of

- *the Designed*: the available meaning-making resources and patterns and conventions of meaning in a particular cultural context;
- *Designing*: the process of shaping emergent meaning, which involves representation and recontextualisation;
- *the Redesigned*: the outcome of designing, something through which the meaning-maker has remade themselves and created a new meaning-making resource.

Kalantis and Cope (2008: 203–204)

According to the New London Group, to support a pedagogy of multi-literacies what is needed is an educationally accessible functional grammar, that is, a metalanguage whose purpose is 'to identify and explain differences between texts, and relate these to the contexts of culture and situation in which they seem to work' (New London Group, 2000: 24). To be useful, a metalanguage should address the following five questions (Kalantis and Cope, 2008: 205):

1 Representational – What do the meanings refer to?
2 Social – How do the meanings connect the persons they involve?
3 Organisational – How do the meanings hang together?
4 Contextual – How do the meanings fit into the larger world of meaning?
5 Ideological – Whose interests are the meanings skewed to serve?

Genre-based pedagogy

One metalanguage that has been useful to multiliteracies education is Halliday's systemic functional linguistics (SFL) (cf. Chapters 1 and 3). SFL considers grammar to be an open-set of resources, the meanings of which are motivated by the functions they serve. James Martin and his colleagues (e.g. Christie, 2008; Christie and Martin, 2007; Martin, 2006, 2009) have applied SFL to the development of the concept of genre, defined as 'a socially sanctioned means of constructing and negotiating meanings' (Christie,

2008: 29) and to the development of a genre-based pedagogy for reading and writing. In this approach, findings from an SFL analysis of the texts that students are expected to read and write are the foundation of the curriculum. Advocates of this approach point out that its pedagogical power comes from the fact in that it offers a systematic means of describing texts and the ways language is used to make meaning and thus offers clear, explicit directions to teachers and learners about what is to be learned.

The approach has also been usefully incorporated into professional development programmes for teachers to enable them 'to analyze texts, think about language at new levels of abstraction, and develop new understanding of the complex meaning-making practices of their subject matter and their pedagogical approaches' (Achugar *et al.*, 2007: 21). In fact, a study (*ibid.*) examining the use of the genre-based approach in three different teacher development contexts revealed that it provided teachers working with English language learners powerful instructional tools for helping learners expand their understandings and use of their bilingual resources.

Quote 6.8 Principles of genre-based pedagogy

Writing is a social activity
Communication always has a purpose, a context, and an intended audience, and these aspects can form the basis of both writing tasks and syllabuses. This means that students need to engage in a variety of relevant writing experiences which draw on, analyse, and investigate different purposes and readers.

Learning to write is needs-oriented
Effective teaching recognises the wants, prior learning, and current proficiencies of students, but in a genre-based course, it also means, as far as possible, identifying the kinds of writing that learners will need to do in their target situations and incorporating these into the course.

Learning to write requires explicit outcomes and expectations
Learning occurs more effectively if teachers are explicit about what is being studied, why it is being studied, and what will be expected of students at the end of the course, representing what Bernstein (1990, p. 73) calls a 'visible pedagogy'.

Learning to write is a social activity
Learning to write is supported within familiar routines, or cycles of activity, and by linking new contexts and understandings to what students already know about writing. Teaching is, therefore, always a series of scaffolded developmental steps in which teachers and peers play a major role.

Learning to write involves learning to use language
Genre teaching involves being explicit about how texts are grammatically patterned, but grammar is integrated into the exploration of texts and contexts rather than taught as a discrete component. This helps learners not only to see how grammar and vocabulary choices create meanings, but to understand how language itself works, acquiring a way to talk about language and its role in texts.

Hyland (2007: 152–153)

While genre-based approaches have focused primarily on the meaning-making functions of language structures, the development of metalanguages for other semiotic resources has been a growing concern for those with interests in multiliteracies pedagogy. A key contribution of SFL to this work is its metafunctional principle, which states,

> semiotic resources simultaneously provide the tools for constructing ideational meaning (i.e. experiential meaning and logical relations) and for enacting social relations (i.e. interpersonal meaning). These metafunctions are enabled through the organization of the discourse, which is the textual metafunction of semiosis.
>
> (O'Halloran, 2008: 444)

The principle provides a theoretical framework for analysing the functions and interactions of semiotic resources in the performance of particular social goals in multimodal discourses. For example, scholars such as Gunther Kress and his colleagues (Kress, 2003; Kress *et al.*, 2005; Kress and Van Leeuwen, 2006; Bezemer and Kress, 2008) and Unsworth (2006) have drawn on this principle to create new metalanguages for visual designs and multimodal texts, which are texts that integrate visual, audio and technological modes of meaning into their designs. Such work affords the continued development of models and strategies for implementing multiliteracies pedagogy in ways that respond to the challenges created by ever-emerging electronic modes of communication and the increasingly diverse populations of classrooms and sites of learning.

6.4 Summary

In learning contexts concerned with teaching language and culture from a sociocultural perspective, the general instructional aim is not to teach language and culture *per se*, as subject matter removed from any specific contexts of activity. Rather it is to help learners to understand the linguistic and other means by which their activities are constructed and the cultural meanings that are embodied in their uses. It is also to help them to understand the roles and identities they are appropriated into by their use of particular resources, the social, cultural and other forces that give shape to these constructions, and how to negotiate with others to position themselves in relation to these roles and identities, and larger social forces in ways that are mutually beneficial.

While there is general agreement with these goals among practitioners operating within a sociocultural perspective, there is still the question of how we define where we are going in terms of development. Even as we acknowledge the importance of expanding learners' worlds, and the usefulness of ethnographies of communication and studies on multiliteracies for illuminating the multiple modes and their affordances for designing meaning, we still know little about the communicative activities of the many linguistically and culturally diverse groups that comprise our worlds. We do know however, that the impact of electronic technologies on the activities they engage in and the resources they draw on to make meaning is huge. For example, they are, on a daily basis, exposed to if not fully participating in video and online games, hypertext and hypermedia narratives and online chat room discussions. As Unsworth (2008) notes, the literacies entailed in such activities 'are multiple, involving not only the comprehension and composition of images and text, separately and in combination, and in paper as well as digital media, but also navigation though cyberspace to locate relevant sites, manipulation of electronic textual material and evaluation of information' (p. 62).

Moreover, not only are means for communicating increasingly multimodal, the modes themselves are increasingly more permeable and hybrid (cf. Canagarajah, 2003). Because the activities that are made available to our students in language classrooms and other contexts fundamentally shape both the direction and substance of learners' knowledge, the choices we make about the kinds of communicative activities to include in the curriculum are highly consequential. Therefore, even having some knowledge about these worlds leaves us with the value-laden decision of whose worlds we are to orient to in our classrooms.

Assuming that we are able to make such decisions, we still know little about the pedagogical effectiveness of the practices described in this chapter for expanding learners' communicative horizons. Arguing that they should be effective, as the approaches discussed in this chapter do, is certainly not the same as documenting not only that they are effective but how they manage to be so as well. There has been some budding attention to this concern, at least with multiliteracies pedagogy, with findings from recent studies providing evidence on the efficacy of using the metalanguage of SFL in literacy development (e.g. Quinn, 2004; Schleppegrell *et al.*, 2004). We also have some evidence on the successful application of a multiliteracies pedagogy in disadvantaged schools (e.g. Newfield and Maungedzo, 2006). Such research efforts need to be expanded to include other approaches and other contexts, and work to tease apart the complex links between teaching and learning practices and the developmental consequences arising from learners' varied trajectories of participation in them. With continued attention to these concerns, we might find that the specific curricular choices we make about the kinds of communicative practices to include in the classroom and the instructional practices we use to socialise students into them are consequential to learners' development in ways we may not have imagined.

Further reading

Berlin, L. (2005) *Contextualizing College ESL Classroom Praxis: A Participatory Approach to Effective Instruction*, Mahwah, NJ: Lawrence Erlbaum. The author describes in detail an approach to adult ESL instruction that is based on Freire's principles of effective pedagogy. Examples of classroom practices are provided from an ethnographic study undertaken by the author in an intensive English programme.

Byrnes, H. (ed.) (2007) *Advanced Language Learning: The Contribution of Halliday and Vygotsky*, London: Continuum. The chapters in this edited volume examine new approaches to the teaching of advanced levels of language ability. Integrating the insights of Halliday, Vygotsky and Bakhtin with empirical data from language classroom, the chapters explore theoretical, descriptive and instructional aspects of advanced language classrooms.

Martin, J. R. and Rose, D. (2008) *Genre Relations: Mapping Culture*, London: Equinox. This book offers an introduction to genre analysis from the perspective of the Halliday-inspired 'Sydney School' of functional linguistics. Included is an introduction to the study of genre, discussions of five major families of genres (stories, histories, reports, explanations and procedures), and a conclusion in which they discuss several issues on genre analysis arising from their model.

Risager, K. (2007) *Language and Culture Pedagogy: From a National to a Transnational Paradigm*, Clevedon: Multilingual Matters. The text offers a view of language and culture teaching that recognises the increasing diversity of communities around the world. It includes a historical overview of language and culture teaching in foreign language education programmes, and proposes a transnational framework for language and culture pedagogy whose goal is to develop intercultural citizens of the world.

Stein, P. (2008) *Multimodal Pedagogies in Diverse Classrooms*, London: Routledge. The text examines how social justice and democratic practices can be promoted in diverse classrooms. Using examples drawn from her research undertaken in post-apartheid South Africa, the author draws on a social semiotic perspective of communication to examine the myriad forms of representations such as image, space and movement, through which learners create meaning in classrooms and how these differences can be used to promote a dynamic and productive site for learning.

Section

III Researching language and culture

The research enterprise

This chapter:

- presents the theoretical foundations of research on language and culture from a sociocultural perspective;
- discusses several issues to be considered when designing and implementing research;
- offers a list of additional readings on the topics covered in this chapter.

7.1   Introduction

Traditional conceptualisations of research in applied linguists draw a distinction between researchers and practitioners. The task of researchers is to produce new knowledge and practitioners are to use the knowledge to address real world issues. As originally conceived, this was the work of applied linguists, to apply findings about the nature of language and culture to the solving of problems concerned with, for example, the teaching of languages, language policy decision making, the assessment of language abilities and disabilities, problems in workplace communication and so on. This perspective is captured in Corder's 1973 definition of applied linguistics as 'the application of linguistic knowledge to some object' (p. 10), with the applied linguist in the role of 'consumer, or user, not a producer, of theories' (*ibid.*).

A sociocultural perspective on research makes no such distinction. Instead, in defining research as a systematic quest for new understandings and new ways of attending to the world, such activity is viewed as a natural component of all applied linguists' activity. The distinction deemed relevant is that which distinguishes expert researchers from less proficient researchers. Rather than being based on one's professional position, the distinction is predicated on an individual's degree of expertise in a range of knowledge, skills and abilities needed to engaged in a complex and demanding task.

The purpose of this chapter is to lay out some of the general issues and concerns embodied in the enterprise of research with which anyone interested in doing research on language and culture from a sociocultural perspective should at least be familiar. The discussion is not meant to turn novice researchers into experts; for this, one needs extensive training and experience. Rather, it aims to highlight some of the basic issues involved in doing 'good' research that are worthy of consideration.

7.2   Foundations of research on language and culture from a sociocultural perspective

One important aspect of research expertise involves being aware of and able to articulate the theoretical premises embodied in different approaches to research. The ways in which we perceive the world and our relationship to it, however tacit these understandings may be, frame our understandings of the nature of research, the purposes for which we engage in it, the kinds of research questions we ask, and the methods we choose to seek answers to those questions. Before undertaking a discussion on possibilities for research on language and culture, it is useful to review some of the more fundamental presuppositions embodied in a sociocultural perspective.

A first premise has to do with the nature of knowledge. As we have discussed in earlier chapters, a more traditional 'linguistics applied' perspective configures knowledge as a rational, universal entity with unchanging properties that exists separate from and independent of the knower. Language and culture knowledge specifically are perceived as abstract representations that, although located in the head of individuals, can be extracted from individual mind, and subjected to enquiry independently of the varied ways in which they are used.

In contrast, a sociocultural perspective defines knowledge not as some rational system existing apart from its users, but as a socially constituted cultural construct. This construct exists not within universal mind but within our communities, and is given shape by the communicative activities in which we engage as members of our communities and, more specifically, their tools and the ways we use the tools to mediate our actions in our activities with others. It is from our mediated actions that knowledge takes shape, including its forms and functions, and from which referential understandings of the world are drawn.

A second premise has to do with the nature of inquiry. A traditional view of the purpose of research is to expand our theoretical understandings of the universal principles by which the world operates so that we may better predict and control what happens in it. In assuming language and culture knowledge to consist of internally coherent systems by which their existence – apart from any context – is governed, the role of such enquiry is to understand the structural specifications, the formal properties, of the knowledge systems as fully as possible so that we can predict how individuals, universally inscribed, make use of them. In such inquiry, sites of language use become sources of data only in that they allow for the collection of samples from which forms can be extracted and isolated, and hypotheses about the formal properties of systems can be made. In the process, the researcher is the scientist, who stands apart from that which is being studied in the aim for value-free 'objective' findings.

A sociocultural perspective on the nature of inquiry differs fairly significantly from the more traditional view. From this perspective, reality is not a fixed, stable entity but multiple and jointly constructed. Thus, the researcher cannot be separated from what is researched. Acknowledging the impossibility of objectivity, the role of the researcher is to maintain a credible, trustworthy voice through 'habitual reflexivity' (Sweetman, 2003: 528), that is, continual critique of his or her involvement in all aspects of the research process.

Moreover, the goal of research is not to reveal some underlying truth or sets of universal principles and properties of human nature and the world. Rather, the goal is multi-purposed. On one level, it is to understand the communicative worlds in which we live and the semiotic means by which we construct and are constructed in our worlds. To reach such understanding entails the examination of our lived experiences, the meanings residing in them, the social, cultural and political forces that give rise to these meanings, and the consequences that participation in these experiences have for individual action and development. Such examinations reveal the intricacies of our communicative worlds and make clear how our worlds, our social identities and the roles we play, are connected to, and partially constructed by, our communicative actions and those of others, and by the larger sociohistorical forces embodied in them.

In addition to enhancing understandings of the 'taken-for-granted' nature of our everyday lives, such research endeavours aim to contribute to the development of a theory of practice (cf. de Certeau, 1984; Lave and Wenger, 1991). The goal of such a theory is to help to explain, on a broader scale, the communicative actions by which individuals within social groups and institutions, and groups and institutions within larger sociocultural communities, (re)create and respond to both their sociohistorical and locally situated interactive conditions, and the consequences – linguistic, social, cognitive and otherwise – of their doing so.

> **Quote 7.1**   On a theory of social practice
>
> Briefly, a theory of social practice emphasizes the relational interdependency of agent and world, activity, meaning, cognition, learning, and knowing. It emphasizes the inherently socially negotiated character of meaning and the interested, concerned character of the thought and action of persons-in-activity. This view also claims that learning, thinking, and knowing are relations among people in activity in, with, and arising from the socially and culturally structured world. This world is socially constituted; objective forms and systems of activity, on the one hand, and agents' subjective and intersubjective understandings of them, on the other, mutually constitute both the world and its experienced forms.
>
> Lave and Wenger (1991: 50–51)

As Ortega (2005) notes, the value of such research is to be judged 'ultimately on the basis of its potential for positive impact on societal and educational problems' (p. 430). Therefore, in addition to enhancing understandings, an additional purpose is to use the findings to engage with individuals, groups, institutions and communities and ultimately contribute to the transformation of understandings, policies and practices 'in ways that can feed forward into society' (Bygate, 2005: 574).

> **Quote 7.2**   On the multiple goals of applied linguistics research
>
> Although applied linguistics has a commitment to its necessary collaborators, it has, also, an equal commitment and obligation to itself. It has constantly to work to develop generalisable principles of theoretical and analytic insights which will enable it to say not only what it does, but why what it does is grounded in coherent and sustainable argument. . . . If applied linguistics is, ultimately, concerned not just with application but with the transformation and recontextualisation of the professional practices with which it engages, it is equally concerned with such continuing respecification of itself.
>
> Candlin and Sarangi (2004a: 3)

7.3   Methodological considerations

7.3.1   Choice of methods

In addition to making one's assumptions clear, doing good research involves choosing appropriate methods for collecting and analysing data, since the methods we choose to use will shape the kinds of data we gather and ultimately what we find. Data generally take two forms: quantitative and qualitative. The basic distinction between the two is that quantitative data are expressed in terms of numbers or amounts while qualitative data are not. Instead, qualitative data can take many forms, including verbal and non-verbal means of social action, pictorial and other kinds of visual representations, and so on.

Although this division is a common one, a closer look reveals that they are not distinct categories. Rather, they are intimately connected in that quantitative data are based upon qualitative judgements, and qualitative data can be 'quantitized' (Sandelowski *et al.*, 2009: 211), described and manipulated numerically. The purpose of research on language and culture is to discern, examine and interpret meaningful communicative patterns and plans, and to explain them in terms of larger ideological themes and topics that emerge from the patterns. To generate well grounded, warranted claims about the patterns and themes detected through analysis of the data, we must rely on counting, which is a basic means for determining quantity. The more often an action takes place, or a form appears, or a concept or idea is generated, the more basis we have for determining whether there is a pattern or theme. Once we have determined the existence of a pattern or a theme, we generally rely on the number of times it occurs to determine its significance. The more often something happens, the more warranted is our claim of conventionality. Similarly, the more a theme appears in particular oral or written texts, the stronger our claim can be as to its significance to the person or persons to whom the texts belong.

The more we build our analysis on the basis of frequency, the less concern there is that the examples we have chosen to illustrate a claim are selective, representing our own hunches, rather than illustrative of the whole body of data from which the examples are drawn. Use of such quantitative methods allows researchers to 'show regularities or peculiarities . . . they might not otherwise see or be able simply to communicate, or to determine that a pattern or idiosyncrasy they thought was there is not' (Sandelowski *et al.*, 2009: 210).

On the other hand, no matter which particular means of quantifying data we choose to use, the meaningfulness of the quantified data can only be determined through qualitative judgements based on the perceptions of those from whose lives the data are drawn. That is to say, detecting patterns of communicative behaviour can tell us how ubiquitous something is in the full body of empirical evidence. However, what it cannot tell us is the meaning such patterns have for those whose patterns they are. It can, as Widdowson (2000: 7) has pointed out, 'only analyze the textual traces of the processes whereby meaning is achieved; it cannot account for the complex interplay of linguistic and contextual factors whereby discourse is enacted'. Without some form of qualitative evaluation of the data, the numbers remain meaningless.

From a sociocultural perspective, both quantitative and qualitative data can help us to gain an understanding of the worlds in which we live, and thus are viewed as complementary rather than competing forms of data. Beginning in the mid 1990s the issue of how to mix or link the two kinds of data to enhance our understanding of our research data was taken up in earnest (Creswell, 2009). Mixed methods research is defined as 'the collection or analysis of both quantitative and qualitative data in a single study in which the data are collected concurrently or sequentially, are given a priority, and involve the integration of the data at one or more stages in the process of research' (Creswell *et al.*, 2003: 212). Mixing methods allows for a pragmatic approach to research design, which focuses on working back and forth between various forms of representation, between induction and deduction, and between specific results and their more general implications (cf. Morgan, 2007).

Quote 7.3   Moving beyond dualisms in research

It does not have to be wrong to focus on quantitative or qualitative research one at a time. . . . But it is wrong to construct a world in which quantitative or qualitative and related dualisms – objective/subjective, laboratory/natural, context bound/context free, hard data/soft data – are choices that leave a person with more foist than choice and often wrong.

McDermott and McDermott (2009: 205)

The choices we make in terms of the kinds of data we collect and the methods we use to analyse them depend on the research questions we ask. Our task as researchers is to choose the most appropriate tools for the study. In the end, what will make our research 'good' is using the methods we have chosen systematically and rigorously so that the data we collect and the claims we make are ecologically valid (Cicourel, 2007), that is, fair and credible representations of the phenomenon of study even if the answers to our questions are not what we thought or hoped they would be.

Quote 7.4   On the value of methodological diversity

Inquiry has always been and will always be a moral, political, value-laden enterprise. We seek only a politics of hopes, models of social justice to lead us forward. As members of a larger moral community, we all need to draw together so we can share our problems and experiences with these new discourses. We need a moral and methodological community that honours and celebrates paradigm and methodological diversity.

Denzin (2010: 424–425)

7.3.2   Transcription issues

Since data for studies of language and culture from a sociocultural perspective are taken from naturally occurring events, collection methods, as noted earlier, often involve video and audio tapings of these events. For the purposes of analysis, these taped events must be transcribed, or represented in another form, which most often is writing. While on the surface the process of re-presenting the activity graphically may seem unproblematic and fairly straightforward, it is, as Elinor Ochs (1979) and others (e.g. Duranti, 2006) have pointed out, a theoretical task in itself.

It is theoretical in that it entails our making consecutive and multiple-layered choices about what to include and what to ignore. That is to say, in the process of transcribing, we select certain actions from a much larger repertoire to re-present in another form. In turn, the specific aspects we select shape what we determine to be relevant in the analysis. For example, using conventional orthography to represent oral discourse renders invisible any accent or dialectic features. Likewise, in noting only verbal cues in our encoding of a communicative activity, we give primacy to these cues as significant tools in the realisation of the event before we have even begun the analysis. The decision to leave out non-verbal and paralinguistic actions makes it impossible to consider communicative acts realised non-verbally, such as a pointed finger to direct attention, raised eyebrows to indicate surprise, eye gaze to signal a change of turns and so on.

Bucholtz provides a compelling example of how different interpretations of actions can arise from variation in transcriptions. Example 7.1 is an illustration of a transcript of spoken discourse taken from her 1998 study on 'nerd girl' identity, presented to represent what she called 'the nerd manifesto' (Bucholtz, 2007: 787), defined as a statement on what it means to be a nerd. In this example, only one person appears to be involved in producing the statement and it is presented as a well-thought out and confidently delivered declaration.

Example 7.1   Version One

Fred: We're always the nerds. We like it. We're glad to be the nerds and the squares. We don't drink, we don't do any drugs, we just get naturally high, we do insane funny things. And we're smart. We get good grades.

Source: Bucholtz (2007: 786)

Example 7.2 is another rendition of a small portion of the same recording. In this version, the contributions of Mary, the interviewer, are included, which indicate that rather than being a single-authored declaration, the statement was a joint production by both the interviewer and the inter-viewee. Also included are features of voice quality such as creakiness (indi-cated by the transcriber's comments contained within the symbols < >), laughter (indicated by @), lengthening of sounds (indicated by a : following the sound), and self-interruption or abrupt cut-off (indicated by -), all of which indicate some hedging and hesitation in the participants' comments. In her analysis of the second version, Bucholtz arrives at a different inter-pretation of Fred's actions. She states:

> Fred's comments are not the product of an autonomous, triumphant voice of nerd pride but are rather the result of considerable co-construction (and obstruction) by me as the researcher. Her stated views, while clearly strongly held, are much more hedged and halting in their expression than my first transcript acknowledged.
>
> (Bucholtz, 2007: 787)

Bucholtz's examples provide persuasive evidence on the effects of differ-ences in transcription on researchers' interpretations of the phenomenon under study.

Example 7.2   Version Two

  1 Mary: [So]
  2 Fred: [We're al]ways the nerds.
  3   We like it.
  4 Mary: You@'re the nerds?
  5 Fred: We're <creaky> {glad} to be the nerds,
  6   a@nd the squa:res and,
  7 Mary: Is that what
  8 Fred: [we don't-]
  9 Mary: [you say] you are?
 10 Fred: <[i?]> Well,
 11   we don't exactly s:-
 12   We don't always say it,=
 13   =I say it. n@

Source: Bucholtz (2007: 787)

Transcription is inherently variable. The point is not that all possible actions be included, since no transcript can fully recapture the totality of experience. What matters is that decisions on what to transcribe have a principled basis. This means that we must choose a set of conventions that makes salient those particular aspects of the event that we are interested in, and are consistent in our use of symbols to render the findings 'readable' by others doing similar kinds of research. Also important, when reporting our findings, is to state our criteria for selecting sections of transcribed data to illustrate an analysis. Where the issue is not even recognised, the question arises as to whether the selected samples of transcribed data are convenient rather than representative examples of the whole body of data. As such, we run the risk of using data to support our own version of reality, whether or not it adequately reflects the reality of those whose communicative experiences they are.

Quote 7.5   On variation in transcription

A transcript is an evolving flexible object; it changes as the transcriber engages in listening and looking again at the tape, endlessly checking, revising, reformatting it. These changes are not simply cumulative steps towards an increasingly better transcript: they can involve adding but also subtracting details for the purposes of a specific analysis, of a particular recipient-oriented presentation, or of compliance with editorial constraints.

Mondada (2007: 810)

Several conventional standards for transcribing audio and video talk data exist, including the conventions developed by Gail Jefferson (2004), used by those working in conversation analysis, and the Santa Barbara discourse conventions (Du Bois, 2006). Recently, the increasing sophistication of digital tools for capturing and annotating naturally occurring communicative experiences along with the increased interest in examining multimodal action (cf. Chapter 6), which includes a focus on semiotic resources such as visual, gestural and spatial in addition to language, has made the process of transcribing video data much more complicated. Also complicating the process is the increasing bi- and multilingual character of communicative experiences, requiring researchers to have a high level of fluency in languages, and the ability to translate from one language to another and to employ the appropriate orthographic representations of languages. One response to managing the growing complexities in capturing, annotating and transcribing video data is *TalkBank*, a worldwide interdisciplinary research project. The project has developed an electronic repository of databases, which can be found at <http://talkbank.org>, to use in the ongoing development of transcription standards and tools.

7.4   Negotiating relationships

Another essential component involved in designing and producing a high-quality research project are the relationships we establish with those involved in the project. Included are not only the primary participants and the individuals and groups from whom we must gain and maintain approval for access to the site, but also those who may not be participating fully in the study but have some official role in the context or setting. At least two factors influence the kinds of relationships we develop. First, as research on social identity theory shows (Tajfel and Turner, 1986; cf. Chapter 2), our social identities, which include demographic features such as gender, age, social class and ethnicity, as well as identities deriving from membership in social groups affiliated with families, workplaces and community organisations, influence not only how we perceive others but also how others perceive us. The more similar we perceive others to be in terms of a valued identity, or the more neutral any differences are perceived to be, the more disposed we are to develop supportive relationships with others. Conversely, the more different or unfamiliar we perceive others to be, the more misgivings about developing relationships of trust are likely to arise. A key dynamic influencing the negotiation of relationships in a research project is how project participants perceive themselves in relation to each other.

Another factor influencing the relationships we establish are the multiple roles project participants may expect us to play in a research project, including for example, roles as friend, advocate, or resource, in addition to the traditional role of researcher (cf. Sarangi and Candlin, 2003). For example, during the process of data collection in a workplace setting for a study of how business meetings are conducted, some participants may expect the researcher to advocate on their behalf for improved working conditions. Negotiating appropriate responses to such expectations as we strive to sustain relationships of collaboration and trust is an ongoing challenge. The challenge can become even more pressing in settings with which we are less familiar. Effective researchers are practised in self-reflection, skilled in developing and managing interpersonal relationships, accommodating, and willing to deal with difficulties as they arise (Garner *et al.*, 2006).

Quote 7.6   Managing relationships in research

As applied linguistics becomes more empirically grounded, managing relationships with research participants becomes more pivotal. Here a key inter-relational dimension involves the negotiation of research findings and their potential applicability with target audiences, as both sources for and recipients of the research data. In short, a call for making applied linguistic processes and products audience-designed. Such a call will require applied linguists to go beyond mere pattern seeking in their methodology and address questions of social, personal and institutional relevance in common with other disciplines in social science. Such a challenge invokes not only research collaboration and partnership as a central practice, but researcher deference, humility and participant respect as core tenets of applied linguistics.

Candlin and Sarangi (2004b: 227)

7.5 Research ethics

A final, important issue in the development of research expertise concerns **research ethics**. Ethical issues involved in doing research can be grouped into three dimensions (Guillemin and Gillam, 2004). The first involves **procedural ethics**, which entails seeking official approval to conduct research from institutional boards or committees. The criteria such boards and committees typically use to judge worthiness of research projects are based on three principles (Kubanyiova, 2008): respect for person; beneficence, that is, 'ensuring that the research project yields substantial benefits while minimizing harm' (*ibid.*: 505); and justice, defined as equitable distribution of benefits.

These boards and committees determine, for example, whether all the components for a well-designed research study are clearly articulated. This includes clear and adequate articulation of the theoretical presuppositions framing the study and the rationale for undertaking it, the questions guiding the study and identification of the kinds of data needed to answer them, and the methods to be used for gathering and analysing the data. The institutional boards also determine whether and how well the rights of the research participants are protected, how well risks to the participants are minimised and whether the anticipated benefits outweigh any potential risk. They also determine the adequacy and appropriateness of the plans for obtaining informed consent and guaranteeing participant confidentiality. Informed consent means that prospective participants must be fully acquainted with the procedures and risks involved in the research before giving their written consent to participate. Guaranteeing confidentiality means ensuring prospective participants that any identifying information will not be made available to anyone who is not directly involved in the study. Finally, the boards determine the adequacy and appropriateness of the qualifications of the researcher to conduct research involving human participants.

A second dimension is **practical ethics**, which encompasses the everyday, locally situated, ethical issues that come up when doing research (Guillemin and Gillam, 2004). As Kubanyiova (2008) notes, in any research endeavour, 'ethically important moments' (p. 506) may arise for which the principles underlying institutional review boards' criteria and codes 'may hold ambiguous, contradictory, or no answers at all' (*ibid.*). Kubanyiova divides practical ethics into two dimensions, the **ethics of care** and **virtue ethics**. The ethics of care demands from researchers a level of sensitivity for, identification with and responsible, caring actions towards the participants in the study. For example, a researcher working from an ethics of care recognises that, although an institutional board may give official approval to the use of certain research methods, unintended effects may arise during their implementation, which will require the researcher to alter some of the procedures to protect the participants. Virtue ethics is broader in that it requires researchers to have the ability to recognise when such dilemmas occur, the willingness to deal with them when they do, and the ability to think through the issues with care and thoughtfulness and to respond appropriately. While some issues may be difficult to resolve, an ethically competent researcher works through the complexities and makes socially and morally responsible and principled decisions.

The third dimension of research ethics, **professional ethics**, comprises the officially sanctioned guidelines and codes of conduct developed by professional associations and government funding agencies. The British Association of Applied Linguistics (BAAL), for example, produced a set of guidelines intended to help applied linguists 'to maintain high standards and to respond flexibly to new opportunities . . . showing due respect to all participants, to the values of truth, fairness and open democracy, and to the integrity of applied linguistics as a body of knowledge and a mode of inquiry' (BAAL, www.baal.org.uk/about_goodpractice-full-5.pdf:2).

Similarly, the government of Canada has an interagency advisory panel devoted to research ethics. The panel comprises members from the Canadian Institutes of Health Research (CIHR), Natural Sciences and Engineering Research Council of Canada (NSERC) and the Social Sciences and Humanities Research Council of Canada (SSHRC). In 2008 and 2009 the Panel revised their *Policy Statement on the Ethical Conduct for Research Involving Humans* (www.pre.ethics.gc.ca/eng/index/) and submitted a final revision to the three councils in mid-2010 for their consideration and approval. Another source of information on research ethics is the website of the Council of European Social Science Data Archives (CESSDA). CESSDA is an umbrella organisation devoted to the archiving and distribution of electronic data for the social science and humanities research community across Europe. The website contains a wide selection of references to professional ethical codes, guidelines and standards from a variety of professional organisations from around the world (www.cessda.org).

While these codes and guidelines are important, they are often written at a level of generality that requires researchers to be skilled in interpreting, evaluating and applying them to their specific contexts. To advance the development of such skills, the Council of Graduate Schools (CGS) recently instituted an initiative called *The Project for Scholarly Integrity*. The CGS is a consortium of over 500 colleges and universities in North America and 16 universities outside North America whose mission is to improve and advance graduate education (www.cgsnet.org). The Project seeks to integrate research ethics and scholarly integrity into the entire graduate school research experience. Towards that end, it is working with several institutions on the development of educational programmes whose goal is to provide comprehensive training in the responsible conduct of research. It is expected that once developed, the programmes and accompanying resources will be used as exemplary models and shared with the wider CGS community and other interested institutions.

Quote 7.7   What do we mean by ethical research practice?

The bases of ethical research practice are a series of obligations – to society, to funders and employers, and to the subjects of the research. Ethical considerations can impinge on the research process from the very beginning – on the decision to carry out the research in the first instance – through the conduct, management and administration of the research, including for example the definitions of the research questions – to the effects on and relationships with the participants; to recognition of limits of competence; and to the effects on larger groups and communities, interpretations, and reporting of the results of research.

CESSDA (www.cessda.org/sharing/rights/4/index.html#codes)

7.6 Summary

As discussed in this chapter, good research depends on one's degree of research expertise. Among other knowledge, skills and abilities, this expertise involves understanding and being able to articulate one's assumptions about the nature of knowledge, of knowing, and of both the nature and purpose of enquiry. It is also a matter of asking relevant questions, choosing the most appropriate tools for answering the questions, skilfully developing and managing interpersonal relationships and adhering to ethical standards of professional behaviour throughout the entire process.

Such expertise does not just happen once we decide to gather data. Rather, it is a life-long practice, involving extensive, active experiences in communities of researchers. Part of the process of becoming bona fide members of these communities involves engaging regularly in professional conferences, reading and contributing to professional journals and books, and connecting with others via professional electronic discussion lists and bulletin boards. It also entails a collective willingness to look past our current understandings, to encourage exploration in unfamiliar territories, and to be open to unexpected experiences and discoveries in these quests.

In the chapters that follow, I present an overview of some of the more common approaches to the study of language, culture and learning from a sociocultural perspective along with a set of basic guidelines for undertaking such research. Also included are suggestions for research projects that individuals at any level of experience in various contexts can undertake, and a collection of additional resources that readers may find useful in their teaching and research endeavours.

Further reading

Creswell, J. (2009) *Research Design: Qualitative, Quantitative, and Mixed Methods Approaches*, 3rd edn, Thousand Oaks, CA: Sage. This text present three approaches to research design: qualitative, quantitative and mixed methods. The chapters are divided into two sections. In the first, the author discusses several matters to consider in selecting a research design. In the second section, the philosophical underpinnings and procedures for designing, undertaking and presenting findings from each of the three approaches are presented.

Dornyei, Z. (2007) *Research Methods in Applied Linguistics*, Oxford: Oxford University Press. The author provides a comprehensive, practical overview of qualitative and quantitative research methods used in applied linguistics. Using examples from classrooms and other settings and drawing on his own experiences, the author guides the reader through the various stages of designing, conducting and reporting research.

Gregory, I. (2003) *Ethics in Research*, London: Continuum. The book discusses the ethical dimensions of social and educational research. It is written especially for novice researchers. The text comprises seven chapters, which address such issues as general principles of ethical research, consent and confidentiality, and moral issues in research.

Locke, L., Silverman, S. and Spirduso, W. (2009) *Reading and Understanding Research*, 3rd edn, Thousand Oaks, CA: Sage. This is a primer to reading, understanding and evaluating qualitative and quantitative research. Written especially for novice researchers, the book provides a step-by-step guide to the critical analysis of research studies and a comprehension discussion on making use of the research findings.

Vogt, W. P. (2005) *Dictionary of Statistics and Methodology: A Nontechnical Guide for the Social Sciences*, 3rd edn, Newbury Park, CA: Sage. This book provides about 2,000 definitions of statistical and methodological terms that are used in the social and behavioural sciences. The definitions are written clearly, and many include examples. All are designed to help readers to understand their use in research reports and articles.

Chapter 8

Approaches to research on language and culture

This chapter:

- describes eight approaches used to research language, culture and learning;
- offers a list of additional readings for each approach.

8.1 Introduction

While one can choose from a variety of research approaches when planning research, eight are most common to research on language, culture and learning from a sociocultural perspective. These include the ethnography of communication, interactional sociolinguistics, conversation analysis, discourse analysis, systemic functional linguistics, critical discourse analysis, linguistic ethnography and the microgenetic approach. While each takes a particular perspective on the study of social action, they share the following features. First, they approach the study of language and culture as one dialogic, mutually constituted unit. Thus, all studies of language are also considered to be studies of culture. Second, they consider social activity to be their unit of analysis. While the size of the unit may vary from one-word actions to larger cultural, institutional and historical activities, the general concern is with uncovering the sociocultural worlds that are constituted in the actions we take and, conversely, uncovering the actions by which our worlds are constituted. This means that the approaches are empirically based, relying on data taken from naturally occurring contexts of action. Finally, while the data are generally qualitative in nature, these approaches recognise the value of using a mix of quantitative and qualitative methods for collecting and analysing data.

The purpose of this chapter is to provide a short overview of each of the eight approaches. The overviews are not meant to be comprehensive, but rather are meant to serve as primers, particularly for novice researchers. For more detailed explanations, readers are encouraged to explore each approach more fully on their own. To help, a list of additional readings is provided after each section. The readings include studies using the approach and essays about the approach itself. The lists are not meant to be inclusive, only illustrative. A search of any database of academic journals and books will surely lead readers to many more examples. A listing of some relevant journals can be found in Chapter 11.

8.2   Ethnography of communication

As discussed in Chapter 1, Dell Hymes developed an approach to the study of language and culture, which he termed the **ethnography of communication**. The objective of this approach is to describe the communicative habits shared by members of a community. Its central unit of analysis is the communicative event. Communicative events occur within social situations such as ceremonies, mealtimes, social gatherings and so on, and are comprised of communicative acts that serve to accomplish the event. For example, a birthday party, an important social situation for many social groups, is comprised of various events, such as opening gifts, playing games, making toasts and eating. Each of these events is comprised of a set of acts by which they are achieved. For example, opening gifts typically include the acts of choosing a gift to open, exclaiming surprise or delight upon opening the gift, and thanking the gift-giver.

Quote 8.1   The focus of ethnography of communication

The starting point is the ethnographic analysis of the communicative habits of a community in their totality, determining what count as communicative events, and as their components, and conceiving no communicative behavior as independent of the set framed by some setting or implicit question. The communicative event is thus central.

Hymes (1962: 13)

As a way to describe the links between the use of language forms and context in a communicative event, Hymes proposed the **SPEAKING** model. This framework was constructed as a guide to researchers to enable systematic descriptions and comparisons of communicative events across groups and communities and, on a broader scale, to uncover the particular ideologies about the participants' worlds embodied in their practices. Each letter of the SPEAKING model represents one of the components of a communicative event to be described; all are interrelated in that each is defined by and helps to define the other. Likewise, the framework itself is contingent on the particular analysis of an event: in other words, as it is used to enhance our understanding of the event, the event itself helps to transform our understanding of the framework. The individual components of the SPEAKING model are:

- **S**ituation, including the physical and temporal setting and scene and its particular cultural definition;
- **P**articipants, including their identities in terms of age, gender, ethnicity, social status and other relevant features, and their roles, relationships and responsibilities as participants in the event;
- **E**nds or outcomes of the event and both group and individual participant goals;
- **A**cts constituting the event, including their form, content and sequential arrangements;
- **K**ey or tone underlying the event, for example, whether it is humorous, serious, or playful;
- **I**nstrumentalities used to realise the event, including the code, e.g. which language or which language variety, and channel, e.g. including vocal and non-vocal (e.g. oral, written, etc.) means, and verbal and non-verbal (e.g. prosodic features, body movements, etc.) means;
- **N**orms of interaction and interpretation of language behaviour including turn-taking patterns;
- **G**enre with which the event is most closely associated, for example, storytelling, gossiping, joking, lecturing, interviewing and so on.

To conduct an ethnography of communication requires researchers to have an in-group member's commonsense understanding of the communicative event of interest and its significance to the group. To gain this knowledge researchers must spend extended time with group members in and around the enactment of the event and this, of course, requires that the researchers develop relationships of trust with the group members. The role of researchers during this time is that of participant-observers, who 'manag[e] ordinary sociability and normal social intercourse' (Walsh, 2004: 233) with the members while maintaining a degree of marginality, that is, 'a poise between a strangeness that avoids over-rapport and a familiarity that grasps the perspectives of the people in the situation' (*ibid.*).

Primary sources of data for ethnographies of communication include multiple audio and video recordings of the focal communicative event gathered during the time that the researcher is acting as participant-observer. Other important sources of data include field notes of the researcher's own experiences and his or her observations of the experiences of the events' participants, interviews with participants, and related documents and written records.

Analysis of communicative events is inductive and typically involves four stages. In the first, regularly occurring features important for the accomplishment of the event are noted. In the second, their patterned uses are described and, in the third stage, the conventional meanings of the patterns are interpreted in light of how they are typically used by the participants to take action. The SPEAKING framework, noted above, serves as a framework for describing the events' significant features and patterns of behaviour and their systematic relationships. In the fourth stage, analysis, the participants' actions, and on a more general level, the events themselves, are explained in light of the larger social, historical and political contexts they help to create. The focus throughout analysis is to develop a complete and accurate account of the event, as witnessed and participated in by the group members.

Closely related to ethnographies of communication are **micro-ethnographies** and **case studies**. While both use similar data collection methods, what distinguishes them from ethnographies of communication is their research focus. In comparison to ethnographies of communication, which entail complete descriptions of the various components of communicative events, a micro-ethnographic approach 'may offer a detailed analysis of only one type of event or even a single instance of an event, perhaps contrasted with a second type of instance found in another context' (Watson-Gegeo, 1997: 138). Similarly, case studies typically focus on behaviours or attributes of a single event or case (Duff, 2007b; Roberts, 2006).

Also related to ethnographies of communication are **critical ethnographies**. While they share a focus on communicative events and use the same methods for data collection and analysis as those used in conventional ethnographies of communication, they differ in that they take an explicitly 'ideologically sensitive orientation' (Canagarajah, 1993: 605) in their analysis. They do so by seeking to address how the patterns and norms of an event index, accommodate to, contest and/or transform larger social structures such as power, social justice, discrimination and so on.

Another related approach is **nexus analysis** (Scollon and Scollon, 2004, 2007). Like critical ethnography, nexus analysis seeks to move past description and understanding to effect real social change. However, it differs from critical ethnography and the other ethnographic approaches in that it takes social action rather than groups of people and communicative events as its focal unit. A nexus analysis begins with the identification of a specific action, e.g. poor classroom performance by a student or group of students, and then seeks to map the complex, socially distributed 'trajectories of people, places, discourses, ideas and objects' (Scollon and Scollon, 2004: viii) that emanate from this action. The aim, according to Scollon and Scollon, is not to create a rich description of the action. It is, instead, to weave connections among the people, events, ideas and resources so that the specific problem embodied in the action can be fully understood and future actions can be shaped to effect positive change.

Quote 8.2   On nexus analysis

Much in a nexus analysis is continuous with both traditional ethnography and with the ethnography of communication, but the starting point is changed and the method for proceeding is also rather different. The purpose of a nexus analysis concerning racism, for example, is not to set out a rational description of racism and its consequences nor to argue that there is no rational basis. Racist acts occur whether or not there is any rational basis. Further, nexus analysis does not presume that we know where we are likely to find racism in a society or even more narrowly within specific events, situations, or actions. Nexus analysis begins where racism is enacted in the experience of real social actors. Then, after some detailed analysis of these actions, the analysis probes outward into the histories of actors, resources, scenes, or settings across time and place – first into the past to see how the actions are constituted and into the future to work toward shaping future actions. Thus the question of 'Where do we start?' is answered quite directly: we start where we are and build out from there.

Scollon and Scollon (2007: 619)

The ethnography of communication approach and its affiliations are also the basis for research on language socialisation practices. As discussed in earlier chapters, the particular concerns of this strand of research are with documenting the patterns of language use, the norms for participation specific to communicative events and the larger cultural understandings embodied in the patterns and norms by which individuals are socialised into their particular groups and communities. Such research has added much to our understanding of the developmental paths that are created within culturally specific ways of using, teaching and learning language and culture.

Because of the broad range, amount and type of data typically collected for the approaches discussed here, it is sometimes easy for researchers to 'get lost' in their data. They may 'lose sight of concrete communication in the sense of actual communities of persons. Forms of formalization, the abstract possibilities of systems, hoped-for keys to mankind as a whole, seem to overthrow the dogged work of making sense of real communities and real lives' (Hymes, 1974: 7). To ensure that the sense being made reflects those whose worlds are being studied, it is especially important for researchers to make clear how data were gathered, including the specific sources used, and that examples used in the research report reflect the entire corpus of data.

Further reading on the ethnography of communication and affiliated approaches

Heath, S. B. and Street, B. (2008) *Ethnography: Approaches to Language and Literacy Research*, New York: Teachers College Press. The authors draw on their own field work and examples of ethnographic studies undertaken in Australia, Iran, South Africa, the United Kingdom, and the United States to provide a highly accessible account on the practicalities of using ethnography to study language and literacy practices.

Gobo, G. (2008) *Doing Ethnography*, London: Sage. The author provides a practical description of the various phases of an ethnographic study, and offers the novice researcher helpful suggestions for conducting research using this approach.

Roberts, C. (2010) 'Language socialization in the workplace' *Annual Review of Applied Linguistics*, 30: 211–227. The article discusses the challenges to understanding and investigating language socialisation of migrant workers and professionals in the workplace of the 21st century. It illustrates these challenges with an in-depth look at the complex linguistic and technical conditions of a high-tech multilingual company.

Scollon, R. and Scollon, S. (2004) *Nexus Analysis: Discourse and the Emerging Internet*, New York: Routledge. The authors offer a detailed summary of the key tenets of nexus analysis and use its methodological resources to examine the links between social practice, culture and technology, and, ultimately, to demonstrate the power of the emerging technologies to transform the socio-cultural landscape.

8.3   Interactional sociolinguistics

As discussed in Chapter 2, **interactional sociolinguistics** (IS) is an approach to the study of language and culture developed by John Gumperz. Where an ethnography of communication approach is focused on the patterns of language use constitutive of a particular communicative event, and the presuppositions held by members of a particular group about the patterns and the event, an IS approach focuses more closely on actual movement in communicative activity and specifically on how participants' use of particular linguistic and other cues affect each other's interpretations of what is happening in the communicative event. The main purpose for undertaking such study is to 'show how diversity affects interpretation' (Gumperz, 1999: 459).

The particular focus of an IS approach is on those cues by which 'speakers signal and listeners interpret what the activity is, how semantic content is to be understood and how each sentence relates to what precedes or follows' (Gumperz, 1982a: 131). Of particular concern are interactions where participants with different cultural presuppositions about seemingly familiar events attempt to interact with each other. Such understanding, Gumperz argues, goes beyond what can be gained from doing only ethnographies of communication since the latter can only tell us what is shared among a group of participants.

Quote 8.3 Objective of IS studies

The aim is to show how individuals participating in such exchanges use talk to achieve their communicative goals in real life situations by concentrating on the meaning making processes and the taken-for-granted background assumptions that underlie the negotiation of shared interpretations.

Gumperz (1999: 454)

This is not to say that IS does not see the value of ethnographies. Quite the contrary, in fact, the IS approach is predicated on findings arising from ethnographies of communication. For researchers to be able to account for intercultural differences in cue use, they must know the conventional meanings that the cues hold for speakers, that is, how they are typically used to create 'culturally realistic scenes' (Gumperz, 1982a: 160). What IS proposes to do is to extend our understanding of the cultural embeddedness of our linguistic actions by demonstrating the consequences that arise from interaction between individuals with different communicative practices for sense making.

Concept 8.1   **Conducting an interactional sociolinguistics study**

An interactional sociolinguistics study involves a two-stage recursive set of procedures.

Stage 1 involves conducting ethnographic research in order to:
(a) become familiar with the local socioculturally constituted environment of the events of interest;
(b) uncover and record recurrent types of communicative events relevant to the research problem at hand;
(c) discover, through participant-observations and interviews with key participants, their expectations and presuppositions for engaging in the activity.

Stage 2 involves analysing recorded events for:
(a) communicative moments of apparent misunderstanding between participants;
(b) prosodic and other cues used by participants to signal their presuppositions and their misunderstandings of each other's intentions at these moments.

Methodologically, IS studies differ slightly from ethnographies of communication in that they involve participants in the data analysis by asking them to listen to or view recordings of the event and point out whatever moments in the recordings they wish to respond to. These moments include times when they felt misunderstood or where they felt they might have misunderstood the other during the time the interaction was actually taking place. These moments are then examined to uncover how differences in the use and interpretation of linguistic cues may have led to unintended consequences in their communicative encounters.

Further readings on interactional sociolinguistics

Auer, P. (ed.) (1998) *Code-Switching in Conversation: Language, Interaction and Identity*, London: Routledge. The studies reported in this volume combine methods of analysis from interactional sociolinguistics and conversation analysis to examine the functions of code-switching in a wide variety of international contexts. In addition to reports of empirical data on the bilingual use of English and Cantonese, French and Italian, Danish and Turkish, and Hebrew and English, contributions include theoretical discussions on the nature of code-switching and bilingual conversation.

Roberts, C., Campbell, S. and Robinson, Y. (2008) *Talking Like a Manager: Promotion Interviews, Language and Ethnicity*, Retrieved from the United Kingdom Department for Work and Pensions website http://campaigns.dwp.gov.uk/asd/asd5/report_abstracts/rr_abstracts/rra_510.asp. This is a report of a study using the research methods of interactional sociolinguistics to examine promotion interviews in ethnically and linguistically diverse areas in order to identify organisational and communicative practices that act as barriers to promotion for ethnic minority candidates.

Sarangi, S. and Roberts, C. (eds) (1999) *Talk, Work and Institutional Order: Discourse in Medical, Mediation, and Management Settings*, Berlin: Mouton de Gruyter. Contributions in this volume take an interdisciplinary approach to the examination of talk and its role in creating workplace practices and relationships. Analyses draw primarily from three approaches: ethnography of communication, conversation analysis, and interactional sociolinguistics. Specific contexts include medical practices, health care delivery, management and social care.

Vine, B., Holmes, J., Marra, M., Pfeifer, D. and Jackson, B. (2008) 'Exploring co-leadership talk through interactional sociolinguistics' *Leadership*, 4: 339–360. The study reported here uses interactional sociolinguistics to examine the ways in which leaders in three organisations display and negotiate leadership in their daily interactions with their workers for the purpose of identifying effective and ineffective leadership practices.

8.4   Conversation analysis

Conversation analysis (CA) is an approach to the study of talk-in-interaction that developed as a field of study in the 1960s around the same time that Dell Hymes and John Gumperz were developing their approaches. It began in sociology as an offshoot of ethnomethodology, the descriptive study of the commonsense reasoning on which people draw to participate in their everyday worlds (Garfinkel, 1967). Drawing on ethnomethodology's interests in the empirical study of social order, CA asserted a fundamental role for interaction as 'the primordial site of human sociality' (Schegloff, 2007: 70), where social life is created and maintained. The specific analytic concern of CA is with describing the procedures by which social group members bring about and maintain social order in their sequentially developed, turn-by-turn actions in talk-in-interaction (Sacks, 1984).

The primary sources of data for conversation analytic studies are naturally occurring activities and events, captured via audio and video recordings. The recordings are then transcribed and analysed for particular resources that participants use to recognise, produce and in other ways coordinate their locally situated actions with each other. Features of the events, in addition to linguistic behaviours, that are typically transcribed include the temporal and sequential organisation of behaviours, such as turns and their distribution, adjacency pairs, overlapping behaviours, pacing and tempo; aspects of speech delivery such as rhythm, intonation, and word stress; and non-verbal behaviours such as body position and eye gaze. Thus, transcriptions of recorded activities can be quite detailed in terms of what is represented.

Example 8.1 contains an example of data transcribed using the conventions of CA. The example is taken from a study by Stivers and Robinson (2006) in which they examined types of preference organisation of responses to questions in multiparty interaction. The excerpt illustrates a type of non-answer response to questions in which one speaker (Mic) first claims an inability to answer another's question (Sha) and then provides an account for his inability to do so (he hasn't, as he states, 'looked at 'em'). The components of this excerpt relevant to the discussion here are the detailed conventions used to mark various features of interaction. These include overlapping or simultaneous talk (indicated by the use of left brackets, [), higher pitch or increased loudness (indicated by the use of underlining), prolongation of sounds (indicated by the use of, after the sound), words that are cut-off (indicated with a hyphen, -, after the word or part of the word, and silence (indicated by numbers in parentheses marking tenths of a second, 0.7 indicates 7/10 seconds of silence).

Example 8.1   Accounting for a non-answer response

```
1 Sha:   [Are those peas any good?

2 Sha:   [((pointing to M's plate))

3        (0.7)

4 Mic:→ [I don' kno:w I- I 'av]en' looked at ['e m. [ I [haven-

5 Nan    [ Ther good for ya,]

6 Sha:                                   [Theh g[ood[faw

7        you? Who knowss:. Wuh wuh u-who aa-oodih you en

8        authority?

9 Nan:   Huh huh huh
```

Stivers and Robinson (2006: 373)

Analyses of talk-in-interaction typically begin with noticing some phenomenon of interest. This can be a simple linguistic token such as 'oh' or the production of a longer behaviour, such as responses to questions, as per Stivers and Robinson's study. The process of deciding on a unit of analysis is inductive in that it is usually identified only after repeated viewings of the recordings. Once an item of interest has been identified, the data are searched for additional occurrences of the phenomenon and the surrounding interactional contexts of each occurrence are described. Cases that appear deviant are important in that they can either confirm the initial analysis or prompt a revision of it. The samples in the collection are then analysed to construct a normative case, the meaning of which is interpreted in light of its use in interaction.

Both the analytic techniques and findings arising from the multiple and varied studies of interaction have been valuable to those interested in researching language and culture from a sociocultural perspective. These studies make visible the multitude of means including, for example, patterns for turn initiations, turn projections, and self- and other-repair strategies in addition to the more traditional syntactic and semantic means we have at our disposal for sense-making in our communicative activities. Although the studies are generally descriptive in nature, they provide a base for taking a more explanatory approach in terms of being able to link the locally situated actions of individuals to the larger institutional and ideological structures embodied in them.

Further readings on conversation analysis

Heritage, J. and Clayman, S. (2010) *Talk in Action: Interactions, Identities, and Institutions*, Malden, MA: Wiley-Blackwell. The text provides a theoretical and methodological overview of CA and an examination of findings on and applications for four institutional domains: calls to emergency numbers, doctor–patient interaction, courtroom trials, and mass communication.

Hutchby, I. and Wooffitt, R. (2008) *Conversation Analysis*, Cambridge: Polity Press. The text provides a comprehensive and accessible overview of the theory and methods of CA. It includes detailed discussions on transcribing and analysing data using a variety of examples to demonstrate the procedures. Also included is a discussion of the relevance of CA to sociology, psychology and linguistics.

Schegloff, E. (2007) *Sequence Organization in Interaction: Volume 1*, Cambridge: Cambridge University Press. The text offers a detailed overview of sequence organisation, defined as the ways in which turns-at-talk are ordered and the actions they accomplish, addressing specifically the sequence organisations for opening, expanding and closing conversations.

Sidnell, J. (2010) *Conversation Analysis: An Introduction*, Malden, MA: Wiley-Blackwell. This text offers an introduction to the methods and analytic techniques of CA. The overview includes real-life examples and step-by-step explanations, making it a useful guide for newcomers to the field.

8.5   Discourse analysis

Discourse analysis is the study of linguistic resources as used in naturally occurring oral and written texts. It is often combined with other approaches such as ethnographies of communication, interactional sociolinguistics and conversation analysis. The linguistic resources of interest can range from single words like 'umm', 'well', and 'ok', to more complex units like speech acts. A discourse analysis of language use usually involves three steps. First, particular lexical, grammatical or discourse features for study are identified in the instances of the collected texts. The patterned uses of the feature or features are then identified and described and their meanings interpreted on the basis of how they are used by those whose texts they are.

In keeping with a sociocultural perspective on language and culture, calls have been made for discourse analysis that is more interpretive and explanatory than merely descriptive, and seeks to explain individuals' uses of their linguistic resources in terms of larger social, political and historical structures (cf. Candlin, 1987). Consequently, in addition to samples of naturally occurring texts for analysis, other sources of data such as participant-observations and participant-perspectives may be drawn on in the analysis.

> **Quote 8.4** On an explanatory approach to discourse analysis
>
> An explanatory approach to discourse analysis seeks to demystify the hidden presuppositions and world-views against which meanings are co-constructed by participants. This approach does so by subjecting the use of particular terms, the choice of phonological and lexico-syntactic realizations, the conversational strategies and routines, the speech act values and the understandings by the participants of the norms of interaction and interpretation in encounters, to analysis and critique. In so doing, this approach seeks to illustrate the degree to which our use of language and our meaning-making, as well as our perceptions of role relationships, are determined by the properties of the social situation, its unstated values and interests, its economy; and from this the degree to which such use confirms the status quo and determines the values of the conversational 'goods' which are being exchanged. . . . It is this attempt to see discoursal features and pragmatic markers characteristic of particular types of encounters . . . as being socially and culturally produced, reflective and reproductive of social relationships between participants, and, importantly, between groups, which marks off an explanatory approach to discourse analysis from one which is merely descriptive or even interpretive.
>
> Candlin (1987: 25–26)

Current advances in electronic software for collecting, storing and analysing large collections or corpora of spoken and written texts have enhanced the kinds of insights that discourse analysis can offer on language use. For example, corpus-based analyses can provide quantitative descriptions of many more variables across a wider range of texts than a traditional analysis can and thus can better account for the representativeness of discourse samples within texts and for distributional patterns across contexts (Conrad, 2002; Upton and Cohen, 2009).

While the types of texts that are analysed by discourse analysts are quite varied, oral and written **narratives** are considered to be a particularly powerful form of discourse. Narratives are considered to be 'retrospective meaning making' (Chase, 2008: 64) by which narrators give shape to and organise past experiences and at the same time display their view of their own and other's positioning within the experiences. Commonly referred to as **narrative inquiry**, the analysis of narratives is based on the premise that stories about one's life experiences offer the analyst a window into understanding how individuals understand themselves and their places in their worlds. It entails eliciting and documenting individual stories through such means as diaries and journals, and oral or written life histories generated through, for example, interviews and memoirs, such as those found in published autobiographies.

According to Pavlenko (2007), narratives are typically analysed for three types of information. The first is **subject reality**, which includes the thoughts and feelings of how the events or phenomena were experienced by the individuals. The second type of information is **life reality**, which comprises repeated events and common themes found in individuals' narrated experiences. The third is **text reality**, which involves how individuals make use of particular linguistic cues in the stories that they tell about themselves to construct themselves as particular kinds of individuals, with particular identities as characters within the story and, at the same time, as individuals who take particular stances in relation to the audience as their stories unfold.

Quote 8.5   Narratives

A narrative can be (a) a short topical story about a particular event and specific characters such as an encounter with a friend, boss or doctor; (b) an extended story about a significant aspect of one's life such as schooling, work, marriage, divorce, childbirth, an illness, a trauma, or participation in a war or social movement; or (c) a narrative of one's entire life, from birth to the present.

Chase (2008: 59)

A recently developed version of discourse analysis is **multimodal discourse analysis**, which incorporates all relevant communicative modes into the analysis. Here, a mode is defined as a 'system with rules and regularities attached to it' (Norris, 2006: 402). The advantage of a multimodal approach is that it makes visible other communicative modes in addition to language used to make meaning, such as gesture, space, objects and visual design. It can also make visible the simultaneity of actions being performed via different modes.

Another alternative is **sociocultural discourse analysis** (Mercer, 2004). This approach is more narrowly framed than the others in that it draws on Vygotskian theory (cf. Chapter 3) to examine how spoken language is used as a tool for thinking collectively in educational settings. It uses both quantitative and qualitative methods of data collection and analysis to describe and, ultimately, assess the intellectual quality of teacher–student and student–student classroom interaction. It differs from conventional discourse analysis in that its focus is less on language itself and 'more on its functions for the pursuit of joint intellectual activity' (*ibid.*: 141). Although developed as a methodology for studying learning in classrooms, sociocultural discourse analysis can be a useful mode of enquiry in other professional and organisational contexts as well.

> **Quote 8.6** Sociocultural discourse analysis
>
> Through a sociocultural discourse analysis we are able to examine and assess the linguistic process whereby people strive for intersubjectivity. We can see how they use language to introduce new information, orientate to each other's perspectives and understandings and pursue joint plans of action . . . [sociocultural discourse analysis] enables those processes of communication to be related to thinking processes and to learning outcomes. In this way, we can examine what is achieved through involvement in discussions, in classrooms and elsewhere – and perhaps offer constructive advice about how discussions can be made more effective.
>
> Mercer (2004: 166)

Further readings on discourse analysis and its variations

Baker, P. (2006) *Using Corpora in Discourse Analysis*, London: Continuum. The author examines how corpus methodologies can be applied to discourse studies. Included in the discussion are descriptions of existing corpora available for research use, steps for building a corpus and techniques for using corpora in discourse analysis.

Biber, D., Connor, U. and Upton, T. (2007) *Discourse on the Move: Using Corpus Analysis to Describe Discourse Structure*, Amsterdam: John Benjamins. The book explores how corpus-based methods can be used for the analysis of the discourse structure of texts. It examines two approaches to the task, top-down and bottom-up, and illustrates them through case studies of the discourse structures found in such genres as fund-raising letters and university classroom teaching.

Clandinin, J. (ed.) (2006) *Handbook of Narrative Inquiry: Mapping a Methodology*, Los Angeles, CA: Sage. This edited volume comprises 24 articles divided into seven sections. Topics addressed include the historical development and philosophical underpinnings of narrative enquiry, different forms of narrative inquiry, ethical issues of doing narrative inquiry and future directions.

LeVine, P. and Scollon, R. (2004) *Discourse and Technology: Multimodal Discourse Analysis*, Georgetown: Georgetown University Press. The volume presents a selection of papers from the fifty-third Georgetown University Round Table (2002) conference, all of which address the impact of new technologies on how discourse data are understood, collected, transcribed and analysed.

8.6   Systemic functional linguistics

Systemic functional linguistics (SFL) is an approach to the study of language that is based on Michael Halliday's theory of language (see Chapters 1 and 3), which considers language to be a social semiotic resource used in specific contexts by individuals to achieve various purposes. One of Halliday's significant contributions is the development of a framework that allows for detailed and systematic descriptions of texts in terms of the functions for which language is used and their relationships to the contexts in which they are used. The framework is *systemic* in that it considers language to be a network of interrelated systems of potential choices. It is *functional* in that it is seeks to account for the functions of linguistic decisions made in particular contexts. The purpose of such a framework is to understand the linguistic choices individuals make in particular contexts and, more generally, to understand 'why a text means what it does, and why it is valued as it is' (Halliday, 1994: xxix).

The unit of analysis for SFL is the text, which is defined as any cohesive stretch of spoken or written language. A key component of the framework which deals with the aspects of context that influence linguistic choices. Register is comprised of three variables and each variable corresponds to a metafunction around which particular lexical and grammatical choices for realising meaning are organised.

The first contextual variable, *field*, has to do with what is being talked or written about. This variable is realised through the ideational function and involves linguistic resources by which we describe, represent or explain our worlds. The second contextual variable, *tenor*, is concerned with the social roles and relationships between the speaker/hearers or writer/readers and their attitudes towards each other. This variable is realised through the interpersonal function of language. *Mode*, the third contextual variable, is the organisational structure of the text, and corresponds to the textual function of language, the linguistic choices for which realise such phenomena as thematic structure and cohesion. Different configurations of lexical and grammatical choices realise different types of texts, which result in different registers.

The strength of the SFL analytic framework is the systematic basis it affords for explaining how texts are similar or different from each other and for making connections between the patterns of linguistic choices in particular texts to their larger social contexts of use. Recently, the use of corpus-based electronic tools for analysing large samples of texts has been incorporated into SFL studies. As noted by Halliday (2005: 130), these tools bring 'a powerful new resource into our theoretical investigations of language'.

A SFL analysis begins with the identification of a text or set of texts of interest and proceeds with the articulation of technical questions to ask about them. Eggins (2004: 330) provides examples of the kinds of questions that can be asked:

• What linguistic evidence is there for claiming that the texts share a common field?

• What linguistic evidence is there for claiming that the texts establish different tenor relationships with their readers?

- Is there any evidence for claiming that one text is more or less cohesive than any other?

Undertaking an SFL analysis can be demanding in that it requires close analyses of patterns of language use in and across entire texts and the use of technical terms to identify and describe the patterns. Thus, it requires a rather high level of skill and an investment of time and effort on the part of the analyst. The payoff, however, is valuable in the understanding it affords of 'how it is that the most ordinary uses of language, in the most everyday situations, so effectively transmit the social structure, the values, the systems of knowledge, all the deepest and most pervasive patterns of the culture' (Halliday, 1973: 43).

Similar to recent movements in discourse analysis to expand the analytic scope to modes other than language, recent research has drawn on the systemic functional framework to analyse the multiple semiotic resources in addition to spoken and written language used to make meaning in discourses. Labelled SF-MDA, the approach has been extended to the analysis of such modes as visual design (e.g. Kress and Van Leeuwen, 2006), gesture (e.g. Martinec, 2004) and displayed art (e.g. O'Toole, 1994).

Further readings on systemic functional linguistics and multimodal analyses

Bednarek, M. and Martin, J. R. (eds) (2010) *New Discourse on Language: Functional Perspectives on Multimodality, Identity, and Affiliation*, London: Continuum. The ten chapters in this volume examine a diverse range of texts from a diverse set of contexts using the systemic functional framework. The volume's key contribution is its extension of systemic-functional theory to the analysis of multimodality, identity and affiliation.

Kress, G. (2009) *Multimodality: A Social Semiotic Approach to Contemporary Communication*, London and New York: Routledge. The author presents a contemporary approach to understanding the multimodality of communication. Topics include multimodality, signs, modes and materiality, design and production, and multimodal analysis.

O'Halloran, K. (ed.) (2004) *Multimodal Discourse Analysis: Systemic Functional Perspectives*, London: Continuum. The nine studies in this volume use a systemic functional framework to investigate multimodal texts and in particular the meanings that emerge from the interaction of two or more modes of communication including language, dynamic and static visual images, electronic media, film and print.

Schleppegrell, M. (2004) *The Language of Schooling: A Functional Linguistics Perspective*, Mahwah, NJ: Lawrence Erlbaum. The author uses systemic functional linguistics to demonstrate the many ways that academic language differs from the language students use outside of school. Included is a discussion of the many challenges that school language presents especially to English language learners who have little exposure to academic language outside of schools.

8.7   Critical discourse analysis

An approach to the study of text features that has its roots in both discourse analysis and SFL is **critical discourse analysis** (CDA). Informed by social theories and a view of language as social action, the purpose of CDA is to move beyond interpretation of the patterned uses of language found in texts to explanation of their ideological underpinnings. More specifically, CDA aims to demonstrate how discourse structures are used to enact, confirm, legitimate, reproduce or challenge dominant ideologies on social issues such as racism and discrimination.

Quote 8.7   Critical discourse analysis

[CDA is] fundamentally interested in analysing opaque as well as transparent structural relationships of dominance, discrimination, power and control, as they are manifested in language.

Baker *et al.* (2008: 279)

In bringing together linguistic theory and social theory, CDA seeks to make visible 'how discourse is shaped by relations of power and ideologies, and the constructive effects that discourse has upon social identities, social relations and systems of knowledge and belief, none of which is normally apparent to discourse participants' (Fairclough, 1992: 12). Moreover, those who engage in CDA do so with the explicit aim of compelling broad social changes by the force of their findings.

Concept 8.2   **Main tenets of CDA**

1   CDA addresses social problems.
2   Power relations are discursive.
3   Discourse constitutes society and culture.
4   Discourse does ideological work.
5   Discourse is historical.
6   The link between text and society is mediated.
7   Discourse analysis is interpretative and explanatory.
8   Discourse is a form of social action.

Source: Fairclough and Wodak (1997)

An affiliated approach to CDA is the **discourse-historical approach** (DHA). Like CDA, it seeks to 'unmask ideologically permeated and often obscured structures of power, political control, and dominance, as well as strategies of discriminatory inclusion and exclusion in language use' (Wodak *et al.*, 1999: 8) and to apply findings of the analysis for social justice and democratic purposes. It differs from CDA in that it addresses the historical dimensions of texts and does so in two ways. First, it situates texts in their historical contexts so as to ascertain the social and political conditions giving rise to them. Second, it explores whether and how the texts change through time, allowing researchers to uncover the social and political conditions which help to preserve the *status quo* and those that facilitate change.

As in discourse analysis, the use of electronic tools for analysing large corpora of texts is playing an increasingly powerful in CDA and DHA by allowing analysts to combine quantitative and qualitative data to build strong empirically based claims about the ideological underpinnings of language use in particular social contexts and, ultimately, to help to bring about social change.

Further readings on critical discourse analysis

Blommaert, J. (2005) *Discourse: A Critical Introduction*, Cambridge: Cambridge University Press. The book provides an accessible, comprehensive overview of the basic principles and methods of critical discourse analysis. It covers topics such as text and context, history and process, and ideology and identity.

Fairclough, N., Cortese, G. and Ardizzone, P. (eds) (2007) *Discourse and Contemporary Social Change*, Bern: Peter Lang. This volume is a collection of 22 papers delivered at an international conference held at the University of Palermo in May 2005. The papers represent a wide variety of theoretical and methodological perspectives, all which address discourse as an aspect of social change.

van Dijk, T. (2010) *Discourse and Power*, Houndsmills: Palgrave. This is a collection of articles written by the author, several of which have been published earlier. Topics include the role of discourse in the reproduction of power and domination in society and the ways in which media and political leaders control access to public discourse.

Wodak, R. and Meyer, M. (eds) (2009) *Methods of Critical Discourse Analysis*, 2nd edn, Thousand Oaks, CA: Sage. This book provides a comprehensive introduction to critical discourse analysis. It includes chapters that discuss the theoretical underpinnings of the approach, describe methods of data collection and analysis, and introduce some of the leading figures in this field of research.

8.8   Linguistic ethnography

A recent addition to contemporary approaches to the study of language and culture is **linguistic ethnography** (LE), defined as 'a cluster of research'

(Tusting and Maybin, 2007: 578) which seeks to better understand the relationships between micro-levels of discourse and text practices and broader social processes and structures. By joining linguistics with ethnography, LE combines 'a formal, abstract discipline and tried-and-tested, finely-tuned methods' (Tusting and Maybin, 2007: 576) for analysing oral and written language practices with 'the more open, reflexive social orientation of ethnographic methods' (*ibid.*) to understand the social processes and structures that give shape to and are shaped by linguistic practices.

Rampton *et al.* (2004) describe five traditions that have given shape to current LE research. Although they are rooted firmly in the socio- and applied linguistics scholarship of the United Kingdom, they also have strong intellectual connections to scholarship in the United States, most centrally that associated with the field of linguistic anthropology. The first tradition is the New Literacy Studies (see, for example, Barton and Hamilton, 1998; and Street, 1993a, b). This tradition draws on Dell Hymes's ethnography of communication approach and other more general ethnographic methods to understand the relationship between local literacy practices and broader social ideologies. A second tradition is the work on ethnicity, language and inequality in the workplace in the UK that has drawn on Gumperz's interactional sociolinguistics approach, reviewed earlier (see, for example, Gumperz and Roberts, 1991; Roberts *et al.*, 1992). Third is the research linking ideology to language and cultural practices as represented in critical discourse analytic studies (cf. Fairclough, 1992, 1995). A fourth tradition has been concerned with examining cognitive development in the classroom, and is represented by work drawing on Vygotsky's theory of development to examine the links between teaching and learning as reflected in teacher–student interaction (e.g. Wells, 1999; Mercer, 2004). The final tradition is what Rampton *et al.* (2004: 11) refer to as 'interpretive applied linguistics for language teaching'. This tradition is characterised by conceptual discussions of rather than empirical research on teaching and learning and is associated with the work of British scholars such as Widdowson (2003) and Brumfit (1984).

Contemporary LE distinguishes itself from the mainly US-based linguistic anthropological approaches of ethnography of communication, IS and micro-ethnography in the following ways. First, it brings a UK research perspective to these lines of research. Second, it is much broader methodologically in that it makes use of various methods for analysing discourse including systemic functional linguistics and critical discourse analysis in addition to those typical of ethnographies of communication and IS studies. A final distinction is that it draws more extensively on social theories, including those of Bakhtin, Bourdieu and Giddens, to uncover the social processes and structures embodied in and constitutive of local discourse practices (cf. Tusting and Maybin, 2007).

Quote 8.8 Key premises of linguistic ethnography

Specifically, associates in linguistic ethnography hold:

1 that the contexts for communication should be investigated rather than assumed. Meaning takes shape within specific social relations, interactional histories and institutional regimes, produced and construed by agents with expectations and repertoires that have to be grasped ethnographically; and

2 that analysis of the internal organization of verbal (and other kinds of semiotic) data is essential to understanding its significance and position in the world. Meaning is far more than just the 'expression of ideas', and biography, identifications, stance and nuance are extensively signalled in the linguistic and textual fine-grain.

Rampton (2007: 585)

Further readings on linguistic ethnography

Creese, A. (2008) 'Linguistic ethnography', in K. A. King and N. H. Hornberger (eds), *Encyclopedia of Language and Education, 2nd edn, Volume 10: Research Methods in Language and Education* (pp. 229–241), New York: Springer. The author provides a very useful summary of the development of this approach, its relationship to similar approaches and its current research directions.

Linguistic Ethnography Forum. Begun as a special interest group of the British Association of Applied Linguistics (BAAL), the UK Linguistic Ethnography Forum (www.ling-ethnog.org.uk) hosts an electronic repository of publications and other resources devoted to the development of work in linguistic ethnography in the UK and elsewhere.

8.9 Microgenetic approach

The **microgenetic approach** differs from the approaches discussed above in that the concern is specifically with the study of learning. However, unlike traditional methods concerned with learning, which seek to study communicative behaviour in its final form, the concern here is with studying social action in the very process of change. This is in keeping with Vygotsky's theory of development, which asserts that the only way to understand human action in its final form is by analysing its development (cf. Chapter 3).

> **Quote 8.9**   On the significance of the historical method for studying development
>
> To encompass in research the process of a given thing's development in all its phases and changes – from birth to death – fundamentally means to discover its nature, its essence, for 'it is only in movement that a body shows what it is'. Thus, the historical study of behavior is not an auxiliary aspect of theoretical study, but rather forms its very base.
>
> Vygotsky (1978: 64–65)

Vygotsky posited four dimensions of historical, or developmental, study of human action: *phylogenesis*, which considers the development of human action in the evolution of the human species; *sociocultural history*, which considers its development over time in a particular culture; *ontogenesis*, which considers its development over the life of an individual; and *microgenesis*, which considers the development of human action over the duration of particular interactions in specific social settings.

Microgenetic studies are small-scale studies in which behaviours of an individual or small group are observed over a period of time to identify changes, and the specific contextual conditions of these changes. Data are collected via observations occurring throughout the specified period of time, using video and audio recordings, collections of other visual, written or electronic records, and additional ethnographic data as relevant. The density of observations should be high enough to capture even the smallest movements. These observations are then subjected to both qualitative and quantitative analyses. Qualitative analyses can uncover the changing shapes of the social actions as they happen. Quantitative measures such as frequency counts, sign tests, and other **non-parametric measures**, can also be employed to detect whether any changes in the observed actions are significant from one point to another, and how the changes relate to specific aspects of the event.

According to Sielger (2006), microgenetic studies address five features of change. The first is the path of change, that is, whether the change is qualitative, resulting in different types of knowledge or ability, or quantitative, resulting in changes in speed or accuracy, or whether both types of change occur. The second feature is the rate of change, defined as the amount of time or length of experience taking place before change appears. A third feature is the breadth of change, which addresses whether the change is domain-specific or applicable to several domains. Microgenetic studies also address the variability of change, that is, how consistent or not patterns of changes are across time, across contexts, across individuals and so on. Finally, microgenetic studies address the sources of change, and more specifically, whether change is facilitated by practice, feedback, social collaboration and so on.

The value of the microgenetic approach is that it allows researchers to understand changes in behaviour in a way that more traditional methods cannot. The intensive collection of repeated observations of individuals' social actions over time, allows researchers to see not only whether change occurs, but what the behaviours look like as they are undergoing change and they allow researchers to link specific changes to specific contextual conditions. Its value as a method for understanding learning is one reason why the prevalence of studies in the field of applied linguistics using this approach to the study of language learning has increased greatly over the last several years.

Quote 8.10 On the value of the microgenetic method

A critical feature of the method is that it allows change to be viewed as 'untidy', rather than the 'tidy' transition suggested by cross-sectional or longitudinal studies. It allows us to identify whether change may be sudden and discrete, or smooth and gradual and, importantly, whether different individuals experience the same transitions. . . . It is only by taking fine-grained measures across the period of change that these elements of change can be identified and measured.

Flynn *et al.* (2007: 4)

Further readings on the microgenetic approach

Flynn, E. and Siegler, R. (2007) 'Measuring change: Current trends and future directions in microgenetic research', *Infant and Child Development*, 16: 135–149. This report is an introduction to a special issue on microgenetic research. The authors summarise five critical features of change – path, rate, breadth, variability and source – and then address several questions on the microgenetic approach including whether the microgenetic approach is a method, a theory or a philosophy and what the next steps are for this approach to the study of learning.

Granott, N. and Parziale, J. (eds) (2002) *Microdevelopment: Transition Processes in Development and Learning*, Cambridge: Cambridge University Press. This edited volume presents studies on development and learning that use microgenetic methods. Four themes are addressed: the nature of variability, mechanisms that create transitions to higher levels of knowledge, interrelations between micro and macro development, and the effect of context.

Kim, D. and Hall, J. K. (2002) 'The role of an interactive book reading programme in the development of L2 pragmatic competence', *Modern Language Journal*, 86: 332–348. The researchers report on a study that used microgenetic methods to explore the connection between the participation of a small group of native-speaking Korean children in an interactive book-reading programme and their development of particular linguistic and conversational resources in English.

van Compernelle, R. A. (2010) 'Incidental microgenetic development in second-language teacher-learner talk-in-interaction', *Classroom Discourse*, 1: 66–81. The study reported here used microgenetic methods to examine the collaborative construction of an object of learning between a learner of French and a teacher during an oral proficiency interview.

8.10 Summary

The approaches presented in this chapter have informed a great deal of research on language, culture and learning in applied linguistics. Those who are new to the field, or at least new to research, are encouraged to seek out additional sources for guidance and information on these and other related approaches. The more familiar we are with options for undertaking investigations, the more likely we are to formulate well-designed research plans whose methods will facilitate finding answers to our questions.

Chapter 9

Guidelines for doing research

This chapter:

- overviews the research cycle for planning and carrying out research projects;
- provides a set of guidelines for evaluating research;
- offers a list of additional readings for understanding and engaging in research.

9.1 Introduction

The scope of research on language and culture from a sociocultural perspective is vast, encompassing studies of myriad culturally situated, semiotically mediated contexts of social life. Contexts of study have ranged in size from one or two individuals to the entire workforce of an organisation, and in levels of formality, ranging from very informal contexts such as telephone chats and family meal conversations to more formal contexts such as professional practices comprising institutions and organisations. The purposes for conducting research are also varied, ranging from enhancing understanding of a particular phenomenon to effecting change to or within the context under study.

Regardless of the type of research we are interested in, to be a professional in the discipline requires the ability to read and evaluate a research study and determine the merits of its findings. This is what Perry (2005) refers to as a discerning consumer, that is, 'one who has self-confidence in his or her own ability to gauge research so that s/he can evaluate the influence a study should have on practical issues of concern' (p. 6). In addition to being informed consumers of research, it is to our collective benefit as a field of professionals that we become skilled in conducting our own investigations. We must be able to ask relevant questions, choose appropriate methods for collecting and analysing data, be rigorous in the process, and be willing to reflect on the findings, making changes to our practices where appropriate, and share what we have learned with others. Toward these ends, this chapter lays a foundation for understanding and engaging in research on language and culture by providing a detailed overview of the research process.

9.2 The research cycle

The research process is best understood as a cycle of six actions. These include identifying concerns and forming questions, choosing the most appropriate research approach for addressing the questions, gathering the data, analysing them, reflecting on the findings and deciding what to do based on what was found, and disseminating or in some way sharing what was learned with others. The process is cyclic in that each step leads to the next, with the findings from one project generating new concerns and questions for further investigation. The six steps, illustrated in Figure 9.1, are explained in greater detail below.

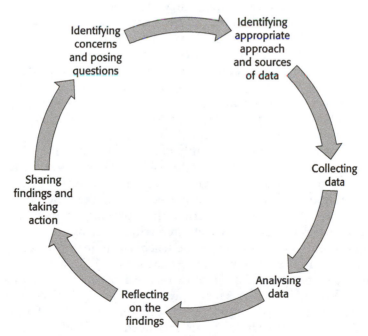

Figure 9.1   **Research cycle**

9.2.1   Identifying concerns and developing research questions

A key component in designing a research project entails identifying particular concerns or issues to address. These concerns can arise from our own personal or professional experiences. For example, those of us with experiences as immigrants may have interests in understanding the varied life trajectories of immigrants within a particular community. Alternatively, those who have experienced the myriad internet-based means of communication may be interested in understanding the kinds of social networks that these means offer to different groups. A desire to effect change in our lives can also inform our research interests. For example, as teachers, we may be concerned with improving language teaching and learning conditions in the particular educational context in which we work. Or, we may be concerned with improving professional relationships among linguistically and culturally diverse individuals in our workplace setting.

Additionally, we can be asked to collaborate on research projects that seek to address problems that have already been identified by others. For instance, professional health caregivers may enlist our efforts in examining caregiver–client consultations for the purposes of improving client care. Finally, concerns can come from issues raised by others in conference or other type of formal presentations, or from our readings of issues discussed in published papers and books.

Once concerns have been generated, we can prioritise them according to their importance or significance, and from this ranked list, a specific topic for investigation can be identified. Reviews of literature can be particularly useful in helping to refine research concerns. Reviews can help us determine what has already been done on the general topic, where discrepancies or disagreements may exist and how the proposed project will complement or enhance current understandings.

Once we have decided on the specific focus, the next step is to generate a list of questions about it. For example, an interest in more macro beliefs about a particular ethnic group embodied in a community-based social institution can lead to the following questions: What official documents produced by the institution refer to or in some way deal with the ethnic group in question? What themes or topics related to the group characterise the documents? Likewise, a concern with improving language pedagogy can lead to questions such as: What interaction patterns are typical of this learning context? What roles does the teacher play in constructing them, and what role do the students play? What kinds of linguistic actions are students becoming appropriated into via their participation in these patterns? And so on. Research questions play a pivotal role in any project in that they give it direction and coherence, they keep the researcher focused, and they make relevant the kinds of data that need to be collected to address them. Thus, it is important that we articulate research questions that are clear, relevant and workable.

Concept 9.1   **Key components of good research questions**

Good questions are:

- *Clear*   They are unambiguous and easily understood.
- *Specific*   They are sufficiently specific for it to be clear what constitutes an answer.
- *Answerable*   We can see what data are needed to answer them and how those data will be collected.
- *Interconnected*   The questions are related in some meaningful way, forming a coherent whole.
- *Substantively relevant*   They are worthwhile, non-trivial questions worthy of the research effort to be expended.

Source: Robson (2002: 59)

Once we have chosen a set of questions on which to focus, we need to consider whether they are reasonable in light of any constraints we may have in terms of time and availability of resources. It may be, for example, that the question asked is both significant and of great interest to us, but we lack the resources needed to address it adequately. A final decision to be made before beginning to collect data is the intended outcome. In other words, we need to consider what we plan to do with the findings. Perhaps the goal is to present the findings at a peer-reviewed conference specifically for feedback on the study, with the ultimate aim of publishing a report of the study in a refereed journal and thereby contribute to professional discussions on that particular topic. Alternatively, we may wish to use the findings to help to justify changes to a particular organisational programme or practice. Whatever the objectives, they will help to guide the implementation of the study, so it is important that they are clear to everyone involved in the research project.

Negotiating access and relationships

Once we have identified the specific setting and participants, we will need to arrange access. Some places require many levels of permission. Many public schools in the United States, for example, require that researchers submit formal applications to district-wide boards of officials for approval before they can seek permission from any particular group of participants in a school. Other professional sites may have similar requirements.

Concept 9.2   Checklist in negotiating access

1 Identify and establish points of contact, and individuals from whom permission is required.

2 Prepare an outline of the study.

3 Formally request permission to carry out the study from all official channels.

4 Discuss the study with 'gatekeepers' and be sure to address potentially sensitive issues.

5 Discuss the study with the likely participants, being sure to address potentially sensitive issues.

6 Be prepared to modify the study based on your discussions.

Source: Based on Robson (2002: 379)

As discussed in Chapter 7, a project's success rests on sustaining mutual goodwill and understanding among all the relevant parties. Thus, the need to maintain good relationships and understandings with various gatekeepers and stakeholders continues well after we have gained access. Candlin and Sarangi (2004a: 3) call this mutual understanding a 'reciprocity of perspectives'. Such a stance, they argue, must extend through the entire project, 'from problematisation at the outset of an inquiry, through the identification of particular and critical moments of focus, the selection of appropriate research tools, through the process of data collection to its analysis and, especially, to the warranting of results and their exploitation and dissemination' (*ibid.*).

9.2.2   Identifying research approach and sources of data

Once the research questions have been articulated, the next step is to formulate a plan for gathering data to help to address them. This entails identifying the approach that we consider to be the most appropriate (cf. Chapter 8). The approach we choose is, of course, very much tied to the questions we are asking. For example, if the concern is uncovering rhetorical patterns typical of a particular collection of oral or written texts, then a discourse analytic or an SFL approach would be appropriate. If the concern is not only with uncovering points at which the use and interpretation of particular linguistic cues by participants in an interaction differ, but also with the effects the differences have on the subsequent unfolding of the communicative event, then an interactional sociolinguistic approach would be appropriate.

Once we have settled on an approach, we must determine the particular sources of data we wish to use (see Figure 9.2). While there are several possible sources of data we can tap into, those we choose are determined in

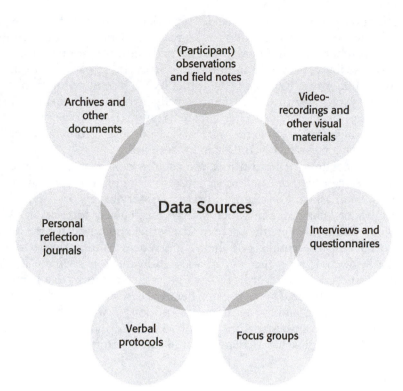

Figure 9.2   **Sources of data**

part by the research approach and questions. An ethnography of communication, for example, will require data from multiple sources, including, videotapes of the communicative event of interest, field notes from long-term observations of the event, and collections of documents that are important to the accomplishment of the event. On the other hand, a micro-analysis of one communicative event may require less data from multiple sources collected over a period of time, and more finely tuned transcriptions of the event itself in order to capture the moment-to-moment movement of actions in the interaction. Several data sources are discussed below.

(Participant) observations and field notes

Observations require us to be present for an extended period of time in the context under study. For example, if we are interested in the routine activities of a classroom community of language learners, we need to spend time in the classroom observing the activities. If, during the observations, we decide to participate in the context, we are considered to be a

participant-observer. We can decide to participate fully in the events, for example, acting either as an aide to the teacher in the classroom context or as the teacher. An advantage to full participation is that our presence is likely to raise few concerns or questions among the other participants in that context. A major disadvantage is the difficulty we face in trying to observe and collect data and at the same time be a fully involved participant. A more reasonable position may be to participate as an interested observer. In this case, the other participants are aware of the purpose of our presence but we do not have to be involved fully in all activities.

Written accounts, or **field notes**, are usually kept on our observations. These notes can be more or less structured, depending on the questions that have been asked. For example, prior to observing a work site, we can make a list of behaviours in which we are particularly interested. While observing, we can then use the list to note whether and how often the behaviours occur and the contexts of their occurrences. Alternatively, interest may be in documenting the myriad ways individuals participate in their workplace interactions, regardless of whether they conform to a particular list. In this case, the field notes become detailed descriptions of the different behaviours observed and the contextual conditions in which they occurred. However we choose to structure our observations and note-taking, it is imperative to have a well-articulated system for recording observations and taking notes.

Video recordings and other visual materials

Video recordings of communicative events and activities are able to capture actions as they occur in real time. They allow us to study the connection between (a) linguistic actions and spatial organisation, (b) linguistic actions and body movements, including gestures, posture and facial movements and (c) communicative stability and change across time in ways that cannot be performed by any other means of data collection.

Decisions about where to place recording devices, how many devices to use, and how often to record are important to the quality of the data collected. For example, placing one camcorder in the corner of a fairly small room may not permit all of the activity to be captured nor is it likely to capture all of the sounds, especially if there are several individuals interacting at the same time. Thus, it is important that we know the setting well enough to be able to set up devices in ways that will allow us to record all the sights and sounds particular to the context. A note of caution: turning recording equipment on or moving the equipment around a room can be distracting to participants. Care should be taken to minimise such intrusions (cf. Clarke, 2003).

Photographs from the context are another source of data. These are subject to the same issues of representation that video recordings are in that decisions made on what and when to photograph need to be systematic and well-articulated. Issues of how to maintain participant confidentiality become paramount when collecting visual records of participation, even more so when recording in contexts where some but not all participants agree to participate. There is no definitive way of addressing these matters, but as discussed in Chapter 7, it is one of the practical issues of ethics that researchers who rely on visual records for data must confront.

A last point concerns the means by which data are collected. Recent developments in digital technologies for capturing the incredible complexity and dynamics of social action are transforming research on language and culture. Not only has the quality of video and photographic recordings improved, but the ways in which we can use the data have as well. Such tools, for example, allow for the direct linking of transcriptions to digitised audio and video recordings, and thus facilitate the instant retrieval of annotations and immediate access to data from annotations. In addition, in supporting the construction of repositories of digitised communication data, the tools allow for sharing and analysis of data across the internet, and thus facilitate cross-institution, geographically distributed, networked collaboration on collection and analysis of data from a wide range of contexts and sites that have not traditionally been part of mainstream research. These cross-case and cross-corpora comparisons are helping to build an international database of samples of social action that can be drawn on for further research and use (see, e.g. Talkbank.org for examples of such databases).

Interviews and questionnaires

Interviews are conversations conducted with participants. They can be a stand-alone source of data or used in conjunction with other methods to help us make sense of data gathered through other means. They are usually audio or video recorded and then transcribed for analysis. Interviews are typically of three types: **structured, semi-structured** and **open**. The purpose of structured interviews is to obtain specific kinds of information on a particular topic. The interview questions are compiled prior to the interview, leaving little opportunity for the interviewee to address other topics. This type of interview is helpful when we have a set of specific questions in mind and are interested in seeking answers to only those questions.

The purpose of semi-structured interviews is also to get answers to specific questions and so here, too, we come to the interview with a set of pre-formulated questions. However, unlike structured interviews, here the interviewee is afforded opportunities to elaborate upon his or her answers. Open interviews are even less structured. In these interactions, we are free to direct the discussion as we wish, expanding on some issues, raising others for discussion and so on. The interviewee also has the freedom to raise additional topics for discussion and in other ways move the conversation in various directions.

An advantage to both semi-structured and open interviews is that they are flexible and thus allow for the possibility of our ending up with unanticipated perspectives on the research topic. They are particularly useful if we are interested in obtaining others' ideas on a general topic, or in uncovering others' understandings of particular concepts or terms. A disadvantage is that the interview data may be difficult to code and analyse, especially if each interviewee addresses a different aspect of the topic or decides to move the conversation towards different topics altogether. Once we have decided upon the structure of the interview, there are several additional issues we must deal with, including identifying willing participants, gaining their trust and establishing rapport, and agreeing on a location for conducting the interviews. It is assumed that those conducting the interview are proficient in the language and culture of the interviewees, and when necessary, are able to draw on the skills of appropriate interpreters during the interview process. In specialised contexts such as medical or legal settings, we may also have to draw on knowledgeable members from that context to make sense of special registers with which we may be unfamiliar.

Questionnaires are similar to structured and semi-structured inteviews in that they solicit specific kinds of information from respondents. An advantage to using questionnaires is that they allow the researcher to gather data from a much greater number of individuals than one can through interviews. A disadvantage is that they create distance between the researcher and the respondents. Lacking the interpersonal nature of interviews, questionnaires do not allow the researcher and respondents to work toward shared understandings of perspectives on questions and responses. Moreover, the kind of information being sought by questions is never fully obvious to respondents; how questions are phrased can influence how respondents think about or remember events, people and objects (Cicourel, 2003).

Emerging electronic technologies have expanded the means for conducting interviews and using questionnaires with video and other internet connections affording both synchronous and asynchronous exchanges that are not limited by geographical or temporal boundaries. Eliminating location and time constraints, in turn, allows for the inclusion of a greater number and diversity of participants as interviewees and respondents to questionnaires.

Focus groups

Focus groups are small groups of about six to ten individuals who undertake a discussion, facilitated by the researcher, of a particular topic or theme. Focus groups are often used to help researchers define and refine themes, concepts, and questions to be used in the research project. They are also used to explore themes and perspectives that are difficult to access through other data sources. Focus group meetings can take place at the site of the study or off-site, in someone's home or a public meeting room and the data are typically collected via audio or video recordings, which are then transcribed.

A challenge to facilitating focus groups successfully is that they require the facilitator to be skilled in managing small group discussions. They must be skilled, for example, in using questions, prompts, and probes to help participants speak to issues they may not have thought about and deal with contradictory statements in their own talk and opposition from other participants (cf. Myers, 2007).They must also be skilled in facilitating the discussion so that one or two members do not dominate, in making space for alternative views and voices while managing inappropriate behaviour, in keeping the discussion on the topic without leading it, and in sustaining an appropriate and adequate pace of talk so that all the topics are covered.

Verbal protocols

Verbal protocols involve asking individuals to verbalise their thoughts while engaged in a particular activity. The purpose is to glean from individuals' comments, the cognitive processes and strategies they are using to accomplish the activity. They are a useful source of data if, for example, one is interested in gaining an understanding of individuals' perceptions of their involvement in a task. Verbal protocols are usually audio or video recorded, and later transcribed for analysis.

A variation of the verbal protocol is the **stimulated recall**. In this version individuals are prompted to recall thoughts they had while engaging in a recently completed activity or to provide comments on their participation in some activity upon being presented with a visual or written selection of their earlier activity. This is often used in an interactional sociolinguistics approach, where participants are brought in to observe their taped participation in an event and asked to stop the tape wherever they think their linguistic actions were being misunderstood by the other participants, or where they might have misunderstood those actions of their interlocutors (cf. Chapter 8). The researcher then begins the analysis of contextualisation cue difference at those points.

Personal reflection journals

Personal journals are documents produced by the researcher in which he or she records his or her feelings and reflections during the time he or she is engaged in the study. They usually contain two parts. In the first, the researcher records detailed descriptions of incidents, readings, observations or other events considered significant to the research context. In the second, the researcher records personal feelings, opinions and reactions to the incidents, readings, observations and events. Journal recording is typically done according to some schedule, for example, at the end of each week of data collection. While journals are often written, they can also be kept as audio or video recordings. In addition to providing the researcher with additional documentation of events and activities taking place in the research context, the journals can help to make apparent whether and how the researcher might have influenced the collection and analysis of data.

Example 9.1   Researcher diary notes

This is an example of a researcher's diary notes, kept while the researcher was involved in a study exploring research capacity in a nursing and midwifery higher education institute in Ireland.

> Following a second interview with the CNMFFa, I was asked 'How is your own work going?' I described the amount of data gathering that I had conducted. I also said laughingly 'Of course, I've nothing written!' I meant by this the type of formal writing of chapters and sections. I felt safe in saying this as this particular CNMFF had described how writing had only commenced in the second half of the third year of the Fellowship.
>
> Researcher Diary 11/1/05 (Condell, 2008: 327)

Archives and other documents

Archives are collections of official documents that provide a historical record of a context. They can include written reports, records, tapes, newsletters, memoranda, physical artefacts and other materials that are typically stored in libraries, offices and other sites designated as official repositories. Such data can provide different viewpoints on a topic, and thus aid in comparative analyses across contexts. It is also useful to identify and collect other documents and artefacts, which may not have official status but may be pertinent to a particular research setting. An ever-expanding source of various types of documents is the internet. Web pages and blogs, for example, have become important sites of online self-representations of individuals, groups, organisations and communities.

Quote 9.1   On the value of web blogs as a source of data

Blogs offer substantial benefits for social scientific research. . . . First, they provide a publicly available, low-cost and instantaneous technique for collecting substantial amounts of data. Further, blogs are naturalistic data in textual form, allowing for the creation of immediate text without the resource intensiveness of tape recorders and transcription . . . they also enable access to populations otherwise geographically or socially removed from the researcher. . . . Moreover, the archived nature of blogs makes them amenable to examining social processes over time, particularly trend and panel type longitudinal research. These qualities of practicality and capacity to shed light on social processes across space and time, together with their insight into everyday life, combine to make blogs a valid addition to the qualitative researcher's toolkit.

Hookway (2008: 92–93)

9.2.3   Collecting data

Once the participants and sources of data have been identified, the next decision to be made concerns the time period during which data will be collected. *When* and *how often* we decide to collect data depends on our research questions. If, for example, we are interested in perceptions of newly arrived adult immigrants in a workplace language programme of their language needs, then, clearly, the data need to be collected when the individuals first enter the programme. Likewise, if we are interested in documenting the changes in individuals' knowledge and skills as they apprentice to a particular programme, then data should be collected over an extended period of time in order to produce enough data to be able to document any changes that occur.

A last point to be considered before the process of data collection can begin is the manner in which we collect the data. No matter what questions are asked, what research approach is taken or what sources of data are used, we must go about the process of collecting data systematically. This requires that we be able to articulate clearly and methodically any and all decisions we make about sources and methods of data collection. If, for example, we decide to ask individuals in a multilingual workplace to generate a list of their concerns, all participants of the group should be involved in the task. If, however, there are time or location constraints, or the number is just too large to be practical and we decide to enlist a small group, we must be able to state the criteria we used in enlisting the participation of individual respondents. Likewise, if we decide to videotape instances of a particular communicative event, the criteria for deciding when and how often to tape must be stated clearly, and the specific methods used to tape followed as systematically as possible for all recordings. Otherwise, as pointed out in Chapter 7, we run the risk of collecting data that support our own version of reality, whether or not it adequately reflects the reality of those whose contexts of experiences are the focus of study.

9.2.4   Analysing the data

Analysis of the data is the fourth step in the research process. This entails coding, or transforming the data into another form. How we code depends on the kind of data we have collected and our larger research questions. For example, coding can involve identifying specific linguistic features of a set of verbal data and transforming them into numerical values, as with corpus-based analyses of texts. Alternatively, if we are working from transcriptions of videotaped interactions, and the concern is with patterns of interaction, we may begin the analysis by coding the function of utterances according to their syntactic structure (e.g. coding the utterance 'what did you say?' as a question) or according to the action they perform in the interaction (e.g. coding the utterance 'what did you say?' as a statement of disapproval). In other cases of interaction, the focus might be on finding specific communicative event boundaries, and coding the cues used by participants to open and close them. Often, we will need to construct our own coding framework, although it is useful to draw on and, where possible, incorporate coding schemes that others have used. Whatever coding framework we decide to use, it is important to define it clearly and to use it consistently across similar sources of data.

Once the data are coded, the next step involves searching across datasets for regularities or patterns of occurrence, and grouping and organising the regularities into larger segments for subsequent qualitative and/or quantitative interpretation. In terms of analysis across large datasets, the larger segments can function as a framework with which to make systematic comparisons with subsequent segments and to identify and interpret individual actions within them. The use of a comparative framework ensures comprehensive treatment of the phenomenon under study.

Quote 9.2   On the comparative method in data analysis

The method begins with a small batch of data. A provisional analytic scheme is generated. The scheme is then compared to other data, and modifications made in the scheme as necessary. The provisional analytic scheme is constantly confronted by 'negative' or 'discrepant' cases until the researcher has derived a small set of recursive rules that incorporate all the data in the analysis.

Mehan (1979: 21)

A last step involves arranging the findings so that they represent the data fairly and accurately. Hymes's (1980) SPEAKING model (cf. Chapter 8) is one example of a framework that can be used to represent and compare findings from investigations of particular communicative events. Qualitative data can also be represented by transcriptions, diagrams, flow charts and pictures, in addition to written descriptions. In the case of quantitative analyses, findings can be represented as numbers and displayed in the form of tables, charts and graphs.

Analysis of the data is a critical component of any research project. All of the claims we make must be based on careful, explicit and systematic analysis. Antaki and his colleagues (2003) have identified a number of pitfalls to avoid when analysing verbal data, some of the more common of which are under-analysis through summary, the use of isolated extracts from the data or simply spotting features. What we as researchers must strive for, they argue, is 'close engagement with one's text or transcripts, and the illumination of their meaning and significance through insightful and technically sophisticated work' (*ibid.*: 18). Our rigorous, comprehensive treatment of data coupled with a 'methodological awareness', that is, an ability 'to anticipate the consequences of methodological decisions while carrying out a research project' (Seale, 2002: 97) helps ensure the credibility of our findings.

9.2.5   Reflecting on the findings

Once the data have been sufficiently analysed and the findings presented, the next step involves reflecting on the findings in relation to the questions originally asked and, where appropriate, identifying steps for using the findings to meet the intended outcomes. Some questions to guide our reflections include: What did we find? Of the findings, which ones did we anticipate and which ones were unexpected? Were our questions answered adequately or were there obstacles that prevented us from completing the project? Could the project have been done differently? How so? What new knowledge or understanding can we take from the study? In what ways can the findings contribute to the real work setting in which or for which the project was undertaken? What might our next steps be?

Figure 9.3 offers a set of criteria for reflecting on and evaluating one's research project.

9.2.6   Sharing findings and taking action where appropriate

The final step in the research process entails sharing what has been learned with others and, where appropriate, taking action. No matter what was found, there will be something worthwhile to report from which others can learn. Ways to share the new knowledge or understandings include more structured, academic activities such as formal presentations of the findings to our colleagues at meetings arranged by local, state, regional, national or international professional organisations. We can also submit reports for publication consideration to professional journals or newsletter.

Figure 9.3   Criteria for evaluating research projects

A. Introduction to problem

Is the stated problem clear and researchable?

> Is the rationale for the problem clearly presented?
> Is the research problem situated in a relevant theoretical framework?
> Are the research questions stated clearly?
> Is it clear what the study will contribute?

Is there a thorough review of literature?

> Are cited references relevant to the problem and up-to-date?
> Does the review make clear the relevance of the problem?

B. Methods

Did selection procedures identify participants and contexts appropriate to the problem?

> Are characteristics of participants and site described?
> Are reasons given for participant and site selection?
> Are selection and identification of participants ethical?

Are methods appropriate and adequate?

> Are the data sources and collection methods adequately described and appropriate
>   for answering the research questions?
> Is it clear how, when, and by whom data were collected?
> Are procedures for analysis, including descriptions of coding procedures, fully
>   described and appropriate for the kinds of data collected?

C. Findings

Are findings appropriate and clearly presented?

> Are the data reported clearly?
> Are connections between the questions asked and the findings clear?
> Is there enough evidence to support claims?
> Are all cases arising from the analysis fully accounted for?

D. Conclusions

Do the findings support the conclusions?

> Are explanations for the findings reasonable, appropriate and adequate?
> Are findings grounded in the theoretical framework that motivated the research?
> Are conclusions supported by the findings?
> Have possible limitations of the study been discussed?
> Is the contribution this study makes to the field clearly stated, and appropriate?

Are there recommendations for future action?

> Are recommendations for future research and practice given?
> Are the recommendations adequate and appropriate?

Additional means that are less traditionally academic can include discussing the project and findings at public meetings run by community or professional groups, and posting them to electronic bulletin boards or websites affiliated with the individuals, groups and communities we wish to reach. How successful we are in communicating information and findings from the project and helping to effect change depends on how responsive we are in our means of presentation to the expectations of our various audiences.

Quote 9.3 Communicating with different audiences

Communication should always be designed for a particular audience:

- Academic colleagues will expect theoretical, factual, or methodological insight.
- Policy makers will want practical information relevant to current policy issues.
- Practitioners will expect a theoretical framework for understanding clients better; factual information; practical suggestions for better procedures; reform of existing practices.
- The general public wants new facts; ideas for reform of current practices or policies' guidelines for how to manage better or get better service from practitioners or institutions; and assurances that others share their own experience of particular problems in life.

Silverman (2010: 422)

9.3 Summary

Research is an essential component of the professional lives of applied linguists. Robson (2002: 18) coined the term 'scientific attitude' to describe research that is undertaken systematically, sceptically and ethically. Researchers who are systematic are clear about what they are doing and why, and can articulate explicitly the basis for any decisions involving data collection and analysis. Sceptical researchers know to scrutinise their work, and lay their work open for scrutiny by other researchers, not just at the end of the project but throughout the entire process. Ethical researchers follow codes of conduct that safeguard the interests and concerns of project participants. Above all, as noted in Chapter 7, our role as researchers is to maintain a credible, trustworthy voice through 'habitual reflexivity' (Sweetman, 2003: 528).

Engaging in research with a scientific attitude can lead to more than just enhanced understandings. As importantly, it can help us to develop the skills we need to articulate more clearly concerns that are of significance to our particular circumstances, interests and needs, their epistemological foundations, and both the theoretical and empirical questions these concerns give rise to. At the same time, the process of engaging in research and the findings arising from our explorations afford us and those with whom and for whom we engage in research opportunities to move past what we already know and towards the development of new perspectives and different lenses for interpreting, understanding and engaging in our worlds.

Further reading

Berg, B. (2008) *Qualitative Research Methods for the Social Sciences*, 7th edn, Boston, MA: Allyn and Bacon. Written for the novice researcher, and using real-life examples, the text provides a comprehensive overview on how to design, collect, and analyse qualitative data.

Denzin, N. and Lincoln, Y. (eds) (2008) *Collecting and Interpreting Qualitative Materials*, 3rd edn, Thousand Oaks, CA: Sage Publications. This is an edited volume of nineteen chapters divided into two sections. The chapters in the first section discuss methods of collecting and analysing data. Chapters in the second section discuss issues involved in interpreting, evaluating and presenting research findings.

Lofland, J., Snow, D., Anderson, L. and Lofland, L. H. (2005) *Analyzing Social Settings: A Guide to Qualitative Observation and Analysis*, 4th edn, Belmont, CA: Wadsworth Publishing. This is a comprehensive and practical guide to the collection and analysis of qualitative data. In their discussions, the authors include a wealth of illustrative examples. It is considered an exemplar of research methods texts.

Silverman, D. (2006) *Interpreting Qualitative Data*, 3rd edn, Los Angeles: Sage. The text is a practical guide written specifically for novice researchers interested in undertaking a research project. Each chapter includes hands-on exercises and a list of related internet links and additional readings.

Chapter 10

Contexts of research

This chapter:

- describes a framework for conceptualising research contexts;
- provides an example of research for each dimension of the framework;
- offers suggestions for research projects.

10.1   Introduction

In the preceding chapters, we have laid out some of the more significant assumptions about language, culture and learning embodied in a sociocultural perspective on human action, and we have reviewed how the concepts have informed teaching practices. In terms of research, we have discussed several issues related to carrying out credible research projects, discussed some of the more typical approaches used by applied linguists to study language and culture from a sociocultural perspective, and offered a set of guidelines for planning, conducting and evaluating research.

In this chapter we look at how we might identify topics and questions that are appropriate for empirical investigations. The discussion is framed around a conceptual map that arranges social activity into four dimensions. I discuss the characteristics and scope of each dimension, and for each I include an example of a research study and suggestions for research projects. The suggestions are presented using the model of the research process described in Chapter 9. They are included as illustrations of how readers might plan and conduct studies of relevance to their personal and professional contexts. Remember, before beginning any study that involves human participants, you must secure approvals from all relevant official groups and informed consent for participation from all participants (cf. Chapter 7).

10.2   Contexts of research

As we have discussed, the general aim of research on language and culture from a sociocultural perspective is on understanding our social worlds, our varied identities and roles as social actors, and the varied consequences arising from long-term engagement in our worlds. Since our social worlds are complex and layered, understanding them involves unfolding or teasing apart the many layers of meanings. We need to understand not just how we act as individuals in any particular moment, but how, as individuals, we construct and are constructed in particular communicative activities. We also need to understand how these activities inform and are informed by the larger social institutions to which they are linked, and the larger beliefs, values and attitudes within which the institution are nested. Figure 10.1, which is an adaptation of a map proposed by Layder (1993) for doing social research, presents a conceptualisation of the many layers involved in research on language and culture from a sociocultural perspective.

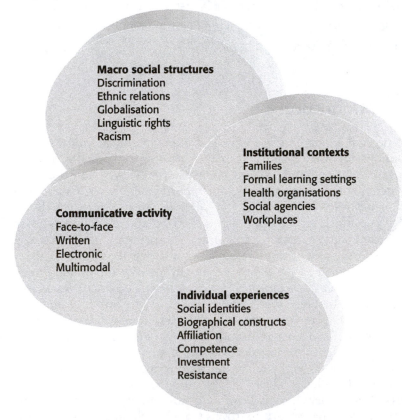

Macro social structures
Discrimination
Ethnic relations
Globalisation
Linguistic rights
Racism

Institutional contexts
Families
Formal learning settings
Health organisations
Social agencies
Workplaces

Communicative activity
Face-to-face
Written
Electronic
Multimodal

Individual experiences
Social identities
Biographical constructs
Affiliation
Competence
Investment
Resistance

Figure 10.1   **Contexts of research**

As shown in the diagram, the framework is composed of four intersecting dimensions: macro social structures, institutional contexts, communicative activities and individual experiences. Such a map is useful in that it 'tie[s] together the interpersonal world of everyday life with the more impersonal world of social institutions' (Layder, 1993: 206), and thus makes apparent the interconnectedness of the more situated aspects of life to the more macro issues of social institutions, beliefs and ideologies. While each dimension has its own distinctive constellations of characteristics, the analysis we engage in for each is similar in that on each level we seek to describe what is going on and interpret the phenomena from the perspectives of those whose worlds we are investigating. We also seek to explain the phenomena by connecting what we have learned on one level to how they are constructed on other levels. This means, then, that uncovering the meanings of individual behaviour requires that we locate them in their larger contexts of action. Likewise, understanding social beliefs and attitudes entails connecting them to their instantiations in real-world contexts of social activity. Limiting our focus to only one level will constrain what we can see, and how we come to understand it. For example, suppose we look only at changes that occur in individual behaviour in classrooms and find that, over a period of time, the behaviours in question change only slightly. If we stay at this level, we may, perhaps wrongly, attribute the lack of change to the individuals themselves, claiming individual inability or disinterest in making the changes. If we include an analysis of the classroom activities in which the individuals were involved, however, we may find that the opportunities for participation in the activities, at least for some individuals, were limited. This lack of opportunities may help to explain, in part, the lack of change in individual behaviour. And so on. The point is that without attempting to understand our findings in light of social activity on other levels, our understandings will remain incomplete.

Quote 10.1   On the interconnectedness of micro and macro elements

[M]acro phenomena make no sense unless they are related to the social activities of individuals who reproduce them over time. Conversely, micro phenomena cannot be fully understood by exclusive reference to their 'internal dynamics', so to speak, they have to be seen to be conditioned by circumstances inherited from the past. In other words, micro phenomena have to be understood in relation to the influence of the institutions that provide their wider social context. In this respect macro and micro phenomena are inextricably bound together through the medium of social activity and thus the assertion of the priority of one over the other amounts to a 'phoney war'.

Layder (1993: 102–103)

10.2.1   Macro social structures

This dimension is generally concerned with the large-scale, society-wide beliefs, values and attitudes towards social phenomena such as discrimination, racism, ethnicity and intergroup relations. Also included are beliefs, values and attitudes of social constructs such as personhood and freedom, and social issues such as linguistic rights and language policies.

The focus of research in this dimension is on the explication of macro social structures as evidenced in language and in particular in public and other official documents, and documenting the linguistic and discursive means by which they are oriented to, distributed and maintained, by those whose documents they are. The purpose for such undertaking is not only to raise awareness of how language is used to create particular viewpoints and particular representations of the world, and of how these views can persuade us to act in particular ways. It is also to clear a pathway to social change. Sources of data can come from a range of oral, written and multi-modal genres, such as official records and other public documents, news discourses, documentaries, speeches and advertising. In addition, they can come from a range of fields such as medicine, law, public policy, education, labour markets and so on.

This macro dimension of sociocultural structure has been of particular interest to applied linguists. A primary focus of research has been on the ways language and other modes of communication are used to create particular visions of social phenomena like gender and class, and social issues such as discrimination and democracy. Here one finds the work of critical discourse analysts such as Jan Blommaert (e.g. Blommaert, 2010; Bloemmart et al., 2006), Norman Fairclough (e.g. 1992, 1995, 2000), Teun van Dijk (e.g. 1993, 2008), and Ruth Wodak and her colleagues (Wodak et al., 1999; Wodak and Wright, 2006) (cf. Chapter 8).

While the goals of this research are in keeping with this dimension, some of the earlier studies have been criticised, and rightly so, for their lack of system and rigour in explicating the criteria for choosing samples of texts to examine (cf. Widdowson, 2000). As noted in Chapter 8 in relation to the analysis of data, if the methods for collecting and analysing data are not clearly stated and systematically utilised, it raises the question as to whether the text samples are chosen to make a point that fits with the researcher's own viewpoint rather than to interpret the particular worldviews embodied in the settings from which the samples are drawn.

In an effort to strengthen the power of CDA to illuminate macro social structures, recent studies have been aided by the use of electronic tools that permit the analysis of large corpora of data. Others have drawn on interactive software tools to expand their analyses to include modes such as images, sound and movement in addition to language and the ways in which the modes interact at different levels to reflect and enact social structures and practices (cf. O'Halloran, 2008; Owyong, 2009). Example 10.1 is an illustration of the kinds of studies undertaken by applied linguists concerned with the dimension of macro social structures. It is a useful illustration of the potential of corpora and corpus-based tools for making visible the ideologies embodied in public documents.

Example 10.1   Macro social structures

Study
O'Halloran, K. (2009) 'Inferencing and cultural reproduction: A corpus-based critical discourse analysis', *Text & Talk*, 29: 21–51.

Purpose
In 2004, the European Union (EU) expanded to twenty-five countries. Eight of the ten new countries were from Eastern Europe. According to O'Halloran, about six weeks before the official expansion of the union, the *Sun*, a well-known British tabloid, began a campaign to draw attention to the harmful effects of immigration from Eastern European countries to the United Kingdom. The purpose of O'Halloran's study was to investigate the semantic patterns or 'strategies' (p. 22) used by the newspaper to promote the campaign and to position readers into acceptance of it.

Approach
Corpus-based critical discourse analysis.

Data sources
The source of data was a corpus of articles published in the *Sun* in which one or more cultural key words were found. Included in the key word search were such terms as *(im)migration*, *(im)migrant(s)*, *EU*, and *European*. The articles were collected from the six-week period leading up to 1 May 2004, the date that the expansion became official. The corpus consisted of 76 texts, comprising a total of 26,350 words.

Data analysis
O'Halloran used the electronic software Wordsmith Tools 5.0 to locate corpus-based, comparative statistical keywords (CCSKs). CCSKs are defined as grammatical and lexical terms that are statistically more frequent in a text or set of texts than in a large reference corpus, and thus can provide a picture of the more salient topics in the corpus. In this case, the reference corpus was BNC-baby, an approximately four million word sample of the British National Corpus which consists of around one million words each of academic prose, conversation, fiction and newspaper text. He examined the extent to which CCSKs '(i) co-occur across stretches of text larger than collocational spans in concordance lines, and (ii) provide text structure' (p. 29).

Findings

The analysis of CCSKs reveals that words such as *immigration, EU, Blair* and *Britain* were among the top ten CCSKs. Examining words that were not only frequent but also well dispersed across the six weeks revealed that *But* (as a sentence starter) appeared more frequently in the corpus of articles than in the BNC-baby corpus.

According to O'Halloran, the use of *But* is significant in that it (1) signals a contrastive relation between the preceding sentence and the one begun with *But*, and thus provides text structure; and (2) starts a sentence and therefore has prominence.

He conjectured that if *But* were providing text structure for strategies on a regular basis, the strategies would have prominence as well. To determine whether this was the case, he examined the number of CCSKs co-occuring with *But* and found several linkages.

In his qualitative examination of these links between *But* and the CCSKs, O'Halloran identified five types of rhetorical strategies. *But* is used:

1 to set up a negative evaluation of the UK government perspective on Eastern European immigration.

2 to set up immigration as a challenge to the government, or a fear or worry for various reasons.

3 to indicate negative contrast, and project that immigration will lead to overstretched UK social services.

4 to set up stories or predictions that there will be illegal immigrants arriving to the UK from Eastern Europe.

5 To signal, through negative contrast, the prospect of serious criminality arising from immigration from Eastern Europe.

Conclusions

O'Halloran concluded that 'because of these repeated lexicogrammatical associations, regular readers [of the *Sun*] … have been positioned into making negative contrastive inferences from repeated exposure to the five strategies, which in turn could lead to cultural reproduction of these meanings' (pp. 37–38).

Suggestions for research projects

To recap, research on macro sociocultural structures involves the systematic collection and analysis of contextually situated oral, written and multimodal texts for the purposes of uncovering the particular ideological assumptions embodied in their linguistic and discursive arrangements. Questions that can guide projects undertaken in this domain include the following: What social, cultural and ideological perspectives about the notions of language and culture are contained in a particular set of classroom texts for English language learners? What are the official language policies embodied in the standard practices of a professional organisation? How are these informed by beliefs about language and language users in the larger social context? What political ideologies about race and ethnicity are found in a particular social organisation and how do they influence the kinds of practices found in that organisation? How do teachers construct learners' identities in their stories about their experiences in their classrooms? How do these constructions reflect the cultural and political ideologies of their educational institution? Below are two examples of research projects that those new to research can undertake.

Research project 10.1

Perspectives on the English-speaking culture(s) found in textbooks used in EFL classrooms

Identifying concerns and posing questions
As we know, the resources and tools we use in our classrooms shape our learners' development in significant ways. Understanding what may be possible for their development in terms of social and cultural understandings requires in part that we understand the social and cultural meanings embodied in the tools and materials we make available to them.

One way we might go about uncovering these meaning is through an analysis of the textbooks that we use. Consider using the following questions as guides: What are the typical images and themes on culture that are found in texts common to EFL classrooms settings? Whose social communities are most commonly represented in these images and themes? How representative are these of our learners' communities? Of the communities in which they aspire to become members?

Identifying appropriate approach and sources of data
A multimodal discourse analysis would be an appropriate approach for this study. The first step is to choose the texts you wish to examine. For example, you may decide to include all the texts used at one level of instruction across subject matters in your educational setting. Alternatively, you may decide to include texts used to teach one subject across all levels of instruction. Whatever you decide, be sure you are able to articulate the criteria you use to make your selections. Since examining every page would make the task unmanageable, choose specific sections from each text to examine. You may choose to look at every other chapter or a certain percentage of chapters from each text. As with the choice of texts, your decisions must be principled, that is, based on some clearly articulated set of criteria.

Collecting data
Create a provisional analytic framework to use on which to note and classify the written and visual content within each selection. Figure 10.2 contains an example of a basic framework that can be used, or you can construct one that addresses your particular concerns.

Topical Content	Representations	
	Words and phrases	Visual representations (Where appropriate, note demographics of individuals (e.g. socioeconomic status, gender, race, age), scene and location (e.g. geographical location, urban, rural), and so on.)
Personal Life		
Family Life		
The Community		
Sports		
Health and Welfare		
Travel		
Education		
The Workplace		
Current Events		
Religion		
Arts, Humanities		
Political Systems		
Science		
Other		

Figure 10.2   Analytic framework for analysis of EFL texts

Analysing data
Examine each selection, identifying, describing and classifying the content of the visual and written content. Once you have examined each selection, look across datasets for recurring themes within each topic. Quantify the number of units that fit within each (as, for example, percentages) and choose the best, most representative examples for each theme. You might construct a diagram to represent the semantic and other relations comprising a theme. Construct a set of statements about the data that you feel best represent what you found.

Reflecting on the findings
What did you find out about the social and cultural content contained in the textbooks? Which findings did you anticipate? Which were most surprising?

What might account for these meanings? How relevant are these meanings for your students? How might you add to or in some way enhance the tools and resources that students will use in the classroom?

Sharing findings and taking action
It is likely that your findings will be of interest to those who teach similar courses. Thus, it would be worth while to share a summary of your findings with your colleagues, either as part of a faculty meeting, or as a posting to an electronic bulletin board for EFL teachers. In addition, you might send your review to a journal for publication consideration.

Research project 10.2

The representation of immigrants in the news

Identifying concerns and posing questions
As we discussed in Chapter 2, our social identities take shape in the social groups to which we belong. Media such as newspapers, television programmes and magazines play an especially significant role in shaping public beliefs and ideologies about these groups and these portrayals give shape to our own perceptions of these groups and their members.

The issue of immigration and immigrants in the United State has always garnered attention in the media. Around presidential election time, the issue takes on special prominence in public discussions. The questions for this project are: How are immigrants portrayed in newspaper articles during a period of time preceding the US presidential elections of 2008? How does this portrayal compare to coverage in the year, or portion of a year, after the election?

Identifying appropriate approach and sources of data
An appropriate approach is discourse analysis. The first step is to choose the newspapers from which data will be collected. Some of the more prominent newspapers in the United States giving national coverage are the *New York Times*, the *Wall Street Journal*, and the *Washington Post*. If you are interested in more local portrayals, then choose newspapers that are regional or community-based. You also need to decide on the section or sections of the newspaper that you will examine. Perhaps you want to look only at front page headline news or you may decide to examine all of the articles in the editorial section of the paper. Alternatively, you may decide to limit your selection in the editorial section to letters to the editor.

You must also specify the time period over which data collection will occur. You may choose to examine all copies of one newspaper the month before and the month after the election or you may decide to examine only the Sunday edition of two or three newspapers for several weeks before and after the election. Whatever choices are made in terms of newspaper selections and periods of collection, be sure you can articulate the rationale behind them.

Collecting data

Copies of newspapers are usually archived in libraries or in internet-based repositories. Once you have located the newspapers, you can gather copies of the selected sections.

Analysing data

Total the number of articles found from each newspaper for the collection period. Use key words such as *immigrant* and *immigration* to determine whether the article is relevant to your study. Calculate the percentage of articles you located on the topic versus the total number of articles examined. Once you have identified the relevant articles, examine each selection, noting the sentences in which the key words appear and identifying those discourse features (e.g. lexical items) used in the story that are related to your key words. Once you have examined each selection, look across datasets for recurring themes or concepts, or categories. Calculate the number of units that fit within each and choose the most representative examples for each theme, concept or category. Construct a set of statements about the data that you feel best represent what you found.

Reflecting on the findings

How were immigrants portrayed in the articles: e.g. Productive contributors to the community? Troublemakers? Sympathetic characters? Law abiding? Did the articles stories vary across the type of newspaper? What can you conclude about the portrayal of immigrants in news stories? How might these images shape the everyday lives of immigrants in your community?

Sharing findings and taking action

If you work for or are familiar with an organisation that provides social services to immigrants in your community, you may decide to share your findings with them. Together you can discuss whether the representations of immigrant work to their advantage or disadvantage and together develop ways to enhance their public portrayals.

10.2.2 Institutional contexts

This dimension has to do with the institutional contexts constituting our social communities. These contexts are shaped by specific goals that are drawn from the larger worldviews in which they are nested. These goals, in turn, give shape to particular kinds of communicative activities and particular kinds of social roles and relationships in those contexts. Families, schools, churches, civic organisations, places of work, professional groups, friendship circles, neighbourhood and other social and special-interest clubs and associations are some of the more significant social institutions in which we hold memberships. The general concern of research in this dimension is with explicating the communicative practices and activities that characterise particular institutional contexts, including the resources and patterns of participation by which the social roles and role relationships within these activities are produced and regulated.

The general approach to such studies is ethnographic. Sources of data typically include notes from long-term participant observations, audio and video recordings, interviews with members of the institution, and collections of official documents. Combining the use of the ethnography of communication framework with discourse and conversation analytic techniques to analyse the data allows us to see how more micro-social actions are connected to larger patterns of use, and how these patterns are embedded within and, on another level, help to constitute particular communicative meanings, beliefs and ideologies. Example 10.2 is an illustration of the kinds of studies that fall within the dimension of institutional context.

Example 10.2   Institutional contexts

Study
Gillen, J. (2009) 'Literacy practices in Schome Park: A virtual literacy ethnography', *Journal of Research in Reading*, 32: 57–74.

Purpose
The focus of the study is on the diverse literacy practices of an out-of-school project called Schome Park, a three-dimensional (3D) virtual island world. Gillen's purpose for undertaking the study was twofold: (1) to understand the kinds of literacy practices afforded by the project and (2) to ascertain the usefulness of a synthesis of methods for exploring literacy practices made possible by new digital technologies.

Approach
A virtual literacy ethnography.

Participants
The virtual community included students from ages 13 to 17 who were invited to join via their school and adult staff members.

Data sources
Data for the ethnographic description of the community were collected over a 15-month period during which time Gillen acted as participant-observer in the virtual community and included field notes and visual and written records of the community taken by the author throughout her participation.

Data analysis

Gillen used general ethnographic methods to become familiar with the virtual community and its literacy practices. To investigate the students' use of written language in Chat Logs, one of the communicative domains Gillen identified as significant to the community (see below), she conducted a corpus analysis of a large, randomised sample of the students' turns in the logs collected over a four-week period. She used the electronic software Wordsmith 4 to create a frequency list of words and then compared the list to the BNC-Baby (subset of the British National Corpus, see Example 10.1) to find out whether any lexical items figured more significantly in the virtual world literacy practices.

Findings

Some findings arising from ethnographic data include the following: Participants used pseudonyms and took on avatar characters as they participated in the Park. Three primary communicative domains found in the community were: chat logs, a wiki, which is a compilation of individually authored web pages, and a forum, designed to allow several asynchronous discussions. Of the various communicative domains available to the students, the forum was the most constantly used means. It was used to plan events and discuss happenings within the project. Also available on the forum were games and discussions on topics such as archaeology, video production, and school dinners.

In terms of the students' use of written language in chat logs compared with the general corpus, findings include the following:

1   The functions of students' turns were mainly questioning and inquiry, marked by a prevalence of a question words such as *how* and *what*.

2   Words such as *time, here, there, now, think* and *because* appeared more frequently in the students turns. According to the author, this suggested that the students spent a great deal of time managaing their 'positioning in space and time' (p. 67).

3   Terms suggesting positive relationship building and collaborative activities were frequent and included *yes, haha, LOL, thanks* and *please*.

4   Frequently appearing terms included *thing, things, make* and *stuff* indicating a prevalence of talk about the construction of objects and scripts.

Conclusion

Participating in Schome Park involves an enormous amount of literate activity which calls for the use of a 'multiplicity of semiotic resources that have to be deployed in combinations that are patterned in ways to make sense to fellow interactants' (p. 72). The various communicative domains such as chat logs, the wiki, and the forum are best understood not as separate domains 'but as opportunities for and shapers of interactions by purposeful designers and communicators of the virtual community' (*ibid.*).

Suggestions for research projects

As noted above, the general concern of research in this dimension is with explicating the communicative practices and activities, including participant roles and role relationships, embodied in particular social institutions. Questions to guide research projects in this domain include the following: What communicative practices and activities comprise a particular institution? What beliefs and assumptions about language and culture are embodied in them? Whose interests do these serve? How compatible are the activities within institutions and how do they compare across institutions? Included here are suggestions for two research projects that fall within this domain.

Research project 10.3

Students' funds of knowledge

Identifying concerns and posing questions
As we know, students come to school with rich reservoirs of cultural and linguistic knowledge developed in the contexts of their families and communities upon which teachers can build to create a more meaningful learning environment in the classroom. To uncover some of the knowledge and skills your students already possess, you can conduct a funds of knowledge project, based on the work done by Luis Moll and his associates and described in Chapter 4. A question that can guide your research is: What funds of knowledge and resources do students bring with them from their home contexts?

Identifying appropriate approach and sources of data
One approach appropriate for this study is ethnography of communication. A primary means for collecting data can be through visits to the homes and neighbourhoods of your students, and through conducting interviews and questionnaires with your students and their families. In addition to being primary sources of data, students can also be involved as co-investigators and asked to conduct interviews or complete questionnaires with their family members. They can also be asked to create multimodal portfolios in which they include written, visual, graphic, audio, video and other kinds of materials that they feel best represent their home and community contexts.

Collecting data
Together with the students, decide on appropriate times to visit their families and neighbourhoods and develop an interview protocol or a questionnaire they can use with their family members and neighbours. Develop a time line for conducting the interviews and completing the questionnaires. Since the findings are to be used to transform your classroom environment, it is advisable to conduct the study early in the school year. Provide students with guidelines for creating home and community portfolios along with a deadline for completing them.

Analysing data
Together with students, discuss what you learned from your visits to their families and neighbourhoods. Together, transcribe the interviews and/or tally the responses to the completed questionnaires, noting recurring themes and topical patterns. Follow the same procedure for the portfolios. Summarise and arrange the findings from the interviews, questionnaires and student portfolios into particular funds of knowledge.

Reflecting on the findings
What funds of knowledge do students bring with them to school? How similar or different are they across students? How do they compare with the school's funds of knowledge as represented in the curricular and instructional practices and policies? What do they tell you about the needs, interests, and abilities of your students? How do they compare with the funds of knowledge you bring from your home context? How might they be incorporated into your classroom learning community?

Sharing findings and taking action
Together with the students, design means for sharing what you have learned with the larger school community. You might also create a web site and invite other school communities to do similar kinds of projects. Also consider presenting your findings to a professional group of teachers. What you have learned may help them to decide to make changes to their own classroom communities.

Research project 10.4

Family literacy practices in multilingual environments

Identifying concerns and posing questions
While we know that many families arriving to our communities come with many languages, often within the same family, we know far less about how families with multiple languages manage their communicative experiences, and more particularly their literacy practices. Thus, the question guiding this project is: What are the literacy practices of one multilingual family?

Identifying appropriate approach and sources of data
The approach to take here is broadly ethnographic, including methods typical of ethnography of communication to capture the range and scope of literacy practices, and discourse analytic methods for analysis of written documents that include transcriptions of taped conversations and interviews with participants, and the materials they use in their literacy practices (e.g. books, newspapers, lists, letters, etc.). Given the range of data to be collected, it is most feasible to begin with one family. The findings here can lead to new questions for exploration with additional multilingual families.

Collecting data

Collecting data involves long-term participation with the group of participants. It can include regular conversations with the family to discuss literacy practices and their perceptions of them; observations of the individual family members as they go about their daily lives to uncover the ways that literacy practices enter into and are used by the individuals to construct their worlds; and collection of materials that are important to the family in terms of what they read and what they write.

Analysing data

Transcribe the videotapes and identify the common features of the literacy practices. Use Hymes's SPEAKING model as a beginning framework. Describe the patterned uses of print, the codes of language they involve, and interpret the conventional meanings in light of how they are used by the family. In addition, analyse your field notes and participant interviews for recurring themes and use them to help explain the literacy activities in light of the larger social and cultural contexts.

Reflecting on the findings

What literacy practices are most commonly engaged in by this family? Do they vary by language? What do the practices mean to the family? Do the meanings vary by family role (e.g. parent vs. child)? How important are they to maintaining their identities as multilinguals? How closely are their practices supported by the larger social community?

Sharing findings and taking action

Your findings will have much to offer teachers and administrators in K–12 schools and adult education programmes, and both local and state policy makers. You might consider offering workshops on your findings for these groups. You might also see if there is interest among families in your community who have similar multilingual backgrounds in organising and participating in literacy-based clubs.

10.2.3   Communicative activities

This third dimension is concerned with the identification and characterisation of the communicative activities sustaining, and sustained by, a particular institutional context. In addition to everyday activities by which institutional members of particular communities live their lives, attention is also given to those practices by which novice members or newcomers are apprenticed into the institution's activities and the specific means by which they are assessed or evaluated as bona fide members. Communicative activities include oral and written events as well as those accomplished with electronic means, such as e-mailing and electronic bulletin board postings.

The aim of research in this dimension is to identify, describe, interpret and ultimately explain the locally situated meanings of the communicative actions by which individuals jointly produce their encounters. The focus here is not on individuals within their activities, but on the particular activities that shape and are shaped by individual involvement.

Several approaches can be used to accomplish the goals of this dimension. Ethnographies of communication are typically used to uncover the conventional linguistic patterns of participation and communicative plans shared by group members and by which they accomplish their activities. If the activity is accomplished through face-to-face interaction, conversation analysis is sometimes combined with the more general ethnographic analyses to uncover the particular interactional features oriented to by the participants to produce order in the conversation. Studies can also take an interactional sociolinguistic approach to examine points of *mis*-communication to uncover differences in meanings attributed to particular cues. Finally, discourse analysis or systemic functional linguistics can be used to uncover particular linguistic cues used to index larger contextual meanings. Examples of studies utilising these approaches can be found in Chapter 8.

Similar to the studies undertaken in the other two dimensions, in addition to audio and video recordings of the encounters, data sources include field notes taken from participant-observations, and interviews with the participants themselves. The sampling of studies of communicative activities cited in Chapter 1, the language socialisation practices reviewed in Chapter 3, and the review of communicative activities particular to classrooms reviewed in Chapter 5, are examples of the kinds of studies typical of this dimension. In addition, Example 10.3 includes a more detailed summary of one study, which investigated the practices of an electrical engineering team and how one novice member was socialised by three core members into practices.

Example 10.3 Communicative activity

Study
Vickers, C. (2007) 'Second language socialization through team interaction among electrical and computer engineering students', *Modern Language Journal*, 91: 621–640.

Purpose
To understand how non-native speaking members of a team of student engineers comprising native and non-native speakers of English become socialised to the team practices.

Approach
Ethnography of communication and interactional sociolinguistics.

Participants

Participants comprised a team of six members. All members were seniors majoring in electrical and computer engineering (ECE) at a major American university. Of the members, five were native English speakers, one was a non-native speaker of English.

Data source

Vickers first drew on Hymes's concepts of speech communities and speech events, and ethnographic methods to familiarise herself with the larger ECE community of which the team meeting was a part. Some of her field work included extensive discussions with ECE professionals, class observations, participation on the ECE department's senior portfolio evaluation committee, and observations of seven teams. She used this information to narrow her focus to one meeting of one team, and ultimately to one component of the team meeting, the joint design of an engineering project.

Data on this component were gathered from seven meetings of the team. In the first two meetings, Vickers observed and collected field notes. She observed and audio recorded the third and fourth meetings and observed and video recorded the last three meetings. Meeting times ranged from one hour to three hours for a total of 12.5 hours.

Data were collected over the course of one academic year.

At the end of the academic year, Vickers conducted stimulated recall sessions with three team members in which they were asked to (1) stop the video when they saw instances of communication that were successful or unsuccessful, (2) evaluate the level of competence of the member or members communicating in that instance and (3) indicate specific behaviours that provided evidence for their assessments.

Data analysis

Vickers first coded the audio and video-taped interactions into several sequences of action and then examined more closely two sequences related to technical content: Questions of Technical Content (QTC) and Explanations of Technical Content (ETC).

She then conducted a frequency count of QTC and ETC sequences for two groups of members, core and full, and compared them over time across the two groups.

Findings

General ethnographic findings were these:

In the ECE team there was no institutionally defined authority figure. Instead, individual members were constructed as experts in the team interactions who operated as core members of the team. Others were constructed as novices who operated on the periphery of the team. On this team, three members were constructed as core and one member, Ramalan, the non-native English speaking member, was constructed as the only peripheral participant. The other two members of the team never spoke in any of the team meetings.

At at the beginning of the team meetings, the three core members provided more ECTs than Ramalan and Ramalan asked more QTCs than the core members did.

By the last meeting, the number of QTC sequences in which Ramalan particpated decreased and there was a marked increase in his participation in ETC sequences, indicating a move from peripheral to core membership on the team.

According to Vickers, the change was linked to (1) the work of two core team members to scaffold Ramalan's involvement in their interactions so that he could display the necessary technical knowledge, and (2) Ramalan's involvement in the design of one aspect of the project work that solved real problems for the team and thus allowed him to position himself as an expert.

Conclusion
The study 'demonstrates that L2 socialization is part of a larger process of socialization in human development, which is dependent on the novice participants' access to opportunities for interaction with socialized members of the community' (p. 621).

Suggestions for research projects

As noted above, this dimension is concerned with identifying, characterising and explaining the meanings of the particular communicative tools and resources used by individuals to produce their communicative activities. Also of concern are the means by which newcomers or novices are socialised into full, competent participation. Research projects seek answers to such questions as: What are the communicative means and plans constitutive of a communicative activity determined to be significant to the lived experiences of the members of a particular institutional context? What social identities and role relationships are made available to the participants in the activity? How are newcomers and other novices oriented to and appropriated into legitimate participation? Where does long-term use of the activity's mediated means lead the participants in terms of what they learn and how they learn it? Included here are suggestions for two projects that offer newcomers practice in undertaking research in this domain.

Research project 10.5

Social activity in a retirement community

Identifying concerns and posing questions
Communicative activities are important means by which individuals and groups enact and construct their everyday worlds. While there has been much

recent work on activities of youths and schooling communities, far fewer studies have been done on adults, and in particular, on adults living in retirement communities. Those interested in this population might consider conducting a project that examines this group more closely. One question to guide the project is: What is one communicative activity by which social affiliation is created and maintained in a retirement community?

Identifying appropriate approach and sources of data
Ethnography of communication would be an appropriate approach. The choice of a particular community depends on your professional and practical interests. The choice of particular activity should be determined after you have spent time with the community.

Collecting data
This study requires long-term involvement in the community as an observer or participant-observer. In addition to making multiple video recordings of the activity of interest, keep field notes of your own observations and experiences, interview the participants for their reflections and observations, and collect all related materials, artifacts, documents and written records.

Analysing data
Transcribe the videotapes and identify the features important to the accomplishment of the activity. Construct a framework of the conventional or typical sequence of communicative actions as they unfold in the activity. Describe the patterned uses of language and interpret their conventional meanings in light of how they are used by the participants to take action.

The SPEAKING framework would be useful here in describing the activity. In addition, analyse your field notes and participant interviews for recurring themes and use them to help to explain the activity in light of the larger social and cultural contexts it helps to (re)create in the community.

Reflecting on the findings
What did you find about the particular communicative activity? How is it typically enacted? What functions does it play in the larger community? Whose interests does it seem to serve? How do participants feel about it? What new knowledge or understanding about this community can you take from your study? What might your next steps be?

Sharing findings and taking action
Depending on your professional role, you can decide to share your findings with those who work in or aspire to work in retirement communities. You can also present your findings to a professional organisation concerned with ageing and language use. More informally, you can post your findings to a professional electronic bulletin board.

Research project 10.6

Classroom discourse and language learning

Identifying concerns and posing questions
As discussed in Chapter 5, the discourse of classrooms is consequential to learners' development in that it helps to shape both the processes and products of learning. If you are concerned with improving classroom conditions for foreign language learning, one place to begin is by examining the discourse of these classrooms. A basic question to guide this project is: What are the intellectual and practical activities that teachers and students construct in and through their discourse in a foreign language classroom?

Identifying appropriate approach and sources of data
Ethnography of communication along with discourse or conversation analysis would be appropriate approaches to uncovering the communicative activities comprising the discourse of a classroom community. The level and grade of the foreign language classroom will depend on your own professional interests.

Collecting data
To get a sense of the conventional practices constituted in the classroom discourse requires long-term involvement in the community. How often you visit the classroom depends on how long the course runs. If, for example, it runs for an entire academic year, you might decide to collect data once a week. If it is much shorter, say an eight-week course, you should probably plan on collecting data a few times a week. In addition to audio- and video-recording the classroom activities, keep field notes, collect related materials and artifacts, and plan to interview the teacher and students for their perceptions.

Analysing data
The first step of the analysis involves transcribing the recordings. The second involves coding the discourse into its constituent activities. You might consider involving the teacher in constructing the official coding scheme. On the transcriptions, ask her to indicate what was happening, that is, the purpose(s) directing the interaction, and label the various activities embedded in the talk accordingly. She might use labels such as 'transitioning', 'disciplining a student' and 'drilling subject/verb agreement'. She can also be asked to indicate points in the talk where these activities began and ended, and where she was unsure of what was going on. Hymes's SPEAKING model would be helpful as a descriptive framework. Another step involves constructing a framework of the conventional or typical sequence of utterances as they unfolded in a particular activity. Here discourse or conversation analysis would be helpful. In addition, analyse your field notes and participant interviews for recurring themes and use them to help explain the significance of the activities to the classroom community.

Reflecting on the findings
What kinds of activities are typical of the discourse of this foreign language community? Were any a surprise to you? To the teacher? What kinds of understandings of language and of themselves as language learners are students being socialised into through participation in these activities?

Sharing findings and taking action
Together with the teacher, you might consider how to change or enhance the classroom discourse so that it provides more opportunities for student involvement and for their using language that is communicatively rich. You might also co-present your findings at a meeting of foreign language educators.

10.2.4   Individual experiences

The final dimension focuses on the 'intersection of biographical experience and social involvements' (Layder, 1993: 9) by examining individuals' experiences within their communicative worlds. This focus differs from a concern with communicative activities, described above, in that it gives attention to 'the way individuals respond to, and are affected by, their social involvements as against a focus on the *nature* of the social involvements themselves' (*ibid.*: p. 74; emphasis in the original).

Such a focus includes concerns with how individuals use the cues available to them in their communicative encounters to both index and construct their everyday worlds. It focuses, in particular, on the ways individuals index and construct their social identities and roles and those of others in light of the kinds of identities and roles into which they have been ascribed or socialised. In addition, attention is given to the ways that individuals use language in the construction of concepts such as motivation, voice, affiliation, agency and competence. Remember, as with social identities and roles, these constructs are considered to be fundamentally social, developed within and thus contingent on individuals' particular experiences in their social worlds.

Like studies of communicative activities, studies here can take different approaches. Sources of data typically include field notes from participant-observations of individuals' biographical experiences, and interviews and conversations with the individuals, in addition to audio- and video-recordings of their experiences. The conventions of language use uncovered by ethnographies of communication can allow closer inspection of how individuals orient to their conventionality. Several studies on individual experiences were discussed in Chapter 2. Example 10.4 contains a short overview of a study by Hanh Ngyugen, which examines an intern's development of interactional skills essential to performing as an expert pharmacist in patient consultations.

Example 10.4   Individual experiences

Study
Nguyen, H. (2006) 'Constructing "expertness": A novice pharmacist's develop-
ment of interactional competence in patient consultations', *Communicaiton
& Medicine*, 3: 147–160.

Purpose
The purpose of Nguyen's study was to trace a pharmacy intern's development of several components of interactional competence related to his ability
to perform as an expert in patient consultations that take place at the pharmacy
counter.

Approach
Conversation analysis.

Participants
The consultations included one male intern and a total of 18 patients. Other
than number, no information on the patients involved in the consultations
is given.

Data source
The primary source of data was a set of 18 videotapes of pharmacist–patient
consultations collected over an eight-week period. The consultations took
place in an independently owned pharmacy in which the student pharmacist
was interning and involved the intern dicussing with the patients the medicines
they were to take. The consultations with the intern included only patients
filling new prescriptions.

Data analysis
Nguyen used conversation analysis to examine how the intern's performance
in the consultations changed over time in terms of the following: responding
to patient's explicit and implicit requests for information, resolving patients'
challenges, and maintaining a balance between transactional and interpersonal
functions.

Findings
Nguyen found that interns' performances in the consultations became more
expert-like in the following ways.

1 His responses to patients' implicit requests for expert advice changed from
   miminal responses to a patient's trouble telling (e.g. nodding) to a displayed orientation to the trouble telling as a patient's implicit request for
   his expert input, followed by appropriate responses.

2 His presentation of expert information changed in that at the beginning,
   he provided it 'in a somewhat automatic manner without orienting to the
   patient's ongoing actions' (p. 151) such as, for example, providing information

when the patient was writing a check and not paying attention. Moreover, in these presentations he used technical terms without regard to the patient's apparent lack of understanding. By the end of the internship, the intern was providing expert information only when contextually appropriate and with much fewer technical terms, displaying, according to Nguyen, 'a *selective* display of expert behaviors' (p. 153, emphasis in the original).

3 His ability to resolve patient challenges to his authority changed, moving from apparent hesitation, indicated by mumblings, and pauses in his talk, to a more expert orientation displayed by a lack of hesitations and use of expert information to resolve the challenges without conflict.

4 His ability to balance the transactional and interpersonal functions of the consultations perspectives changed in that with time, the intern produced more behaviours that indicated an alignment with a layperson's pespective, such as using more casual expressions (e.g. a whole bunch of medicine).

Conclusions

The experience of the internship afforded the intern a unique opportunity to develop the interactional competences needed to perform as an expert in the context of pharmacist–patient consultations. More generally, the study demonstrates that while the acquisition of professional knowledge is essential to professional development of expertise, the development of interactional competence is crucial to being be an expert in social interaction.

Suggestions for research projects

To recap, the concern of this dimension is with individuals' experiences within their communicative worlds and, in particular, with how they use the cues available to them to both index and construct their everyday worlds, and their social identities and roles and those of others in light of the kinds of identities and roles into which they have been ascribed or socialised. In addition, attention is given to the ways that individuals use language in the construction of socially mediated concepts such as motivation, voice, affiliation, accommodation, agency and competence. Questions that studies in this dimension seek to answer include: How are the communicative resources of a practice used by participants to index their individual, social and cultural identities? How do individuals position themselves linguistically and otherwise in terms of the kinds of identities and role relationships made available to them in their communicative practices? Which voices seem more privileged or engender more authority, and which social identities are being made relevant? How are these identities reshaped by individuals as they make their way in their activities and with what communicative means? How do the participants appropriate the resources of others for their own purposes? What are the different means by which individuals accommodate to, resist, or actively oppose their involvement in particular communicative activities? What are the social, cognitive, linguistic and other consequences arising from an individual's long-term participation in particular communicative activities? What do individuals believe about their roles as participants and how, if at all, do these beliefs shape what they do? The following are suggestions for two projects to give novice researchers practice in doing research on individual experiences.

Research project 10.7

Perceptions of identity and agency in narratives of multilingual speakers

Identifying concerns and posing questions
The ways in which we use language in our communicative activities depend in part on our notions of identity and agency, that is, who we perceive ourselves to be, how we think others see us and how we would like others to perceive us. Understanding the everyday worlds of multilingual speakers requires in part our coming to understand their own understandings of themselves as language users. The question guiding this project is: How does a group of adult multilingual speakers perceive themselves as language users, and how do they construct their identities in the stories they tell about themselves?

Identifying appropriate approach and sources of data
Narrative analysis would be an appropriate approach. The sources of the narratives depend on the group you are interested in studying. If you are a teacher, you might want to gather life stories from a group of students. If your interest is the workplace, consider gathering narratives from multilingual individuals who hold positions in your field. The number of narratives collected depends on the context in which you are conducting your study and the kinds of claims you hope to make.

Collecting data
You can generate narratives through interviews with your participants or you can ask them to provide written narratives. Some questions you might ask include 'What are some qualities you possess that you feel are unique to bilingual speakers?' 'Can you describe your experiences as a multilingual speaker?' 'What have been some of the pivotal moments in your becoming multilingual?'

Analysing data
First, decide on the features you wish to examine. They can include, for example, themes and topics, or use of pronouns and other linguistic markers to index in-group versus out-group identities, or to create themselves as characters in plots of their stories. You can also examine words they use to describe themselves and others as certain kinds of individuals in relation to particular contexts or events and the particular languages they speak. You might choose to quantify the number of units that fit within each feature. Next, identify,

describe and interpret the meanings of the patterned uses of the features. Construct a set of statements about the data that you feel best represent what you found.

Reflecting on the findings
How do these individuals perceive themselves as users of multiple languages? What identities are relevant to them? How do they position themselves in relation to others in their worlds? To the social contexts they consider significant? How do their perceptions compare to other individuals' narratives?

Sharing findings and taking action
There are several electronic websites devoted to multilingualism and/or globalisation where you can post your findings. You may also wish to share the findings with a professional organisation interested in the topic of language and identity. If your participants were also your students, you might discuss the implications of the findings with them.

Research project 10.8

A bilingual child's use of language in play activities

Identifying concerns and posing questions
While there is much evidence on the linguistic features of child bilingual development, less is known about their communicative development in specific contexts of language use. In order to understand more fully the directions the language development of children who are raised as simultaneous bilinguals can take, these contexts need closer examination. Thus, a question to guide this research project is: How does a child being raised bilingually use her two languages to constitute her involvement in play?

Identifying appropriate approach and sources of data
A microethnographic analysis of play events is an appropriate approach. Because of the detailed focus on language use, the number of participants can be small. In this case, one focal child and her involvement in play events with her adult caregivers can be used. If each caregiver interacts with the child in one of the two languages (e.g. mother interacts in English, the father in German), the dataset should include an equal number of play events for each language.

Collecting data
Set up a video recorder in the room where the child plays and record the play events as they take place. Decide on a time period for collecting the data. You should have enough data to be able to justify claims about the typicality of the child's language use in her play events.

Analysing data
After first transcribing the recordings, code each utterance according to language code (i.e. German or English). Utterances containing morphological or lexical items from both languages should be coded as mixed. Also code each utterance for its communicative function (e.g. agreeing, confirming, directing, requesting). Quantify codings for each event, and search across datasets for regularities or patterns in terms of language code use and function and choose examples from the data that best illustrate the patterns found. Construct a set of statements about the data that you feel best represent them.

Reflecting on the findings
What languages did the child use in her interactions with the adult caregivers? How closely did her code use correspond to the language used by each interlocutor? What functions typify her utterances? Do they vary by code use? By interlocutor? By play event? How might you characterise the child's involvement with each interlocutor? What conclusions can you draw about the child's communicative development in the two languages?

Sharing findings and taking action
Consider writing up your report of the study and submitting to a journal concerned with bilingualism and child development.

10.3   Summary

The ideas presented in this chapter are meant to help newcomers to the field and others who are not familiar with a sociocultural perspective to get some idea of the range of possibilities for exploration. The framework highlighting the multiple dimensions of research contexts not only helps us to conceptualise the multiple layers of our social worlds, it also provides a guide for identifying possible topics and questions for undertaking research. While the possibilities are unlimited, the focus of any investigation depends on one's particular circumstances, interests and needs.

Without a doubt, conducting research on language and culture learning from a sociocultural perspective is both labour and time intensive, and thus, requires a fairly strong commitment to engaging in 'the dogged work of making sense of real communities and real lives' (Hymes, 1974: 7). Such work is typically not for those who are looking for quick studies, with simple answers. Rather, it is for those who enjoy exploring, who are not discouraged by what can sometimes seem to be unruly ways of living, and who are willing to persevere despite the bumps and obstacles they are likely to encounter in their journeys. Chapter 11 contains lists of relevant journals, professional organisations and websites where readers can find additional materials, resources and tools to aid them in their explorations.

Section

IV Resources

Resources for teaching and researching language and culture

This chapter:

- provides a list of journals that publish studies on language and culture;
- provides a list of professional organisations for applied linguistics;
- provides a list of web-based resources for researching and teaching language and culture.

11.1 Introduction

Increased worldwide access to electronic network capabilities such as the world-wide web has changed the ways in which we stay in touch with current practices in the field and communicate and connect with others. We can now gain entry to myriad research and teaching sites, connect with colleagues around the world, and both present and respond to innovations almost as quickly as they are developed. The purpose of this chapter is to provide some web-based resources to get readers started on their own explorations in the researching and teaching of language and culture. The information here is in no way meant to be comprehensive. Rather, the intent is to provide a preliminary chart of possible connections and linkages readers can pursue according to their interests and needs. No doubt readers will uncover additional sites in their journeys.

What follows, then, is this: First is an annotated list of journals that publish articles on matters related to researching and teaching language and culture. Included for each is the website address where additional information including submission and subscription guidelines can be found. Also included is an annotated list, including website addresses, of some of the major professional organisations for applied linguists. Membership information and other material can be found at each organisation's website. Finally, the chapter includes an annotated list of web-based resources for researching and teaching language and culture. Each site contains fairly extensive sets of links to a variety of topics on the researching and teaching of language and culture that, for the most part, are geared specifically to applied linguists.

11.2   Journals

Included here is an abridged annotated list of journals where the reader is likely to find articles that treat the topics discussed in the text.

Annual Review of Applied Linguistics, http://journals.cambridge.org/action/ displayJournal?jid=APL. Published once a year, the journal provides a comprehensive, up-to-date review of research in key areas in the broad field of applied linguistics. Each issue is thematic, covering the topic by means of critical summaries, overviews and bibliographic citations.

Anthropology & Education Quarterly, www.wiley.com/bw/journal.asp?ref=0161-7761. This peer-reviewed journal publishes scholarship on schooling in social and cultural contexts and on human learning both inside and outside of schools. Articles rely primarily on ethnographic research to address immediate problems of practice as well as broad theoretical questions. It is the journal of the Council on Anthropology and Education, a professional association of anthropologists and educational researchers and a section of the American Anthropological Association.

Applied Linguistics, http://applij.oxfordjournals.org/. This quarterly journal that publishes research on language with relevance to real-world problems. It encourages principled and multidisciplinary approaches to research on language-related concerns and welcomes contributions that reflect critically on current practices in applied linguistic research in the various fields encompassed by applied linguistics.

Australian Journal of Language and Literacy, http://alea.edu.au/html/ publications/16/australian-journal-of-language-and-literacy. This is the journal of the Australian Literacy Educators' Association. It is produced three times a year with articles examining national and international literacy practices and theories. According to the website, its purpose is to provide a forum in which literacy professionals from all settings can exchange and discuss ideas and practices relevant to their work.

Canadian Modern Language Review, www.utpjournals.com/cmlr/cmlr.html. This quarterly journal publishes peer-reviewed articles on all aspects of language learning and teaching. Article topics range from ESL, to French immersion, to international languages, to native languages. The journal's issues include reviews of relevant books and software, along with helpful teaching techniques and plans.

Critical Discourse Studies, www.tandf.co.uk/journals/titles/17405904.asp. An international and interdisciplinary journal its primary aim is to publish critical research that advances understandings of how discourse figures in social processes, social structures, and social change. It is published four times a year.

Critical Inquiry in Language Studies, www.isls-inc.org/pubs.htm. This is peer-reviewed journal of the International Society for Language Studies. Published four times a year, it focuses on research that addresses issues of language, power, and community within educational, political and sociocultural contexts with reference to international and/or historical perspectives.

Discourse & Society, http://das.sagepub.com/. Multidisciplinary journal that publishes research at the boundaries of discourse analysis and the social sciences. It focuses in particular on the discursive dimensions of social and political issues and problems, and encourages contributions that relate the situational micro-context of verbal interaction, discourse and communication to the macro-context of social, political and cultural structures.

Discourse Studies, http://dis.sagepub.com/. This multidisciplinary and international journal for the general study of text and talk, it is published six times a year. Its focus is on research in any domain of the study of spoken and written discourse, with special attention given to interdisciplinary studies in linguistics, anthropology, ethnomethodology, cognitive and social psychology, communication studies and law.

The ELT Journal, www3.oup.co.uk/eltj/scope/. Quarterly publication for those in the field of teaching English as a second or foreign language, its goal is to provide an interdisciplinary forum for discussion of the pedagogical principles and practices that shape the ways in which the English language is taught around the world.

Intercultural Pragmatics, www.degruyter.de/journals/intcultpragm/detailEn.cfm. This peer-reviewed quarterly journal publishes research on major issues in pragmatics, including empirical explorations of the ways in which language is both shaped by and helps to shape culture and implications of pragmatics research for practical applications in the fields of language acquisition and intercultural communication.

International Journal of Bilingualism, http://ijb.sagepub.com/. Published four times a year, the journal disseminates research on linguistic, psychological, neurological, and social issues emerging from language contact, with particular interests in the language behaviour of bi- and multi-lingual individuals.

International Journal of Bilingual Education and Bilingualism, www.tandf.co.uk/ journals/1367-0050. Published six times a year, this journal disseminates high-quality theoretical and empirical research with the aim of fostering international understandings of bilingualism and bilingual education.

Issues in Applied Linguistics, www.humnet.ucla.edu/humnet/teslal/ial/ial/ home.html. Started in November 1989, this refereed journal is managed, edited and published by graduate students of the UCLA Department of Applied Linguistics. Published twice a year, it disseminates research in the broad areas of discourse analysis, sociolinguistics, language acquisition, language analysis, language assessment, language education, language use, and research methodology.

Journal of Applied Linguistics, www.equinoxjournals.com/JAL. The purpose of this journal is to advance research and practice in Applied Linguistics as a principled and interdisciplinary endeavour. It is especially concerned with research methodology and, specifically, matters related to research tools, issues of ethics and research participation.

Journal of Language, Identity and Education, www.tandf.co.uk/journals/titles/ 15348458.asp. The focus of this peer-reviewed quarterly journal is on interdisciplinary research and critical scholarship concerned with educational issues related to language and identity. Of particular interest are studies reflecting diverse theoretical and methodological frameworks and dealing with areas such as research on schooling practices for linguistically and culturally diverse student populations, and multilingualism and multiliteracy.

Journal of Language and Politics, www.benjamins.com/cgi-bin/t_seriesview. cgi?series=jlp. Published four times a year, this journal focuses on discussions and analyses of the various dimensions in the interplay of language and politics. Articles bring together sociological concepts, political theories, and historical analysis in their attention to different dimensions of political discourse.

Journal of Linguistic Anthropology, http://linguisticanthropology.org/ journal/. This is a semi-annual publication of the Society for Linguistic Anthropology, a section of the American Anthropological Association. In addition to research studies, the journal publishes critical essays, interviews, commentaries, discussions and brief translations of relevance to the field of linguistic anthropology.

Journal of Multilingual and Multicultural Development, www.tandf.co.uk/ journals/0143-4632. Published six times a year, this journal contains articles that address the many aspects of multilingualism and multiculturalism, and includes theoretical essays and research studies on such topics as ethnicity and nationalism, multicultural and pluralist accommodations in heterogeneous societies, educational provisions for language and culture, language and group rights.

Journal of Second Language Writing, www.jslw.org/. This peer-reviewed international journal appears four times a year and features theoretically grounded empirical reports of research and discussions of issues in second language and foreign language writing and writing instruction.

Language Awareness, www.tandf.co.uk/journals/0965-8416. This is a quarterly journal that publishes articles exploring the role of explicit knowledge about language in the process of language learning and teaching and the role of explicit knowledge about language in language use.

Language and Communication, www.elsevier.com/wps/find/journaldescription. cws_home/616/description#description. This journal provides an interdisciplinary forum for theoretical and empirical discussions on topics and issues related to verbal and non-verbal communication with an emphasis on the many ways in which language is integrated with other forms of communicational activity and interactional behaviour.

Language, Culture and Curriculum, www.tandf.co.uk/journals/0790-8318. Publishes articles three times a year, articles in this journal discuss the diverse social, cultural, cognitive and organisational factors that are relevant to the design and implementation of language curricula. Second languages and minority and heritage languages are a special concern.

Language and Intercultural Communication, www.tandf.co.uk/journals/ 1470-8477. The goal of this journal, which produces four issues per year, is to promote an understanding of the relationship between language and intercultural communication. It publishes theoretical and empirical work exploring new ways of understanding cultural practices and intercultural relationships and their pedagogical implications.

Language in Society, http://journals.cambridge.org/action/displayJournal?jid =LSY. Published quarterly, the journal includes empirical articles of general theoretical, comparative or methodological interest to those in sociolinguistics, linguistic anthropology, and related fields.

Language Teaching, http://journals.cambridge.org/action/displayJournal?jid =LTA. This journal publishes survey articles and original research articles on second and foreign language teaching and learning. It also includes recent plenary conference speeches and research-in-progress reports.

Linguistics and Education, www.elsevier.com/wps/find/journaldescription. agents/620373/description#description. This journal publishes articles that apply theory and method from areas of language study to the study of education. Areas of language study include text/corpus linguistics, sociolinguistics, functional grammar, discourse analysis, critical discourse analysis, conversational analysis, linguistic anthropology/ethnography, language acquisition and language socialisation.

Mind, Culture and Activity, www.tandf.co.uk/journals/authors/hmcaauth.asp. Published quarterly, this interdisciplinary, international journal publishes articles that address the relationship among mind, culture, and activity. Readership is quite broad and includes anthropologists, psychologists, applied linguists, sociologists and educators.

The Modern Language Journal, http://mlj.miis.edu/. A quarterly refereed journal devoted to discussions about the teaching and learning of foreign and second languages, it publishes essays, research studies, editorials, reports, book reviews and professional news and announcements pertaining to modern languages, including TESL.

Pragmatics, http://ipra.ua.ac.be/main.aspx?c=*HOME&n=1267. This is the peer-reviewed quarterly publication of the International Pragmatics Association. It includes scientific articles, research reports and discussions on language and communication from a functional perspective.

Research on Language and Social Interaction, www.tandf.co.uk/journals/journal.asp?issn=0835-1813&linktype=44. This quarterly journal publishes empirical research on language as it is used in interaction that is based on close analysis of naturally occurring interaction. It is also open to theoretical essays and quantitative studies where they are tied closely to the results of naturalistic observation.

Social Semiotics, www.tandf.co.uk/journals/carfax/10350330.html. Published five times a year, this journal publishes reports of research studies using textual analysis, discourse analysis, ethnography or combinations of these and/or other methods to examine the economy of signs in contemporary social activity.

TESOL Quarterly, www.tesol.org/s_tesol/seccss.asp?cid=209&did=1679. Published by the international TESOL organisation, the journal includes contributions on topics of significance to the broad field of English language teaching. Topics can include the psychology and sociology of language teaching and learning, issues in research and research methodology and the preparation of language teachers.

Text & Talk, www.degruyter.de/journals/text/detail.cfm. Published six times a year, this journal disseminates interdisciplinary scholarship in language, discourse and communication studies, with special emphasis given to under-represented domains such as communication science, professional communication, stylistics, narratives and institutional ethnography.

Written Communication, http://wcx.sagepub.com/. Published quarterly, this interdisciplinary journal publishes theoretical and empirical research on writing. Topics of interest include the nature of writing ability, the impact of technology on writing and literacy, including workplace literacy.

11.3   Professional organisations

Listed here are just a few of the many organisations for applied linguists. Readers who are interested in locating and joining a national or regional organisation specifically for applied linguists should consult the website of AILA, the International Association of Applied Linguistics, for a list of worldwide affiliates.

AILA – International Association of Applied Linguistics/Association Internationale de Linguistique Appliquée, www.aila.info/. Founded in 1964, AILA is the premier international association for applied linguists worldwide linking over 35 national and regional applied linguistics associations. Its purpose is to promote research, scholarship and practice in applied linguistics and foster language pluralism. It holds a triennial world congress, organised by a different national or regional affiliate each time, supports the research of more than 20 scientific commissions, and collaborates with other organisations on related objectives and goals.

AAAL – American Association of Applied Linguistics, www.aaal.org. Founded in 1977, AAAL organises annual conferences and promotes research on language-related concerns, including language education, acquisition and loss, bilingualism, discourse analysis, literacy, language for special purposes, psycholinguistics, second and foreign language pedagogy, and language policy and planning. It is an affiliate of AILA.

ALAA – Applied Linguistics Association of Australia, www.alaa.org.au/. Established in 1976, ALAA is the national organisation for applied linguists in Australia. ALAA organises an annual conference, produces the journal *Australian Review of Applied Linguistics*, edits occasional papers in applied linguistics, and provides scholarships for high quality student research in areas of applied linguistics. It is an affiliate of AILA.

BAAL – British Association of Applied Linguistics, www.baal.org.uk/. BAAL is a professional association of applied linguists based in the UK. In addition to organising regularly scheduled scientific meetings, BAAL publishes a newsletter and conference proceedings, and awards an annual Book Prize. It is an affiliate of AILA.

Council of Europe, Language Policy Division, www.coe.int/t/dg4/linguistic/. This Division is responsible for designing and implementing initiatives for the development and analysis of language education policies aimed at promoting linguistic diversity and plurilingualism. The programmes cover all languages including mother tongue/first language/language(s), and foreign, second and minority languages.

ECML – The European Centre for Modern Languages, www.ecml.at/. Based in Graz, Austria, the ECML is an institution of the Council of Europe. It works in cooperation with the Language Policy Division of the Council and organises a programme of international projects on language education that serve to promote reform in the teaching and learning of languages.

ISCAR – The International Society for Cultural and Activity Research, www.iscar.org/. ISCAR is an international association whose purpose is to foster the development of multidisciplinary theoretical and empirical research on societal, cultural and historical dimensions of human practices. It organises an international conference every three years.

ISLS – The International Society for Language Studies, www.isls-inc.org/. Established in 2002, ISLS is an interdisciplinary association of scholars interested in critical perspectives on language. The association hosts a bi-annual conference, disseminates a weekly newsletter with language news from around the world to its members, and produces the journal *Critical Inquiry in Language Studies*.

IPrA – International Pragmatics Association, http://ipra.ua.ac.be/. IPrA is an international scientific organisation established in 1986 that is devoted to the study of language use. It has over 1,200 members in over 60 countries. It hosts a biannual conference and produces the journal *Pragmatics*.

ISFLA – International Systemic Functional Linguistics Association, www.isfla.org/. ISRLA is the international organising body for Systemic Functional Linguistics (SFL). It organises an annual conference, called the International Systemic-Functional Congress (ISFC), which rotates between the regions of Australia, Asia, the Americas and Europe. The site has resources and links to publications, conferences, and other information of interest to those who work with SFL.

LSA – Linguistic Society of America, www.lsadc.org. The purpose of the LSA is to advance the scientific study of language. It publishes *Language*, a quarterly journal, hosts an annual conference, a biennial summer Linguistic Institute and occasional summer meetings on issues of interest to graduate students.

TESOL – Teachers of English to Speakers of Other Languages, Inc., www.tesol.org. Incorporated in 1966, TESOL is an international education association, with over 12,000 members worldwide. In addition to sponsoring an annual convention, the association offers seminars and workshops on topics of interest to teachers. It also produces the quarterly journal *TESOL Quarterly* and the monthly electronic newsletter *TESOL Connections*, in addition to books on a wide range of topics.

11.4　Web-based resources

Included here is a list of web-based repositories containing an extensive range of links to resources, materials, and tools useful for researching and teaching language and culture.

CAL – Center for Applied Linguistics, www.cal.org/. CAL is a private, non-profit organisation for scholars and educators interested in how findings from linguistics and related sciences are being used to address language-related problems. The site includes links to a wide range of topics including research, teacher education, design and development of instructional materials, technical assistance, programme evaluation, and policy analysis.

CIOS – The Communication Institute for Online Scholarship, www.cios.org/. CIOS is a not-for-profit organisation whose goal is to support research and education in communications-related disciplines by providing online access to an electronic bibliographic index to the field's literature, a database that identifies the discipline's leading research centres, departments and scholars, and a database of abstracts of articles published in communication journals. It also produces and hosts the *Electronic Journal of Communication*.

CoRD – Corpus Resource Database, www.helsinki.fi/varieng/CoRD/. This is an online open-access resource through which academic corpus compilers can make available basic information about their corpora. It is maintained by the Research Unit for Variation, Contacts and Change in English, which is supported by the Universities of Helsinki and Jyväskylä and the Academy of Finland.

ERIC – The Educational Resources Information Center, www.eric.ed.gov/. ERIC is an information system that provides users unlimited electronic access to more than 1.3 million bibliographic records of journal articles and other education-related materials from a variety of sources, with hundreds of new records added several times per week. ERIS is sponsored by the Institute of Education Science, which is run by the US Department of Education.

Ethno/CA News, www2.fmg.uva.nl/emca/. This site is an electronic medium for the exchange of information relevant to the disciplines of Ethno-methodology and Conversation Analysis. It included regularly updated information on publications, conferences, resources and individual scholars who work in the field or have a strong interest in it.

The Language Varieties Web Site, www.une.edu.au/langnet/index.html. This site contains information on varieties of languages worldwide including Creoles, regional and minority dialects, and indigenous varieties that differ from the standard varieties that are typically used in the media and taught in schools.

The Linguistic Data Consortium, www.ldc.upenn.edu/. Hosted by the University of Pennsylvania, the Linguistic Data Consortium is an open association of universities, companies and government research laboratories. Its purpose is to create, collect and distribute speech and text databases, lexicons, and other tools and resources for language-related research and development purposes.

LRCs – Language Resource Centers, http://nflrc.msu.edu/. LRCs were established by the United States Department of Education to promote the development of expertise in the teaching and learning of foreign languages in the United States. Led by nationally and internationally recognised language professionals, the centres create and disseminate language-learning materials, offer professional development workshops, and conduct research on foreign language learning. There are currently 15 LCRs nationwide. The website provides electronic access to the centres and their materials, workshops and research initiatives.

Mind, Culture, and Activity Homepage, http://lchc.ucsd.edu/MCA/. This site provides an interactive forum for those interested in the study of human mind in its cultural and historical contexts. It is hosted by the Laboratory of Comparative Human Cognition (LCHC) at University of California, San Diego. On the homepage are links to XMCA, an e-mail discussion group, digital video discussions and papers published by the journal *Mind, Culture and Activity*.

Multimodal Analysis Lab, http://multimodal-analysis-lab.org/. This is the website of the Multimodal Analysis Lab. The Lab is a collaborative research venture comprising computer scientists and social scientists focused on the development of new approaches for analysing visual imagery and video texts in the complex multimodal sites afforded by interactive digital technology. The site has links to the various projects and publications produced by team members.

OLAC – The Open Language Archives Community, www.language-archives. org/. OLAC is an international partnership of institutions and individuals who are creating a worldwide virtual library of language resources by developing consensus on best current practice for the digital archiving of language resources, and developing a network of interoperating repositories and services for housing and accessing such resources.

Social Research Methods, www.socialresearchmethods.net/. This website has resources and links to other locations on the Web that deal with applied social research methods. Included is an online textbook on applied social research methods and a resource guide for learning about structured conceptual mapping.

The Subject Centre for Languages, Linguistics and Area Studies, www.lang.ltsn. ac.uk/index.html. The Subject Centre for Languages, Linguistics and Area Studies is part of the UK-wide Learning and Teaching Support Network. The mission of the centre is to act as a repository of information and service and to promote high-quality learning and teaching of languages, linguistics and area studies across higher education institutions in England, Northern Ireland, Scotland and Wales.

Terralingua, www.terralingua.org. Formed in 1996, Terralingua is an international, nonprofit organisation concerned about the future of the world's biological, cultural and linguistic diversity. It contains links supporting the perpetuation and continued development of the world's linguistic diversity and the exploration of connections between linguistic, cultural and biological diversity.

Glossary

affinity spaces Informal contexts of learning, where individuals from a variety of backgrounds come together to pursue a common goal.

agency One's socioculturally negotiated ability or willingness to take action within specific sociocultural contexts.

appropriation Term usually used to describe the process by which children or novice members of an activity move from their roles as less expert participants to more expert participants. In the process, they borrow or model other, more expert members' ways of participating. Eventually, the novices take on these ways as their own, transforming them into ways that are specifically theirs.

classroom discourse The language of the classroom, used by teachers and students to create and participate in their classroom communities. See **discourse**, **IRE** and **IRF**.

co-construction The joint creation of a culturally meaningful reality between two or more individuals.

communicative competence Term first proposed by Dell Hymes in response to Chomsky's notion of linguistic competence. It comprises the knowledge and ability one needs to understand and use linguistic resources in ways that are structurally well formed, socially and contextually appropriate, and culturally feasible in communicative contexts constitutive of the different groups and communities of which one is a member.

communicative event A central unit of analysis in an **ethnography of communication** approach to the study of language use.

communities of inquiry Particular **communities of learners** based on the premise that learning takes place in the process of exploring with others answers to questions that arise from shared experiences. Classroom activities are organised around the open-ended, exploratory study of questions or topics that are generated from real experiences of the group members and thus are of genuine interest to them.

communicative plans Socially shared understandings about the conventional nature of communicative activities – and the means for participating in them – that are of sociocultural significance to the groups to which we belong.

communities of learners Particular **communities of practice** in which expert and novice members share goals centred on moving learners from limited participatory roles as novices to full participatory roles as experts in socioculturally important activities and practices.

communities of practice Groups of individuals who come together with shared purposes structured around professional, social, community, religious or other type of goals.

contextualisation cues Symbolic resources imbued with contextually significant meaning. They provide individuals with recognisable markers for signalling and interpreting **contextual presuppositions**. See **interactional sociolinguistics** and **linguistic indexes**.

contextual presuppositions Foregrounding information or understandings used by individuals to interpret and respond appropriately to communicative interactions with other social group members.

conversation analysis An approach to the study of talk-in-interaction. Its focus is on uncovering the socially constituted means or mechanisms by which social order is produced in interaction.

critical discourse analysis An approach to the study of language use whose concern is with how language use is shaped by relations of power and ideologies, and how such relations affect individuals' understandings of themselves, of others, and of their larger social worlds. See **discourse analysis**.

critical framing One of four types of learning opportunities associated with the **multiliteracies pedagogy**, whose aim is to help learners to understand the historical, social, cultural, political and ideological dimensions of their communicative activities. See **situated practice**, **overt instruction** and **transformed practice**.

critical pedagogy A general approach to education that focuses centrally on the issue of power in teaching and learning contexts. It considers the ideal goal of education to be emancipatory.

design A key concept in **multiliteracies pedagogy** that defines learners' knowledge and abilities in terms of their future outcomes. It is considered a more forward-looking alternative to **communicative competence**.

dialogicality Refers to the relational character of meaning whereby meaning is defined as emerging from the (non-static or fluid) interrelationship between the use of a linguistic resource at a locally situated moment and its historical/conventional use, not purely from any one source.

dialogic inquiry A theory of pedagogy which views knowledge to be co-constructed by teacher and students as they engage in joint activities, which are negotiated rather than imposed.

discourse analysis A broad approach to the study of language use whose focus is on uncovering the contextually based meanings of linguistic resources.

discourse-historical approach A variation of **critical discourse analysis**. Its focus is on studying how oral and written texts reflect particular power systems and ideologies from a historical perspective, and exploring the ways in which they change through time.

emergent grammar A view on language in which grammar is understood as arising from regularities in language use rather than existing as a set of *a priori* mental categories.

encode To arrange or transform thoughts into a code such as language.

ethics of care A component of **practical ethics**. Used in research to refer to researchers' level of sensitivity for, identification with, and responsible, caring actions towards the participants of the study. See also, **research ethics**.

ethnography of communication An approach to the study of language use developed by linguistic anthropologist Dell Hymes. Its focus is on capturing patterns of language use and understandings conventionally associated with sociocultural events and activities typical of particular sociocultural groups and contexts.

ethnomethodology An approach to the study of social life that examines how individuals together create social order in real-world activity. See **conversation analysis**.

formulaic competence A component of **communicative competence**. It includes knowledge of prefabricated chunks of language that speakers use regularly in everyday interactions.

funds of knowledge Historically developed, significant sociocultural practices, activities, skills, abilities, beliefs and bodies of knowledge embodied in households. It is a key concept of a pedagogical innovation in which learners' funds of knowledge are used to transform curricular and instructional practices.

globalisation The ongoing process by which sociocultural groups sustain engagement with each other through a worldwide network of communication, transportation and trade.

habitus The sets of beliefs, knowledge and skills that predispose one's way of being, including behaving, believing, thinking, feeling, interacting with others. One's habitus is largely determined by one's sociocultural environments (i.e. economic status, ethnicity, religion and groups or communities to which one belongs).

indexicality The process by which particular (contextual) meanings are assigned to forms.

interactional competence A component of **communicative competence**. It refers to the skills and knowledge needed for successful interaction. These include knowledge of and skills to perform speech acts and speech act sets, and to open and close conversations, establish and change topics, and so on.

interactional sociolinguistics An approach to the study of language use, the development of which is most often attributed to John Gumperz. A primary aim is to uncover differences in use of cues to signal and interpret meaning in particular contexts of interaction.

intercultural communicative competence The knowledge, skills and abilities needed to understand cultures and communicate successfully with individual from other cultures.

IRE The three-part interactional pattern typical of **classroom discourse**. It involves a teacher-initiated question (I), followed by a student response (R), followed by a teacher evaluation of the response (E). See **IRF**.

IRF Variation of the three-part interactional pattern of **classroom discourse**. It involves a teacher-initiated question (I), a student response (R), and a teacher follow-up to the response in the form of, for example, a comment, an elaboration, or a request for additional information (F). See **IRE**.

language awareness curriculum A curricular component whose purpose is to enhance individuals' awareness of or sensitivity to linguistic variations. An example of such a component is dialect education where learners from non-mainstream language backgrounds explore the structural and communicative features of their own varieties.

language crossing A form of speech stylisation that suggests a stronger sense of social or ethnic boundary transgression in the use of exaggerated linguistic markers. See **speech stylisation**.

language games Established, conventionalised patterns of action, ways of knowing, valuing and experiencing the world, agreed upon and shared in by members of a culture group. The term is most often associated with the writings of Ludwig Wittgenstein.

language socialisation practices Activities or **communicative events** that are realised primarily through language, by which individuals are socialised into roles as legitimate members of particular communities.

legitimate peripheral participation Process of providing increased opportunities to individuals recognised as bona fide novice members of a community or sociocultural group for developing expertise they need in order to be considered accomplished, expert members in the community or group. See **communities of practice** and **communities of learners**.

linguistic ethnography A broadly construed research method for the study of oral and written language practices.

linguistic indexes or indexicals Linguistic resources whose uses index or invoke particular contextual meanings. See **contextualisation cues**.

linguistic indexing The act of indexing or invoking meanings conventionally associated with particular linguistic forms. See **linguistic indexes** and **contextualisation cues**.

linguistic relativity A core concept of the Sapir–Whorf hypothesis. Its basic assertion is that language is a social system based on agreement among speech community members. Since members perceive the world using the resources of their systems, people who live in different linguistic systems see the world differently to the extent that their linguistic systems are different.

literacy practices Communicative activities involving the skills of reading and writing and oriented to by members of a group or community associo-culturally meaningful activities.

micro-ethnography An approach to the study of language use, the focus of which is on the close analysis of one communicative event with particular interest in the specific means by which the event is jointly constructed.

microgenetic approach An approach to the study of language development, the focus of which is on tracking changes in behaviour as they occur over the duration of a particular event in specific settings.

multiliteracies pedagogy A general approach to pedagogy the goal of which is to develop in learners the knowledge, skills and abilities that will expand their communicative options for bringing their cultural worlds into existence, maintaining them, and transforming them for their own socially meaningful purposes. See **design**, **situated practice**, **overt instruction**, **critical framing** and **transformed practice**.

multimodal discourse analysis An approach to research that incorporates into the analysis all relevant communicative modes including gesture, space, objects and visual design in addition to language. See **discourse analysis**.

narrative inquiry A research approach that seeks to understand individuals through the stories they tell about themselves and their experiences.

New Literacies Studies An approach to the study of literacy practices that understands literacy as a social achievement rather than a mental skill and seeks to understand a group's practices in their social, cultural, historical and institutional contexts.

non-parametric measures Typically used in studies where the parameters of the variables of interest in the population are unknown. They are most appropriately used when the sample sizes are small.

overt instruction One of four types of learning opportunities associated with the **multiliteracies pedagogy**, the aim of which is to provide opportunities for learners to focus on, practice and take control of the various linguistic and other relevant conventions needed for competent engagement in their communicative activities. See **situated practice**, **critical framing** and **transformed practice**.

participant-observation A method for collecting data in a qualitative approach to research. The researcher collects data at the same time that he/she participates in and observes the target contexts or communicative activities.

participatory pedagogy A general approach to language education that draws on the work of Brazilian educator Paulo Freire. Its general aim is to help learners to develop their own voices in response to their local conditions and circumstances and, in so doing, transform their lives in socially meaningful ways.

practical ethics A component of research ethics that addresses principled ways of dealing with everyday, locally situated, ethical issues that come up when doing research. See **research ethics**.

pragmatic ethnography A type of project-based learning that involves learners in the ethnographic exploration of the sociocultural patterns and practices of cultural groups.

procedural ethics A component of research ethics that addresses in principled ways the process of seeking official approval to conduct research from institutional boards or committees. See **research ethics**.

project-based learning A pedagogical approach that organises learning around extended tasks or projects that seek to address a challenging question or problem. See **pragmatic ethnography**.

research ethics The application of ethical principles in the design and implementation of a research project.

situated practice One of four types of learning opportunities associated with the **multiliteracies pedagogy**, the purpose of which is to afford learners the possibility to develop a familiarity, or a 'feel' for communicative activities in which they aspire to become active, legitimate members. See **overt instruction**, **critical framing** and **transformed practice**.

social identity The social roles, positions, relationships, reputations and other dimensions of social character as related to our various group memberships, along with the values, beliefs and attitudes associated with them.

sociocultural discourse analysis A research approach that uses both quantitative and qualitative methods of data collection and analysis to describe and assess the intellectual quality of teacher–student and student–student classroom interaction.

sociolinguistic relativity Hymes's reformulation of Whorf's notion of **linguistic relativity**, in which primacy is given to language use and function rather than linguistic code and form.

speech stylisation Refers to the production of speech that is marked by exaggerated representations of languages, dialects, and styles that lie outside the speaker's repertoire. See **language crossing**.

SPEAKING Analytic framework proposed by Dell Hymes for describing systematically the links between the use of language forms and context in a communicative event. Each letter stands for one component of the communicative event to be described.

structuration The process by which social structures or systems – conventionalised ways of doing things – are established. Once established, social structures give shape to individual actors' **communicative events** or activities, and at the same time are reproduced through them. This concept underlies Anthony Giddens's theory.

systemic functional linguistics A theory of language formulated by Michael Halliday, which posits that meanings of language forms are located in their systematic connections between their functions and the contexts of use.

thinking-for-speaking A hypothesis developed by Dan Slobin, a professor of psychology and linguistics, which asserts that languages afford users preferred perspectives for encoding their lived experiences.

transformed practice One of four types of learning opportunities associated with the **multiliteracies project**, the purpose of which is to provide learners with opportunities to take the lead in their own learning. See **situated practice**, **overt instruction** and **critical framing**.

transnational communities Groups comprised of individuals living and working in countries that are not their countries of origin who maintain ties to their countries of origin.

utterance A complete meaningful unit of language use. It is a fundamental unit of analysis in research on language from a sociocultural perspective.

virtue ethics A component of **practical ethics** which entails an ability on the part of the researcher to recognise when ethical dilemmas occur, to think through the issues with care and thoughtfulness and to respond appropriately. See **practical ethics** and **research ethics**.

References

Achugar, M., Schleppegrell, M. and Oteíza, T. (2007) 'Engaging teachers in language analysis: A functional linguistics approach to reflective literacy', *English Teaching: Practice and Critique*, 6: 8–24.

Ahearn, L. (2000) 'True traces: Love letters and social transformation in Nepal', in D. Barton and N. Hall (eds), *Letter Writing as Social Practice* (pp. 199–207), Amsterdam: John Benjamins.

Ahearn, L. (2001) 'Language and agency', *Annual Review of Anthropology*, 30: 109–137.

Alexander, R. (2008) *Towards Dialogic Teaching: Rethinking Classroom Talk*, 4th edn, York: Dialogos.

Alfred, M. (2010) 'Transnational migration, social capital and lifelong learning in the USA', *Journal of Lifelong Education*, 29: 219–235.

Allen, J. P. B. and Corder, S. P. (1973) *The Edinburgh Course in Applied Linguistics*, London: Oxford University Press.

Allport, G. (1954) *The Nature of Prejudice*, Cambridge: Addison Wesley.

Altieri, C. (1994) *Subjective Agency*, Cambridge, MA: Blackwell.

Andrews, L. (1998) *Language Exploration and Awareness*, Mahwah, NJ: Lawrence Erlbaum Associates.

Antaki, C., Billig, M., Edwards, D. and Potter, J. A. (2003) 'Discourse analysis means doing analysis: A critique of six analytic shortcomings', *Discourse Analysis Online*, 1. Available from: www.shu.ac.uk/daol/articles/v1/n1/a1/antaki2002002-paper.html.

Archer, W. (2010) 'Beyond online discussions: Extending the community of inquiry framework to entire courses', *Internet and Higher Education*, 13: 69.

Aronson, E. and Patnoe, S. (1997) *The Jigsaw Classroom: Building Cooperation in the Classroom*, 2nd edn, New York: Addison Wesley Longman.

Aronson, E. and Yates, S. (1983) 'Cooperation in the classroom: The impact of the jigsaw method on inter-ethnic relations, classroom performance and self-esteem', in H. Blumberg and P. Hare (eds), *Small Groups*, London: John Wiley and Sons.

Au, K. H.-P. (1980) 'Participation structures in a reading lesson with Hawaiian children: Analysis of a culturally appropriate instructional event', *Anthropology & Education Quarterly*, 11: 91–115.

Au, K. H.-P. and Mason, J. M. (1983) 'Cultural congruence in classroom participation structures: Achieving a balance of rights', *Discourse Processes*, 6: 145–167.

Auer, P. (ed.) (2007) *Style and Social Identities: Alternative Approaches to Linguistic Heterogeneity*, Berlin: Mouton de Gruyter.

Auerbach, E. R. (2000) 'Creating participatory learning communities: Paradoxes and possibilities', in J. K. Hall and W. Eggington (eds), *The Sociopolitics of English Language Teaching* (pp. 143–163), Clevedon: Multilingual Matters.

Bachman, L. F. (1990) *Fundamental Considerations in Language Testing*, Oxford: Oxford University Press.

Bachman, L. F. and Palmer, A. S. (1996) *Language Testing in Practice*, Oxford: Oxford University Press.

Bailey, B. (2000) 'Communicative behavior and conflict between African-American customers and Korean immigrant retailers in Los Angeles', *Discourse & Society*, 11: 86–108.

Baker, P., Gabrielatos, C., Khosravinik, M., Krzyzanowski, M., McEnery, T. and Wodak, R. (2008) 'A useful methodological synergy? Combining critical discourse analysis and corpus linguistics to examine discourses of refugees and asylum seekers in the UK press', *Discourse & Society*, 19: 273–306.

Bakhtin, M. (1981) *The Dialogic Imagination: Four Essays by M.M. Bakhtin*, trans. C. Emerson and M. Holquist, Austin, TX: University of Texas Press.

Bakhtin, M. (ed.) (1986) *Speech Genres and Other Essays*, Austin, TX: University of Texas Press.

Bakhtin, M. (1990) *Art and Answerability*, Austin, TX: University of Texas Press.

Baquedano-Lopez, P. (2001) 'Creating social identities through Doctrina narratives', in A. Duranti (ed.), *Linguistic Anthropology: A Reader* (pp. 343–358), Oxford: Blackwell.

Barnes, D. (1992) *From Communication to Curriculum*, Portsmouth, NH: Boynton/Cook.

Barton, D. (1991) 'The social nature of writing', in D. Barton and R. Ivanič (eds), *Writing in the Community* (pp. 1–13), Newbury Park: Sage.

Barton, D. and Hamilton, M. (1998) *Local Literacies: Reading and Writing in One Community*, London: Routledge.

Bauman, R. (2000) 'Language, identity, performance', *Pragmatics*, 10: 1–5.

Bayley, R. and Schecter, S. R. (eds) (2003) *Language Socialization in Bilingual and Multilingual Societies*, Clevedon: Multilingual Matters.

Baynham, M. (2006) 'Agency and contingency in the language learning of refugees and asylum seekers', *Linguistics and Education*, 17: 24–39.

Begay, S., Dick, G. S., Estell, D. W., Estell, J., McCarty, T. and Sells, A. (1995) 'Change from the inside out: A story of transformation in a Navajo community school', *Bilingual Research Journal*, 19: 121–139.

Bezemer, J. and Kress, G. (2008) 'Writing in multimodal texts: A social semiotic account of designs for learning', *Written Communication*, 25: 166–195.

Bhabha, H. (1994) *The Location of Culture*, London: Routledge.

Blackledge, A. and Creese, A. (2008). 'Contesting "language" as "heritage": Negotiation of identities in late modernity', *Applied Linguistics*, 29(4): 533–554.

Blommaert, J. (2010) *The Sociolinguistics of Globalization*, Cambridge: Cambridge University Press.

Blommaert, J., Creve, L. and Willaert, E. (2006) 'On being declared illiterate: Language-ideological disqualification in Dutch classes for immigrants in Belgium', *Language and Communication*, 26: 34–54.

Blum-Kulka, S. (1997) *Dinner Talk: Cultural Patterns of Sociability and Socialization in Family Discourse*, Mahwah, NJ: Lawrence Erlbaum.

Boal, A. (1995) *The Rainbow of Desire: The Boal Method of Theatre and Therapy*, New York: Routledge.

Bongartz, C. and Schneider, M. (2003) 'Linguistic development in social contexts: A study of two brothers learning German', *Modern Language Journal*, 87: 13–37.

Bourdieu, P. (1977) *Outline of a Theory of Practice*, Cambridge: Cambridge University Press.

Bourdieu, P. (1980) *The Logic of Practice*, Stanford, CA: Stanford University Press.

Bourdieu, P. (2000) *Pascalian Meditations*, Stanford, CA: Stanford University Press.

Bowerman, M. (1996) 'The origins of children's spatial semantic categories: Cognitive vs. linguistic determinants', in J. J. Gumperz and S. C. Levinson (eds), *Rethinking Linguistic Relativity* (pp. 145–176), Cambridge: Cambridge University Press.

Bowerman, M. and Choi, S. (2001) 'Shaping meanings for language: Universal and language-specific in the acquisition of spatial semantic categories', in M. Bowerman and S. C. Levinson (eds), *Language Acquisition and Conceptual Development* (pp. 475–511), Cambridge: Cambridge University Press.

Bowerman, M. and Levinson, S. C. (2001) 'Introduction', in M. Bowerman and S. C. Levinson (eds), *Language Acquisition and Conceptual Development* (pp. 1–18), Cambridge: Cambridge University Press.

Boxer, D. and Cortés-Conde, F. (2000) 'Identity and ideology: Culture and pragmatics in content-based ESL', in J. K. Hall and L. S. Verplaetse (eds), *Second and Foreign Language Learning through Classroom Interaction* (pp. 203–220), Mahwah, NJ: Lawrence Erlbaum.

Boyd, M. and Maloof, V. M. (2000) 'How teachers can build upon student-proposed intertextual links to facilitate student talk in the ESL classroom', in J. K. Hall and L. S. Verplaetse (eds), *Second and Foreign Language Learning through Classroom Interaction* (pp. 163–182), Mahwah, NJ: Lawrence Erlbaum.

Boyd, M. and Rubin, D. (2002) 'Elaborated student talk in an elementary ESL classroom', *Research in the Teaching of English*, 36: 495–530.

Boyland, J. (2001) 'Hypercorrect pronoun case in English? Cognitive processes that account for pronoun usage', in J. Bybee and P. Hopper (eds), *Frequency and the Emergence of Linguistic Structure* (pp. 383–404), Amsterdam: John Benjamins.

Breen, M. P. (2001) 'Navigating the discourse: On what is learned in the language classroom', in C. N. Candlin and N. Mercer (eds), *English Language Teaching in Its Social Context: A Reader* (pp. 306–322), London: Routledge.

Brison, K. J. (1992) *Just Talk: Gossip, Meetings, and Power in a Papua New Guinea Village*, Berkeley, CA: University of California Press.

Brown, P. (1998) 'Conversational structure and language acquisition: The role of repetition in Tzeltal adult and child speech', *Journal of Linguistic Anthropology*, 8: 197–221.

Brown, P. and Levinson, S. C. (2010) 'Language as mind tools: Learning how to think through speaking', in J. Guo, E. V. M. Lieven, N. Budwig, S. Ervin-Tripp, K. Nakamura and S. Ozcaliskan (eds), *Crosslinguistic Approaches to the Psychology of Language: Research in the Traditions of Dan Slobin* (pp. 451–464), New York: Psychology Press.

Brumfit, C. (1984) *Communicative Methodology in Language Teaching*, Cambridge: Cambridge University Press.

Bucholtz, M. (2004) 'Styles and stereotypes: The linguistic negotiation of identity among Laotian American youth', *Pragmatics*, 14: 127–147.

Bucholtz, M. (2007) 'Variation in transcription', *Discourse Studies*, 9: 784–808.

Bucholtz, M. and Hall, K. (2005) 'Identity and interaction: A sociocultural approach', *Discourse Studies*, 7: 585–614.

Butler, J. (2006) *Gender Trouble: Feminism and the Subversion of Identity*, New York: Routledge.

Bybee, J. L. (2002) 'Consequences for the nature of constructions', in J. Bybee and M. Noonan (eds), *Complex Sentences in Grammar and Discourse* (pp. 1–17), Amsterdam: John Benjamins.

Bybee, J. and Hopper, P. (2001) 'Introduction to frequency and the emergence of linguistic structure', in J. Bybee and P. Hopper (eds), *Frequency and the Emergence of Linguistic Structure* (pp. 1–24), Amsterdam: John Benjamins.

Bygate, M. (2005) 'Applied Linguistics: A pragmatic discipline, a generic discipline?', *Applied Linguistics*, 26: 568–581.

Byram, M. (1997) *Teaching and Assessing Intercultural Communicative Competence*, Clevedon: Multilingual Matters.

Byram, M. (2008) *From Foreign Language Education to Education for Intercultural Citizenship*, Clevedon: Multilingual Matters.

Byram, M. (2010) 'Linguistic and cultural education for Bildung and citizenship', *Modern Language Journal*, 94: 317–321.

Byram, M. and Feng, A. (2004) 'Culture and language learning: Teaching, research and scholarship', *Language Teaching*, 37: 149–168.

Byram, M. and Fleming, M. (eds) (1998) *Language Learning in Intercultural Perspective: Approaches through Drama and Ethnography*, Cambridge: Cambridge University Press.

Byram, M. and Zarate, G. (eds) (1997) *The Sociocultural and Intercultural Dimension of Language Learning and Teaching*, Strasbourg: Council of Europe.

Cameron, D. (2005) 'Language, gender, and sexuality: Current issues and new directions', *Applied Linguistics*, 26: 482–502.

Cammarota, J. and Romero, A. (2009) 'A social justice epistemology and pedagogy for Latina/o students: Transforming public education with participatory action research', *New Directions for Youth Development*, 123: 53–65.

Campbell, S. and Roberts, C. (2007) 'Migration, ethnicity and competing discourses in the job interview: Synthesizing the institutional and personal', *Discourse & Society*, 18: 243–271.

Canagarajah, A. S. (1993) 'Critical ethnography of a Sri Lankan classroom ambiguities in student opposition to reproduction through ESOL', *TESOL Quarterly*, 27: 601–626.

Canagarajah, A. S. (2003) 'Foreword', in G. Smitherman and V. Villanueva (eds), *Language Diversity in the Classroom: From Intention to Practice* (pp. ix–xiv), Carbondale, IL: Southern Illinois University Press.

Canagarajah, A. S. (2004) 'Subversive identities, pedagogical safe houses, and critical learning', in B. Norton and K. Toohey (eds), *Critical Pedagogies and Language Learning* (pp. 116–137), Cambridge: Cambridge University Press.

Canagarajah, A. S. (2006) 'The place of world Englishes in composition: Pluralization continued', *College Composition and Communication*, 57: 586–619.

Canagarajah, A. S. (2007) 'Multilingual academic literacies: Pedagogical foundations for code meshing in primary and higher education', *Journal of Applied Linguistics*, 4: 55–77.

Canale, M. (1982) 'From communicative competence to communicative language pedagogy', in J. C. Richards and R. Schmidt (eds), *Language and Communication* (pp. 2–27), London: Longman.

Canale, M. and Swain, M. (1980) 'Theoretical bases of communicative approaches to second language teaching and testing', *Applied Linguistics*, 1: 1–47.

Candlin, C. N. (1987) 'Beyond description to explanation in cross-cultural discourse', in L. Smith (ed.), *Discourse across Cultures: Strategies in World Englishes* (pp. 22–35), New York: Prentice Hall.

Candlin, C. and Sarangi, S. (2004a) 'Making applied linguistics matter', *Journal of Applied Linguistics*, 1: 1–8.

Candlin, C. and Sarangi, S. (2004b) 'Making inter-relationality matter in applied linguistics', *Journal of Applied Linguistics*, 1: 225–228.

Candlin, S. (2002) 'Taking risks: An indicator of expertise?', *Research on Language and Social Interaction*, 35: 173–193.

Candlin, S. and Candlin, C. (2007) 'Nursing over time and space: Some issues for the construct "community of practice"', in R. Iedema (ed.), *The Discourse of Hospital Communication: Tracing Complexities in Contemporary Health Care Organizations* (pp. 244–267), London: Palgrave Macmillan.

Carbaugh, D. (1988) *Talking American: Cultural Discourses on DONAHUE*, New York: Ablex.

Cazden, C. (1988) *Classroom Discourse: The Language of Teaching and Learning*, Portsmouth, NH: Heinemann.

Cazden, C., John, V. P. and Hymes, D. (eds) (1972) *Functions of Language in the Classroom*, New York: Teachers College Press.

Cekaite, A. (2009) 'Soliciting teacher attention in an L2 classroom: Affect displays, classroom artefacts, and embodied action', *Applied Linguistics*, 30: 26–48.

Cekaite, A. and Aronsson, K. (2004) 'Repetition and joking in children's second language conversations: Playful recyclings in an immersion classroom', *Discourse Studies*, 6: 373–392.

Celce-Murcia, M. (2007) 'Rethinking the role of communicative competence in language teaching', in E. Soler and M. Safont Jordà (eds), *Intercultural Language Use and Language Learning* (pp. 7–22), Dordrecht: Springer.

Celce-Murcia, M., Dornyei, Z. and Thurrell, S. (1995) 'Communicative competence: A pedagogically motivated model with content specification', *Issues in Applied Linguistics*, 6: 5–35.

Chaiklin, S. and Lave, J. (eds) (1993) *Understanding Practice: Perspectives on activity and context*, New York: Cambridge University Press.

Chakhorn, O.-O. (2006) 'Persuasive and politeness strategies in cross-cultural letters of request in the Thai business context', *Journal of Asian Pacific Communication*, 16: 103–146.

Chase, S. (2008) 'Narrative inquiry: Multiple lenses, approaches, voices', in Y. Lincoln and N. Denzin (eds), *The SAGE Handbook of Qualitative Research 3rd edn* (pp. 651–688). Thousand Oaks, CA: Sage.

Chomsky, N. (1957) *Syntactic Structures*, The Hague: Mouton.

Chomsky, N. (1965) *Aspects of the Theory of Syntax*, Cambridge, MA: MIT Press.

Chomsky, N. (1966) *Topics in the Theory of Generative Grammar*, The Hague: Mouton.

Christian, D., Wolfram, W. and Dube, N. (1988) *Variation and Change in Geographically Isolated Communities: Appalachian English and Ozark English*, Tuscaloosa, AL: University of Alabama Press.

Christie, F. (2008) 'Genres and institutions: Functional perspectives on educational discourse', in M. Martin-Jones, A. M. de Mejia and N. Hornberger (eds), *Encyclopedia of Language and Education, Volume 3: Discourse and Education* (2nd edn, pp. 29–40), The Netherlands: Springer Science.

Christie, F. and Martin, J. R. (eds) (2007) *Language, Knowledge and Pedagogy: Functional Linguistic and Sociological Perspectives*, London: Continuum.

Chun, E. (2001) 'The construction of White, Black, and Korean American identities through African American vernacular English', *Journal of Linguistic Anthropology*, 11: 52–64.

Cicourel, A. (2003) 'On contextualizing applied linguistics research in the workplace', *Applied Linguistics*, 24: 360–373.

Cicourel, A. (2007) 'A personal, retrospective view of ecological validity', *Text & Talk*, 27(5/6): 735–752.

Clancy, P. (1999) 'The socialization of affect in Japanese mother-child conversation', *Journal of Pragmatics*, 31: 1397–1421.

Clarke, A. (2003) 'On being an object of research: Reflections from a professional perspective', *Applied Linguistics*, 24: 374–385.

Clarke, M. (2008) *Language Teacher Identities: Co-constructing Discourse and Community*, Clevedon: Multilingual Matters.

Cole, M. (1996) *Cultural psychology*, Cambridge, MA: Harvard University Press.

Collins, J. (2007) 'Migration & multiligualism: Implications for linguistic anthropology and educational research', [Electronic Version], *Working Papers in Urban Language & Literacies*, 47, from http://www.kcl.ac.uk/schools/sspp/education/research/groups/llg/wpull.html.

Condell, S. (2008) 'Writing field notes in an ethnographic study of peers: Collaborative experiences from the field', *Journal of Research in Nursing*, 13: 325–335.

Conrad, S. (2002) 'Corpus linguistic approaches for discourse analysis', *Annual Review of Applied Linguistics*, 22: 75–95.

Consolo, D. (2000) 'Teachers' action and student oral participation in classroom interaction', in J. K. Hall and L. S. Verplaetse (eds), *Second and Foreign Language Learning through Classroom Interaction* (pp. 91–108), Mahwah, NJ: Lawrence Erlbaum.

Cook, G. (2000) *Language Play, Language Learning*, Oxford: Oxford University Press.

Cook, V. (1999) 'Going beyond the native speaker in language teaching', *TESOL Quarterly*, 33: 185–209.

Cope, B. and Kalantis, M. (2000) 'Multiliteracies: The beginnings of an idea', in B. Cope and M. Kalantis (eds), *Multiliteracies: Literacy Learning and the Design of Social Futures* (pp. 3–8), London: Routledge.

Corder, S. P. (1973) *Introducing Applied Linguistics*, Harmondsworth: Penguin Books.

Cotter, C. and Marschall, D. (2006) 'The persistence of workplace ideology and identity across communicative contexts', *Journal of Applied Linguistics*, 3(1): 1–24.

Council of Europe (2001) *Common European Framework of Reference for Languages*, Cambridge: Cambridge University Press.

Creese, A., Bhatt, A., Bhojani, N. and Martin, P. (2006) 'Multicultural, heritage and learner identities in complementary schools', *Language and Education*, 20: 23–43.

Creswell, J. W. (2009) 'Editorial: Mapping the field of mixed methods research', *Journal of Mixed Methods Research*, 3: 95–108.

Creswell, J. W., Plano Clark, V. L., Gutmann, M. L. and Hanson, W. E. (2003) 'Advanced mixed methods research designs', in A. Tashakkori and C. Teddlie (eds), *Handbook of Mixed Methods in Social and Behavioral Research* (pp. 209–240), Thousand Oaks, CA: Sage.

Crowley, T. (1996) *Language in History*. London: Routledge.

Curry, M. (2008) 'Critical friends groups: The possibilities and limitations embedded in teacher professional communities aimed at instructional improvement and school reform', *Teachers College Record*, 110: 733–774.

Dagenais, D., Toohey, K. and Day, E. (2006) 'A multilingual child's literacy practices and contrasting identities in the figured worlds of French Immersion classrooms', *International Journal of Bilingual Education and Bilingualism*, 9: 205–218.

Damen, L. (1987) *Culture Learning: The Fifth Dimension in the Language Classroom*, Reading, MA: Addison-Wesley.

Davis, K. A., Bazzi, S. and Cho, H. (2005) ' "Where I'm from": Transforming education for language minorities in a public high school in Hawai'i.', in B. V. Street (ed.), *Literacies across Educational Contexts: Mediating Learning and Teaching* (pp. 188–212), Philadelphia: Calson.

Day, D. (1998) 'Being ascribed, and resisting, membership in an ethnic group', in C. Antaki and S. Widdicombe (eds), *Identities in Talk* (pp. 151–170), London: Sage.

de Certeau, M. (1984) *The Practice of Everyday Life*, Berkeley, CA: University of California Press.

Denzin, N. (2010) 'Moments, mixed methods, and paradigm dialogs', *Qualitative Inquiry*, 16: 419–427.

Dien, T. (1998) 'Language and literacy in Vietnamese American communities', in B. Perez (ed.), *Sociocultural Contexts of Language and Literacy* (pp. 123–162), Mahwah, NJ: Lawrence Erlbaum.

Dong, J. and Blommaert, J. (2009) 'Space, scale and accents: Constructing migrant identity in Beijing', *Multilingua*, 28: 1–23.

Doughty, C. and Williams, J. (1998) 'Pedagogical choices in focus on form', in C. Doughty and J. Williams (eds), *Focus on Form in Second Language Acquisition* (pp. 197–261), Cambridge: Cambridge University Press.

Du Bois, J. W. (2006) *Representing Discourse: Transcription in Action*, available online at: www.linguistics.ucsb.edu/projects/transcription/representing.

Duchan, J. F. and Kovarsky, D. (eds) (2005) *Diagnosis as Cultural Practice*. Berlin: Mouton de Gruyter.

Duff, P. A. (1995) 'An ethnography of communication in immersion classrooms in Hungary', *TESOL Quarterly*, 29: 505–537.

Duff, P. A. (2002) 'The discursive co-construction of knowledge, identity, and difference: An ethnography of communication in the high school mainstream', *Applied Linguistics*, 23: 289–322.

Duff, P. A. (2007a) 'Second language socialization as sociocultural theory: Insights and issues', *Language Teaching*, 40: 309–319.

Duff, P. (2007b) *Case Study Research in Applied Linguistics*, London: Routledge.

Duff, P. A., Wong, P. and Early, M. (2000) 'Learning language for work and life: The linguistic socialization of immigrant Canadians seeking careers in healthcare', *Canadian Modern Language Review*, 57: 9–57.

Duranti, A. (1997) *Linguistic Anthropology*, Cambridge: Cambridge University Press.

Duranti, A. (2006) 'Transcripts, like shadows on a wall', *Mind, Culture and Activity*, 13: 301–310.

Eggins, S. (2004) *An Introduction to Systemic Functional Linguistics*, 2nd edn, New York: Continuum.

Eisenberg, A. (1986) 'Teasing: Verbal play in two Mexican homes', in B. B. Schieffelin and E. Ochs (eds), *Language Socialization Across Cultures*, Cambridge: Cambridge University Press.

Ellis, N. and Cadierno, T. (2009) 'Constructing a second language', *Annual Review of Cognitive Linguistics*, 7: 111–139.

Ellis, N. and Ferreira-Junior, F. (2009) 'Construction learning as a function of frequency, frequency distribution, and function', *Modern Language Journal*, 93: 370–385.

Ellis, R. (1997) 'SLA and language pedagogy', *Studies in Second Language Acquisition*, 19: 69–92.

Ellis, R. (2003) *Task-based Language Learning and Teaching*, Oxford: Oxford University Press.

Engle, R. and Conant, F. (2002) 'Guiding principles for fostering productive disciplinary engagement: Explaining an emergent argument in a community of learners classroom', *Cognition and Instruction*, 20: 399–483.

Erickson, E. and Schultz, J. (1982) *The Counselor as Gatekeeper: Social Interaction in Interviews*, New York: Academic Press.

Eskildsen, S. (2009) 'Constructing another language: Usage-based linguistics in second language acquisition', *Applied Linguistics*, 30: 335–357.

Fairclough, N. (1992) *Discourse and Social Change*, Cambridge: Polity Press.

Fairclough, N. (1995) *Critical Discourse Analysis: The Critical Study of Language*, London: Longman.

Fairclough, N. (2000) *New Labour, New Language?* New York: Routledge.

Fairclough, N. and Wodak, R. (1997) 'Critical discourse analysis', in T. A. van Dijk (ed.), *Discourse as Social Interaction* (pp. 258–284), London: Sage.

Félix-Brasdefer, C. (2009) 'Pragmatic variation across Spanish(es): Requesting in Mexican, Costa Rican and Dominican Spanish', *Intercultural Pragmatics*, 6: 473–515.

Field, M. (2001) 'Triadic directives in Navajo language socialization', *Language in Society*, 30: 249–263.

Fishman, A. (1991) 'Because this is who we are: Writing in the Amish community', in D. Barton and R. Ivanič (eds), *Writing in the Community* (pp. 14–37), Newbury Park: Sage.

Fitch, K. L. (2002) 'A ritual for leave-taking in Colombia', in J. N. Martin, T. K. Nakayama and L. A. Flores (eds), *Readings in Cultural Contexts*, 2nd edn (pp. 149–155), Mountain View, CA: Mayfield.

Flynn, E., Pine, K. and Lewis, C. (2006) 'The microgenetic method: Time for change?', *The Psychologist*, 19: 152–155.

Ford, C. E. (2008) *Women Speaking Up: Getting and Using Turns in Workplace Meetings*, New York: Palgrave Macmillan.

Ford, C., Fox, B. and Thompson, S. (2003) 'Social interaction and grammar' in M. Tomasello (ed.), *The New Psychology of Language* (Vol. 2, pp. 119–144), Mahwah, NJ: Lawrence Erlbaum Associates.

Foster, M. (1989) '"It's cooking now": A performance analysis of the speech events of a Black teacher in an urban community college', *Language in Society*, 18: 1–29.

Foucault, M. (1972) *The Archaeology of Knowledge*, trans. A. M. Sheridan Smith, New York: Pantheon.

Freeman, D. (2006) *Connecting Teacher and Student Learning Through Research*, Paper presented as part of colloquium sponsored by the TESOL Teacher Education SIG, TESOL Convention, Tampa, Florida.

Freire, P. (1972) *Pedagogy of the Oppressed*, New York: Continuum.

Freire, P. (1973) *Pedagogy for Critical Consciousness*, New York: Seabury Press.

Furstenberg, G. (2010) 'Making culture the core of the language class: Can it be done?', *Modern Language Journal*, 94: 329–332.

Gallimore, R., Boggs, J. W. and Jordan, C. (1974) *Culture, Behavior, and Education: A Study of Hawaiian-Americans*, Beverly Hills, CA: Sage.

Garfinkel, H. (1967) *Studies in Ethnomethodology*, Englewood Cliffs, NJ: Prentice Hall.

Garner, M., Raschka, C. and Sercombe, P. (2006) 'Sociolinguistic minorities, research, and social relationships', *Journal of Multilingual and Multicultural Development*, 27: 61–78.

Garrison, D., Anderson, T. and Archer, W. (2010) 'The first decade of the community of inquiry framework: A retrospective', *Internet and Higher Education*, 13: 5–9.

Gee, J. K. (2004) *Situated Language and Learning*, London: Routledge.

Gee, J. (2007) *What Video Games Have To Teach Us About Learning And Literacy*, 2nd edn, New York: Palgrave Macmillan.

Gee, J. P. (2008) 'A sociocultural perspective on opportunity to learn', in P. Moss, D. Pullin, J. P. Gee, E. Haertel and L. Young (eds), *Assessment, Equity, and Opportunity to Learn* (pp. 76–108), Cambridge: Cambridge University Press.

Gee, J. and Green, J. (1998) 'Discourse analysis, learning, and social practice: A methodological study', *Review of Educational Research*, 23: 119–169.

Giddens, A. (1984) *The Constitution of Society: Outline of the Theory of Structuration*, Berkeley, CA: University of California Press.

Giddens, A. (1991) *Modernity and Self-identity: Self and Society in the Late Modern Age*, Stanford, CA: Stanford University Press.

Gillies, R. (2008) 'The effects of cooperative learning on junior high school students' behaviours, discourse, and learning during a science-based learning activity', *School Psychology International*, 29: 328–347.

González, N. and Amanti, C. (1992) *Teaching Ethnographic Methods to Teachers: Successes and Pitfalls*, Paper presented at the annual meeting of the American Anthropological Association, San Francisco, CA.

González, N., Moll, L., Floyd-Tenery, M., Rivera, A., Rendon, P., González, R. and Amanti, C. (1993) 'Teacher research on funds of knowledge: Learning from households', *Educational Practice Report* 6, National Center for Research on Cultural Diversity and Second Language Learning.

González, N., Moll, L., Floyd-Tenery, M., Rivera, A., Rendon, P., González, R. and Amanti, C. (1995) 'Funds of knowledge for teaching in Latino households', *Urban Education*, 29: 443–470.

Goodenough, W. (1964) 'Cultural anthropology and linguistics', in D. Hymes (ed.), *Language in Culture and Society: A Reader in Linguistics and Anthropology* (pp. 36–39), New York: Harper and Row.

Goodwin, M. H. (2006) *The Hidden Life of Girls: Games of Stance, Status, and Exclusion*, Oxford: Blackwell.

Guillemin, M. and Gillam, L. (2004) 'Ethics, reflexivity, and "ethically important moments" in research', *Qualitative Inquiry*, 10: 261–280.

Gumperz, J. J. (1981) 'The linguistic bases of communicative competence', in D. Tannen (ed.), *Analyzing Discourse: Text and Talk* (pp. 323–334), Washington, DC: Georgetown University Press.

Gumperz, J. J. (1982a) *Discourse Strategies*, Cambridge: Cambridge University Press.

Gumperz, J. J. (1982b) *Language and Social Identity*, Cambridge: Cambridge University Press.

Gumperz, J. J. (1992) 'Contextualization and understanding', in A. Duranti and C. Goodwin (eds), *Rethinking Context: Language as an Interactive Phenomenon* (pp. 230–252), Cambridge: Cambridge University Press.

Gumperz, J. J. (1999) 'On interactional sociolinguistic method', in S. Sarangi and C. Roberts (eds), *Talk, Work and Institutional Order* (pp. 453–471), Berlin: Mouton de Gruyter.

Gumperz, J. and Roberts, C. (1991) 'Understanding in intercultural encounters', in J. Blommaert and J. Verschueren (eds), *The Pragmatics of Intercultural Communication* (pp. 51–90), Amsterdam: John Benjamins.

Gumperz, J. J., Jupp, T. and Roberts, C. (1979) *Crosstalk: A Study of Cross-Cultural Communication*, London: The National Centre for Industrial Language Training.

Gutierrez, K. (1994) 'How talk, context, and script shape contexts for learning: A cross-case comparison of journal sharing', *Linguistics and Education*, 5: 335–365.

Gutierrez, K. (2002) 'Studying cultural practices in urban learning communities', *Human Development*, 45: 312–321.

Hall, J. K. (1993a) '*Tengo una bomba*: The paralinguistic and linguistic conventions of the oral practice *Chismeando*', *Research on Language and Social Interaction*, 26: 57–85.

Hall, J. K. (1993b) 'The role of oral practices in the accomplishment of our everyday lives', *Applied Linguistics*, 14: 145–166.

Hall, J. K. (1993c) 'Oye, oye lo que ustedes no saben: Creativity, social power and politics in the oral practice of chismeando', *Journal of Linguistic Anthropology*, 3: 75–98.

Hall, J. K. (1995) ' "Aw, man, where we goin?": Classroom interaction and the development of L2 interactional competence', *Issues in Applied Linguistics*, 6: 37–62.

Hall, J. K. (1998) 'Differential teacher attention to student utterances: The construction of different opportunities for learning in the IRF', *Linguistics and Education*, 9: 287–311.

Hall, J. K. (1999) 'A prosaics of interaction: The development of interactional competence in another language', in E. Hinkel (ed.), *Culture in Second Language Teaching and Learning* (pp. 137–151), Cambridge: Cambridge University Press.

Hall, J. K. (2002) *Methods for Teaching Foreign Languages: Creating a Community of Learners in the Classroom*, Columbus, OH: Prentice-Hall.

Hall, J. K. (2004) ' "Practicing speaking" in Spanish: Lessons from a high school foreign language classroom', in Boxer, D. and Cohen, A. (eds), *Studying Speaking to Inform Second Language Learning* (pp. 68–87), Clevedon: Multilingual Matters.

Hall, J. K. (2008) 'Language education and culture', in S. May (ed.), *Encyclopedia of Language and Education, Volume 1: Language Policy and Political Issues in Education* (2nd edn, pp. 1–11), New York: Springer Science.

Hall, J. K. (2009) 'Interaction as method and result of language learning', *Language Teaching*, 43: 1–14.

Halliday, M. A. K. (1973) *Explorations in the Functions of Language*, London: Edward Arnold.

Halliday, M. A. K. (1975) *Learning How to Mean: Explorations in the Development of Language*, London: Edward Arnold.

Halliday, M. A. K. (1978) *Language as Social Semiotic: The social interpretation of language and meaning*, London: Edward Arnold.

Halliday, M. A. K. (1993) 'Toward a language-based theory of learning', *Linguistics and Education*, 5: 93–116.

Halliday, M. A. K. (1994) *An Introduction to Functional Grammar*, 2nd edn, London: Edward Arnold.

Halliday, M. A. K. (2005) *Computational and Quantitative Studies* (ed. J. Webster), London: Continuum.

Halliday, M. A. K. and Matthiessen, C. (2004) *An Introduction to Functional Grammar*, 3rd edn, London: Edward Arnold.

Halliday, M. A. K., McIntosh, A. and Strevens, P. (1965) *The Linguistic Sciences and Language Teaching*, Bloomington, IN: Indiana University Press.

Hanks, W. F. (1996) *Language and Communicative Practices*, Boulder, CO: Westview Press.

Harkness, S., Super, C. M. and Keefer, C. H. (1992) 'Learning to be an American parent: How cultural models gain directive force', in R. G. D'Andrade and C. Strauss (eds), *Human Motives and Cultural Models* (pp. 163–178), New York: Cambridge University Press.

Harris, R. (2003) 'Language and new ethnicities: Multilingual youth and diaspora' [Electronic Version], *Working Papers in Urban Language & Literacies*, 22, from www.kcl.ac.uk/schools/sspp/education//research/groups/llg/wpull.html.

Hartmann, D. and Zerbian, S. (2009) 'Rhoticity in Black South African English: A sociolinguistic study', *Southern African Linguistics and Applied Language Studies*, 27: 135–148.

He, A. W. (2003) 'Novices and their speech roles in Chinese heritage classrooms', in R. Bayley and S. R. Schecter (eds), *Language Socialization in Bilingual and Multilingual Societies* (pp. 128–146), Clevedon: Multilingual Matters.

He, A. W. (2004a) 'CA for SLA: Arguments from the Chinese language classroom', *Modern Language Journal*, 88: 568–582.

He, A. W. (2004b) 'Identity construction in Chinese heritage language classes', *Pragmatics*, 14: 199–216.

Heath, S. B. (1983) *Ways with Words: Language, Life, and Work in Communities and in Classrooms*, Cambridge: Cambridge University Press.

Hellermann, J. (2003) 'The interactive work of prosody in the IRF exchange: Teacher repetition in feed-back moves', *Language in Society*, 32: 79–104.

Hellermann, J. (2005) 'Syntactic and prosodic practices for cohesion in series of three part sequences in classroom talk', *Research on Language and Social Interaction*, 38: 105–130.

Hellermann, J. (2008) *Social Actions for Classroom Language Learning*, Clevedon: Multilingual Matters.

Heritage, J. (1984) *Garfinkel and Ethnomethodology*, Cambridge: Polity Press.

Heritage, J. (2004) 'Conversation analysis and institutional talk', in K. Fitch and R. E. Sanders (eds), *Handbook of Language and Social Interaction* (pp. 103–137), Mahwah, NJ: Lawrence Erlbaum.

Heritage, J. and Maynard, D. (eds) (2006) *Communication in Medical Care*, Cambridge: Cambridge University Press.

Higgins, C. (2009) *English as a Local Language: Post-Colonial Identities and Multilingual Practices*, Bristol: Multilingual Matters.

Hilberg, R. S., Tharp, R. G. and DeGeest, L. (2000) 'Efficacy of CREDE's standards-based instruction in American Indian mathematics classes', *Equity and Excellence in Education*, 33: 32–40.

Holmes, J. (2005) 'Story-telling at work: a complex discursive resource for integrating personal, professional and social identities', *Discourse Studies*, 7: 671–700.

Hookway, N. (2008) '"Entering the blogosphere": Some strategies for using blogs in social research', *Qualitative Research*, 8: 91–113.

Hopper, P. (1987) 'Emergent grammar', *Berkeley Linguistics Society*, 13: 139–157.

Hopper, P. (1998) 'Emergent grammar', in M. Tomasello (ed.), *The New Psychology of Language* (pp. 155–166), Mahwah, NJ: Lawrence Erlbaum.

Hopper, P. and Thompson, S. (1993) 'Language universals, discourse pragmatics and semantics', *Language Sciences*, 15: 357–376.

Hornberger, N. (2009) 'Hymes' linguistics and ethnography in education', *Text & Talk*, 29: 347–358.

Huffaker, D. A. and Calvert, S. L. (2005) 'Gender, identity, and language use in teenage blogs', [Electronic Version], *Journal of Computer-Mediated Communication*, 10, from http://jcmc.indiana.edu/vol10/issue2/huffaker.html.

Hyland, K. (2007) 'Genre pedagogy: Language, literacy and L2 writing instruction', *Journal of Second Language Writing*, 16: 148–164.

Hymes, D. (1962) 'The ethnography of speaking', in T. Gladwin and W. Sturtevant (eds), *Anthropology and Human Behavior* (pp. 15–53), Washington, DC: Anthropological Society of Washington.

Hymes, D. (1964) 'Formal discussion', *The Acquisition of Language: Monographs of the Society for Research in Child Development*, 29: 107–111.

Hymes, D. (1971) 'Competence and performance in linguistic theory', in R. Huxley and E. Ingram (eds), *Language Acquisition: Models and Methods*, London: Academic Press.

Hymes, D. (1972a) 'On communicative competence', in J. B. Pride and J. Holmes (eds), *Sociolinguistics* (pp. 269–293), Harmondsworth: Penguin.

Hymes, D. (1972b) 'Models of the interaction of language and social life', in J. J. Gumperz and D. Hymes (eds), *Directions in Sociolinguistics: The Ethnography of Communication* (pp. 35–71), New York: Holt, Rinehart and Winston.

Hymes, D. (1974) *Foundations in Sociolinguistics: An Ethnographic Approach*, Philadelphia: University of Pennsylvania Press.

Hymes, D. (1980) *Language in Education: Ethnolinguistic Essays*, Washington, DC: Center for Applied Linguistics.

Hymes, D. H. (1981) 'Ethnographic monitoring', in H. Trueba, G. Guthrie and K. Au (eds), *Culture and the Bilingual Classroom: Studies in classroom ethnography* (pp. 56–68), Rowley, MA: Newbury House.

Ivanič, I. R. (1998) *Writing and Identity: The Discoursal Construction of Identity in Academic Writing*, Philadelphia: John Benjamins.

Ivanič, I. R. and Satchwell, C. (2007) 'Boundary crossing: Networking and transforming literacies in research processes and college courses', *Journal of Applied Linguistics*, 4: 101–124.

Jefferson, G. (2004) 'Glossary of transcript symbols with an introduction', in G. H. Lerner (ed.), *Conversation Analysis: Studies from the First Generation* (pp. 13–31), Amsterdam: John Benjamins.

Johnson, D. W. and Johnson, F. (1997) *Joining Together: Group Theory and Group Skills*, 6th edn, Englewood Cliffs, NJ: Prentice Hall.

Johnson, D. W. and Johnson, R. T. (2002) 'Learning together and alone: Overview and meta-analysis', *Asia Pacific Journal of Education*, 22: 95–105.

Johnson, D. W. and Johnson, R. T. (2009) 'An educational psychology success story: Social interdependence theory and cooperative learning', *Educational Researcher*, 38: 365–379.

Johnson, D. W., Johnson, R. T. and Holubec, E. J. (2008) *Cooperation in the Classroom*, 8th edn, Edina, MN: Interaction Book.

Johnstone, B. (1999) 'Uses of Southern speech by contemporary Texas women', *Journal of Sociolinguistics*, 3: 505–522.

Johnstone, B. (2007) 'Linking identity and dialect through stancetaking', in R. Englebretson (ed.), *Stancetaking in Discourse* (pp. 49–68), Amsterdam: John Benjamins.

Kalantis, M. and Cope, B. (2008) 'Language education and multiliteracies', in S. May and N. Hornberger (eds), *Encyclopedia of Language and Education, Volume 1: Language Policy and Political Issues in Education* (2nd edn, pp. 195–211), New York: Springer.

Kandiah, T. (1991) 'Extenuatory sociolinguistics: Diverting attention from issues to symptoms in cross-cultural communication studies', *Multilingua*, 10: 345–379.

Kiesling, S. F. (2005) 'Variation, stance, and style: Word final –er, high rising tone, and ethnicity in Australian English', *English World Wide*, 26: 1–44.

Kramsch, C. (1986) 'From language proficiency to interactional competence', *Modern Language Journal*, 70: 366–372.

Krashen, S. D. and Terrell, T. D. (1983) *The Natural Approach*, Hayward, CA: Alemany Press.

Kress, G. (2003) *Literacy in the New Media Age*, New York: Routledge.

Kress, G. (2010) *Multimodality: A Social Semiotic Approach to Contemporary Communication*, London: Routledge.

Kress, G. and Van Leeuwen, T. (2006) *Reading Images: The Grammar of Visual Design*, 2nd edn, London: Routledge.

Kress, G., Jewitt, C., Bourne, J., Franks, A., Hardcastle, J., Jones, K. and Reid, E. (2005) *English in Urban Classrooms: A Multimodal Perspective on Teaching and Learning*, London: Routledge.

Krieger, D. (2003) 'Corpus linguistics: What it is and how it can be applied to teaching', [Electronic Version], *The Internet TESL Journal*, from http://iteslj.org/Articles/Krieger-Corpus.html.

Kubaniyiova, M. (2008) 'Rethinking research ethics in contemporary applied linguistics: The tension between macroethical and microethical perspectives in situated research', *Modern Language Journal*, 92: 503–518.

Kubota, R. (2004) 'Critical multiculturalism and second language education', in B. Norton and K. Toohey (eds), *Critical pedagogies and language learning* (pp. 30–52), Cambridge: Cambridge University Press.

Kyratzis, A. (2004) 'Talk and interaction among children and the co-construction of peer groups and peer culture', *Annual Review of Anthropology*, 33: 625–649.

Labov, W. (1972) *Language in the Inner City: Studies in the Black English Vernacular*, Philadelphia: University of Pennsylvania Press.

Lam, W. S. E. (2004) 'Border discourses and identities in transnational youth culture', in J. Mahiri (ed.), *What They Don't Learn In School: Literacy in the Lives of Urban Youth*, New York: Peter Lang.

Lam, W. S. E. (2009) 'Multiliteracies on instant messaging in negotiating local, translocal, and transnational affiliations: A case of an adolescent immigrant', *Reading Research Quarterly*, 44: 377–397.

Lam, W. S. E. and Rosario-Ramos, E. (2009) 'Multilingual literacies in transnational digitally mediated contexts: An exploratory study of immigrant teens in the United States', *Language and Education*, 23: 171–190.

Larsen-Freeman, D. (2006) 'The emergence of complexity, fluency, and accuracy in the oral and written production of five Chinese learners of English', *Applied Linguistics*, 27: 590–619.

Lave, J. and Wenger, E. (1991) *Situated Learning: Legitimate peripheral participation*, Cambridge: Cambridge University Press.

Layder, D. (1993) *New Strategies in Social Research: An Introduction and Guide*, Cambridge: Polity Press.

Leander, K., Phillips, N. and Taylor, H. (2010) 'The changing social spaces of learning: Mapping new mobilities', *Review of Research in Education*, 34: 329–394.

Lee, P. (1996) *The Whorf Theory Complex: A Critical Reconstruction*, Philadelphia: John Benjamins.

Lee, Y.-A. (2007) 'Third turn position in teacher talk: Contingency and the work of teaching', *Journal of Pragmatics*, 39: 180–206.

Leeds-Hurwitz, W. (1984) 'On the relationship of the "Ethnography of Speaking", to the "Ethnography of Communication"', *Papers in Linguistics*, 17: 7–32.

Leontiev, A. A. (1981) *Psychology and the Language Learning Process*, Oxford: Pergamon Press.

Leontiev, A. N. (1981) *Problems of the Development of the Mind*, Moscow: Progress.

Levinson, S. (2003) *Space in Language and Cognition*, Cambridge: Cambridge University Press.

Levinson, S. (2006a) 'Cognition in the heart of human interaction', *Discourse Studies*, 8: 85–93.

Levinson, S. (2006b) 'On the human "interaction engine"', in N. J. Enfield and S. Levinson (eds), *Roots of Human Sociality* (pp. 39–69), Oxford: Berg.

Li, D. (2000) 'The pragmatics of making requests in the L2 workplace: A case study of language socialization', *Canadian Modern Language Review*, 57: 58–87.

Lin, A. (1999a) 'Resistance and creativity in English reading lessons in Hong Kong', *Language, Culture and Curriculum*, 12: 285–296.

Lin, A. (1999b) 'Doing-English-Lessons in the reproduction or transformation of social worlds?', *TESOL Quarterly*, 33: 393–412.

Lin, A. (2000) 'Lively children trapped in an island of disadvantage: Verbal play of Cantonese working-class schoolboys in Hong Kong', *International Journal of the Sociology of Language*, 143: 63–83.

Louis, R. (2005) 'Performing English, performing bodies: A case for critical performative language pedagogy', *Text and Performance Quarterly*, 25: 334–353.

Luckmann, T. (1995) 'Interaction planning and intersubjective adjustment of perspectives by communicative genre', in E. Goody (ed.), *Social Intelligence and Interaction* (pp. 175–186), Cambridge: Cambridge University Press.

Lüdi, G. (2006) 'De la compétence linguistique au répertoire plurilingue', *Bulletin VALS/ASLA*, 84: 172–189.

Lussier, D. (2007) 'Theoretical bases of a conceptual framework with reference to intercultural communicative competence', *Journal of Applied Linguistics*, 4: 309–332.

Majid, A., Bowerman, M., Kita, S., Huan, D. and Levinson, S. (2004) 'Can language restructure cognition? The case for space', *Trends in Cognitive Science*, 8: 108–114.

Marshall, E. and Toohey, K. (2010) 'Representing family: Community funds of knowledge, bilingualism, and multimodality', *Harvard Educational Review*, 80: 221–242.

Martin, J. R. (2006) 'Metadiscourse: Designing interaction in genre-based literacy programs', in R. Whittaker, M. O'Donnell and C. McCabe (eds), *Language and Literacy: Functional Approaches* (pp. 95–122), London: Continuum.

Martin, J. R. (2009) 'Genre and language learning: A social semiotic perspective', *Linguistics and Education*, 20: 10–21.

Martin-Jones, M. (2003) 'Bilingual resources and "funds of knowledge" for teaching and learning in multi-ethnic classrooms in Britain', *International Journal of Bilingual Education and Bilingualism*, 6: 267–282.

Martin-Jones, M. and Bhatt, A. (1998) 'Literacies in the lives of young Gujarati speakers in Leicester', in L. Verhoeven and A. Y. Durgunoglu (eds), *Literacy Development in a Multilingual Context* (pp. 37–50), Mahwah, NJ: Lawrence Erlbaum.

Martin-Jones, M. and Jones, K. (eds) (2000) *Multilingual Literacies: Reading and Writing Different Worlds*, Amsterdam: John Benjamins.

Martinec, R. (2004) 'Gestures that co-concur with speech as a systematic resource: The realization of experiential meanings in indexes', *Social Semiotics*, 14: 193–213.

McCarty, T. L. (1989) 'School as community: The Rough Rock demonstration', *Harvard Educational Review*, 59: 484–503.

McCarty, T. and Watahomigie, L. (1998) 'Language and literacy in American Indian and Alaska native communities', in B. Perez (ed.), *Sociocultural Contexts of Language and Literacy* (pp. 69–98), Mahwah, NJ: Lawrence Erlbaum.

McDermott, R. and McDermott, M. (2009) 'Quantentative and Squalortative', *Mind, Culture and Activity*, 16: 203–208.

McKay, S. and Wong, S. L. (1996) 'Multiple discourses, multiple identities: Investment and agency in second-language learning among Chinese adolescent immigrant students', *Harvard Educational Review*, 66: 577–608.

McLaren, P. (1995) *Critical Pedagogy and Predatory Culture*, London: Routledge.

McNamara, T. and Roever, C. (2006) *Language Testing: The Social Dimension*, Malden, MA: Blackwell.

Mehan, H. (1979) *Learning Lessons: Social Organization in the Classroom*, Cambridge, MA: Harvard University Press.

Mehan, H. (2008) 'A sociological perspective on opportunity to learn and assessment', in P. Moss, D. Pullin, J. P. Gee, E. Haertel and L. Young (eds), *Assessment, Equity, and Opportunity to Learn* (pp. 42–75), Cambridge: Cambridge University Press.

Melville, W. and Bartley, A. (2010) 'Mentoring and community: Inquiry as stance and science as inquiry', *International Journal of Science Education*, 32: 807–828.

Mercer, N. (2004) 'Sociocultural discourse analysis: Analysing classroom talk as a social mode of thinking', *Journal of Applied Linguistics*, 1: 137–168.

Michael-Luna, S. and Canagarajah, S. (2007) 'Multilingual academic literacies: Pedagogical foundations for code meshing in primary and higher education', *Journal of Applied Linguistics*, 4: 55–77.

Miller, J. (2000) 'Language use, identity and social interaction: Migrant students in Australia', *Research on Language and Social Interaction*, 33: 69–100.

Miller, K. and Schmitt, C. (2010) 'Effects of variable input in the acquisition of plural in two dialects of Spanish', *Lingua*, 120: 1178–1193.

Mindt, D. (1997) 'Corpora and the teaching of English in Germany', in G. Knowles, T. Mcenery, S. Fligelstone and A. Wichman, (eds.) *Teaching and Language Corpora* (pp. 40–50), London: Longman.

Moll, L. C. (1992) 'Bilingual classroom studies and community analysis: Some recent trends', *Educational Researcher*, 21: 20–24.

Moll, L. C., Amanti, C., Neff, D. and González, N. (1992) 'Funds of knowledge for teaching: Using a qualitative approach to connect homes and classrooms', *Theory into Practice*, 31: 132–141.

Mondada, L. (2004) 'Ways of "doing being plurilingual" in international work meetings', in R. Gardner and J. Wagner (eds), *Second Language Conversations* (pp. 18–39), London: Continuum.

Mondada, L. (2007) 'Commentary: Transcript variations and the indexicality of transcribing practices', *Discourse Studies*, 9: 809–821.

Montgomery, M. (2006) 'The morphology and syntax of Ulster Scots', *English World Wide*, 27: 295–329.

Moore, L. C. (1999) 'Language socialization research and French language education in Africa: A Cameroonian case study', *Canadian Modern Language Review*, 52: 329–350.

Morgan, D. (2007) 'Paradigms lost and pragmatism regained: Methodological implications of combining qualitative and quantitative methods', *Journal of Mixed Methods Research*, 1: 48–76.

Mori, J. (2002) 'Task-design, plan and development of talk-in-interaction: An analysis of a small group activity in a Japanese language classroom', *Applied Linguistics*, 23: 323–347.

Morson, G. and Emerson, C. (1990) *Mikhail Bakhtin: Creation of a Prosaics*, Stanford, CA: Stanford University Press.

Myers, G. (2007) 'Enabling talk: How the facilitator shapes a focus group', *Text & Talk*, 27: 79–105.

Nassaji, H. and Wells, G. (2000) 'What's the use of "triadic dialogue"?: An investigation of teacher–student interaction', *Applied Linguistics*, 21: 376–406.

National Research Council (1999) *How People Learn: Brain, Mind, Experience, and School*, Washington, DC: National Academy Press.

Newfield, D. and Maungedzo, R. (2006) 'Mobilising and modalising poetry in a Soweto classroom', *English Studies in Africa*, 49: 71–93.

New London Group (1996) 'A pedagogy of multiliteracies: Designing social futures', *Harvard Educational Review*, 66: 60–92.

New London Group (2000) 'A pedagogy of multiliteracies: Designing social futures', in B. Cope and M. Kalantzis (eds), *Multiliteracies: Literacy Learning and the Design of Social Futures* (pp. 9–38), London: Routledge.

Nguyen, H. T. (2004) 'The development of communication skills in the practice of patient consultation among pharmacy students', Unpublished doctoral dissertation, University of Wisconsin-Madison, Madison, WI.

Nguyen, H. T. (2006) 'Constructing "expertness": A novice pharmacist's development of interactional competence in patient consultations', *Communication and Medicine*, 3: 147–160.

Nguyen, H. (2007) 'Rapport building in language instruction: A microanalysis of the multiple resources in teacher talk', *Language and Education*, 21: 284–303.

Nguyen, H. T. and Kellogg, G. (2005) 'Emergent identities in discussion for second language learning', *The Canadian Modern Language Review*, 62: 111–136.

Nielsen, M. (2009) 'Interpretative management in business meetings: Understanding managers' interactional strategies through conversation analysis', *Journal of Business Communication*, 46: 23–56.

Ninio, A. and Snow, C. (1996) *Pragmatic Development*, Boulder, CO: Westview Press.

Norris, S. (2006) 'Multiparty interaction: A multimodal perspective on relevance', *Discourse Studies*, 8: 401–421.

Norris, S. (2007) 'The micropolitics of personal national and ethnicity identity', *Discourse & Society*, 18: 653–674.

Norton, B. (2000) *Identity and Language Learning*, Harlow: Pearson Education.

Nystrand, M. (2006) 'Research on the role of classroom discourse as it affects reading comprehension', *Research in the Teaching of English*, 40: 392–412.

Nystrand, M., Gamoran, A., Kachur, R. and Prendergast, C. (1997) *Opening Dialogue: Understanding the Dynamics of Language and Learning in the English Classroom*, New York: Teachers College Press.

Nystrand, M., Wu, L., Gamoran, A., Zieser, S. and Long, D. (2003) *Questions in Time: Investigating the structure and dynamics of unfolding classroom discourse*, Albany, NY: University at Albany, State University of New York.

O'Halloran, K. L. (2008) 'Systemic functional-multimodal discourse analysis (SF-MDA): Constructing ideational meaning using language and visual imagery', *Visual Communication*, 7: 443–475.

Ochs, E. (1979) 'Transcription as theory', in E. Ochs and B. B. Schieffelin (eds), *Developmental Pragmatics* (pp. 43–72), New York: Academic Press.

Ochs, E. (1988) *Culture and Language Development: Language Acquisition and Socialization in a Samoan Village*, New York: Cambridge University Press.

Ochs, E. (1996) 'Linguistic resources for socializing humanity', in J. J. Gumperz and S. Levinson (eds), *Rethinking Linguistic Relativity* (pp. 407–437), Cambridge: Cambridge University Press.

Ochs, E. and Schieffelin, B. B. (1982) *Language Acquisition and Socialization: Three Developmental Stories and their Implications* (Vol. 105), Austin, TX: Southwest Educational Developmental Laboratory.

Ochs, E. and Schieffelin, B. B. (2008) 'Language socialization: An historical overview', *Encyclopedia of Language and Education, Volume 8: Research Methods in Language and Education* (pp. 3–16), The Netherlands: Kluwer Academic Publishers.

Ortega, L. (2005) 'For what and for whom is our research? The ethical as transformative lens in instructed SLA', *Modern Language Journal*, 89: 427–443.

Ortner, S. (1989) *High Religion: A Cultural and Political History of Sherpa Buddhism*, Princeton, NJ: Princeton University Press.

O'Toole, M. (1994) *The Language of Displayed Art*, London: Leicester University Press.

Owyong, M. (2009) 'Clothing semiotics and the social construction of power relations', *Social Semiotics*, 19: 191–211.

Pang, V. O. (2005) *Multicultural Education: A caring-centered approach*, 2nd edn, Boston: McGraw-Hill.

Park, J.-E. (2007) 'Co-construction of nonnative speaker identity in cross-cultural interaction', *Applied Linguistics*, 28: 339–360.

Pauwels, A. (1994) 'Applying linguistic insights in intercultural communication to professional training programmes: An Australian case study', *Multilingua*, 13: 195–212.

Pavlenko, A. (2007) 'Autobiographic narratives as data in applied linguistics', *Applied Linguistics*, 28: 163–188.

Pennycook, A. (2001) *Critical Applied Linguistics: A Critical Introduction*, Mahwah, NJ: Lawrence Erlbaum.

Perry, F. (2005) *Research in Applied Linguistics: Becoming a Discerning Consumer*, Mahwah, NJ: Lawrence Erlbaum.

Peters, A. M. and Boggs, S. T. (1986) 'Interactional routines as cultural influences upon language acquisition', in B. B. Schieffelin and E. Ochs (eds), *Language Socialization Across Cultures* (pp. 80–96), Cambridge: Cambridge University Press.

Philipsen, G. (1992) *Speaking Culturally*, Albany, NY: State University of New York Press.

Phillips, S. (1983) *The Invisible Culture: Communication in Classroom and Community in the Warm Springs Indian Reservation*, White Plains, NY: Longman.

Pierce, B. N. (1995) 'Social identity, investment and language learning', *TESOL Quarterly*, 29: 9–31.

Pomerantz, A. and Bell, N. (2007) 'Learning to play, playing to learn: FL learners as multicompetent language users', *Applied Linguistics*, 28: 556–578.

Pratt, M. L. (1987) 'Linguistic utopias', in N. Fabb, D. Attridge, A. Durant and C. McCabe (eds), *The Linguistics of Writing: Arguments Between Language and Literature* (pp. 48–66). New York: Methuen.

Quinn, M. (2004) 'Talking with Jess: Looking at how metalanguage assisted explanation writing in the middle years', *Australian Journal of Language and Literacy*, 27: 245–261.

Radway, J. (1984) *Reading the Romance: Women, Patriarchy, and Popular Literature*, Chapel Hill, NC: University of North Carolina Press.

Rajadurai, J. (2007) 'Out-group phonological markers and the negotiation of identity', *International Journal of Multilingualism*, 4: 282–299.

Rampton, B. (2005) *Crossing: Language and Ethnicity among Adolescents*, 2nd edn, Manchester: St. Jerome.

Rampton, B. (2007) 'Neo-Hymesian linguistic ethnography in the United Kingdom', *Journal of Sociolinguistics*, 11: 584–607.

Rampton, B. (2009) 'Interaction ritual and not just artful performance in crossing and stylization', *Language in Society*, 38: 149–176.

Rampton, B., Tusting, K., Maybin, J., Barwell, R., Creese, A. and Lytra, V. (2004) *UK Linguistic Ethnography: A Discussion Paper*, available at www.ling-ethnog.org.uk/publications.html.

Richards, K. (2006) ' "Being the teacher": Identity and classroom conversation', *Applied Linguistics*, 27: 51–77.

Rine, E. F. (2009) 'Development in dialogic teaching skills: A micro-analytic case study of a pre-service ITA', Unpublished doctoral dissertation, Penn State University, University Park.

Roberts, C. (1998) 'Awareness in intercultural communication', *Language Awareness*, 7: 109–119.

Roberts, C. (2006) 'Figures in a landscape: Some methodological issues in adult ESOL research', *Linguistics and Education*, 17: 6–23.

Roberts, C. and Sarangi, S. (1995) 'But are they one of us?', *Multilingua*, 14: 363–390.

Roberts, C. and Sarangi, S. (1999) 'Hybridity in gatekeeping discourse: Issues of practical relevance for the researcher', in S. Sarangi and C. Roberts (eds), *Talk, Work and Institutional Order: Discourse in Medical, Mediation and Management Settings* (pp. 473–503), Berlin: Mouton de Gruyter.

Roberts, C. and Sayers, P. (1998) 'Keeping the gate: How judgements are made in interethnic interviews', in P. Trudgill and J. Cheshire (eds), *The Sociolinguistics Reader, Volume 1: Multilingualism and Variation* (pp. 25–43), London: Edward Arnold.

Roberts, C., Davies, E. and Jupp, T. (1992) *Language and Discrimination: A Study of Communication in Multi-Ethnic Workplaces*, London: Longman.

Roberts, C., Byram, M., Barro, A., Jordan, S. and Street, B. (2001) *Language Learners as Ethnographers*, Clevedon: Multilingual Matters.

Robson, C. (2002) *Real World Research*, Oxford: Blackwell.

Rogoff, B., Matusov, E. and White, C. (1996) 'Models of teaching and learning: Participation in a community of learners', in D. Olson and N. Torrance (eds), *The Handbook of Education and Human Development: New Models of Learning, Teaching, and Schooling* (pp. 388–415), Cambridge: Basil Blackwell.

Rogoff, B., Moore, L., Najafi, B., Dexter, A., Correa-Chávez, M. and Solís, J. (2007) 'Children's development of cultural repertoires through participation in everyday routines and practices', in J. E. Grusec and P. D. Hastings (eds), *Handbook of Socialization: Theory and Research* (pp. 490–515), New York: Guilford Press.

Sacks, H. (1984) 'Notes on methodology', in D. Atkinson, J. Maxwell and J. Heritage (eds), *Structures of Social Action: Studies in Conversation Analysis* (pp. 2–27), Cambridge: Cambridge University Press.

Sailaja, P. (2009) *Indian English*, Edinburgh: Edinburgh University Press.

Samuda, V. and Bygate, M. (2008) *Tasks in Second Language Learning*, New York: Palgrave Macmillan.

Sandelowski, M., Voils, C. and Knafi, G. (2009) 'On quantitizing', *Journal of Mixed Methods Research*, 3: 208–222.

Santamaria, L. (2009) 'Culturally responsive differentiated instruction: Narrowing gaps between best pedagogical practices benefiting all learners', *Teachers College Record*, 111: 214–247.

Sapir, E. (1985[1929]) 'The status of linguistics as a science', in D. G. Mandelbaum (ed.), *Selected Writings of Edward Sapir in Language, Culture and Personality* (pp. 160–166), Berkeley, CA: University of California Press.

Sarangi, S. (1994) 'Intercultural or not? Beyond celebration of cultural differences in miscommunication analysis', *Pragmatics*, 4: 409–427.

Sarangi, S. and Candlin, C. (2003) 'Trading between reflexivity and relevance: New challenges for applied linguistics', *Applied Linguistics*, 24: 271–285.

Sarangi, S. and Clarke, A. (2002) 'Zones of expertise and the management of uncertainty in genetics risk communication', *Research on Language and Social Interaction*, 35: 139–171.

Sarangi, S. and Roberts, C. (1999) 'The dynamics of interactional and institutional orders in work-related settings', in S. Sarangi and C. Roberts (eds), *Talk, Work and Institutional Order* (pp. 1–57), Berlin: Mouton de Gruyter.

Saville-Troike, M. (1987) 'Dilingual discourse: The negotiation of meaning without a common code', *Linguistics*, 25: 81–109.

Saville-Troike, M. and Kleifgen, J. (1986) 'Scripts for school: Cross-cultural communication in elementary classrooms', *Text*, 6: 207–221.

Scarino, A. (2010) 'Assessing intercultural capability in learning languages: A renewed understanding of language, culture, learning, and the nature of assessment', *Modern Language Journal*, 94: 324–329.

Schegloff, E. A. (2007) *Sequence Organization in Interaction: Volume 1: A Primer in Conversation Analysis*, Cambridge: Cambridge University Press.

Schieffelin, B. B. (1990) *The Give and Take of Everyday Life: Language Socialization of Kaluli Children*, Cambridge: Cambridge University Press.

Schleppegrell, M., Achugar, M. and Oteíza, T. (2004) 'The grammar of history: Enhancing content-based instruction through a functional focus on language', *TESOL Quarterly*, 38: 67–93.

Scollon, R. (2001) *Mediated Discourse*, London: Routledge.

Scollon, R. and Scollon, S. (2004) *Nexus Analysis: Discourse and the Emerging Internet*, London: Routledge.

Scollon, R. and Scollon, S. (2007) 'Nexus analysis: Refocusing ethnography on action', *Journal of Sociolinguistics*, 11: 608–625.

Scribner, S. (1997) 'A sociocultural approach to the study of mind', in E. Tobach, R. J. Falmagne, M. Parlee, L. Martin and A. S. Kapelman (eds), *Mind and Social Practice: Selected Writings of Sylvia Scribner* (pp. 266–280), Cambridge: Cambridge University Press.

Seale, C. (2002) 'Quality issues in qualitative inquiry', *Qualitative Social Work*, 1: 97–110.

Sefton-Green, J. (2006) 'Youth, technology, and media cultures', *Review of Research in Education*, 30: 279–306.

Sharan, S. (1980) 'Cooperative learning in small groups: Recent methods and effects on achievement, attitudes and ethnic relations', *Review of Educational Research*, 50: 241–271.

Sharan, S. (1984) *Cooperative Learning in the Classroom: Research in Desegregated Schools*, Hillsdale, NJ: Lawrence Erlbaum.

Shea, D. (1994) 'Incorporating ideology and structuring mismatch in cross cultural discourse', Paper presented at meeting of the American Association for Applied Linguistics.

Shotter, J. (1996) 'Living in a Wittgensteinian world: Beyond theory to a poetics of practices', *Journal for the Theory of Social Behavior*, 26: 292–311.

Siegler, R. S. (2006) 'Microgenetic analyses of learning', in D. Kuhn and R. S. Siegler (eds), *Handbook of Child Psychology: Volume 2: Cognition, Perception, and Language* (6th edn, pp. 464–510), Hoboken, NJ: Wiley.

Silverman, D. (2010) *Doing Qualitative Research*, 3rd edn, Los Angeles: Sage.

Sinclair, J. and Coulthard, M. (1975) *Towards an Analysis of Discourse: The English used by teachers and pupils*, London: Oxford University Press.

Slavin, R. E. (1980) 'Cooperative learning in teams: State of the art', *Educational Psychologist*, 15: 93–111.

Slavin, R. E. (1989/1990) 'Research on cooperative learning: Consensus and controversy', *Educational Leadership*, 47: 52–55.

Slavin, R. E. (1995) *Cooperative Learning: Theory, Research and Practice*, 2nd edn, Boston: Allyn and Bacon.

Slobin, D. (1996) 'From "thought and language" to "thinking for speaking"', in J. J. Gumperz and S. C. Levinson (eds), *Rethinking Linguistic Relativity* (pp. 70–96), Cambridge: Cambridge University Press.

Slobin, D. (ed.) (1997) *The Crosslinguistic Study of Language Acquisition: Expanding the Contexts*, Mahwah, NJ: Lawrence Erlbaum.

Slobin, D. (2003) 'From "thought" and "language" to "thinking for speaking"', in J. J. Gumperz and S. Levinson (eds), *Rethinking Linguistic Relativity* (pp. 70–96), Cambridge: Cambridge University Press.

Slobin, D. (2003) 'Language and thought online: Cognitive consequences of linguistic relativity', in D. Gentner and S. Goldin-Meadow (eds), *Language in Mind: Advances in the Study of Language and Thought* (pp. 157–192), Cambridge, MA: MIT Press.

Slobin, D., Bowerman, M., Brown, P., Eisenbeiss, S. and Narasimhan, B. (2009) 'Putting things in places: Developmental consequences of linguistic typology', in J. Bohnemeyer and E. Pederson (eds), *Event Representation in Language and Cognition*, Cambridge: Cambridge University Press.

Smagorinsky, P. and Fly, P. (1993) 'The social environment of the classroom: A Vygotskyan perspective on small group process', *Communication Education*, 42: 159–171.

Smith, W. (2010) 'Footing, resistance and control: Negotiating a traffic citation', *Critical Inquiry in Language Studies*, 7: 173–186.

Smythe, S. and Toohey, K. (2009) 'Investigating sociohistorical contexts and practices through a community scan: A Canadian Punjabi–Sikh example', *Language and Education*, 23: 37–57.

Snow, C., Cancino, H., de Temple, J. M. and Schley, S. (1991) 'Giving formal definitions: A linguistic or metalinguistic skill?', in E. Bialystok (ed.), *Language Processing in Bilingual Children* (pp. 90–112), Cambridge: Cambridge University Press.

Song, J. (2010) 'Language ideology and identity in transnational space: Globalization, migration, and bilingualism among Korean families in the USA', *International Journal of Bilingual Education and Bilingualism*, 13: 23–42.

Stein, P. (2004) 'Representation, rights, and resources: Multimodal pedagogies in the language and literacy classroom', in B. Norton and K. Toohey (eds), *Critical Pedagogies and Language Learning* (pp. 95–115), Cambridge: Cambridge University Press.

Stivers, T. and Robinson, J. (2006) 'A preference for progressivity in interaction', *Language in Society*, 35: 367–392.

Stivers, T., Enfield, N. J., Brown, P., Englert, C., Hayashi, M. and Heinemann, T. (2009) 'Universals and cultural variation in turn-taking in conversation', *Proceedings of the National Academy of Sciences of the United States of America*, 106: 10587–10592.

Stoller, F. (2006) 'Establishing a theoretical foundation for project based learning in second and foreign language contexts', in G. H. Beckett and P. C. Miller (eds), *Project-based Second and Foreign Language Education: Past, Present, and Future* (pp. 19–40), Greenwich, CT: Information Age Publishing.

Street, B. (1993a) *Cross-Cultural Approaches to Literacy*, Cambridge: Cambridge University Press.

Street, B. (1993b) 'Culture is a verb: Anthropological aspects of language and cultural process', in D. Graddol, L. Thompson and M. Byram (eds), *Language and Culture* (pp. 23–43), Clevedon: Multilingual Matters.

Street, B. (2003) 'What's "new" in New Literacy Studies? Critical approaches to literacy in theory and practice', *Current Issues in Comparative Education*, 5: 77–91.

Street, B. (ed.) (2004) *Literacies Across Educational Contexts: Mediating Learning and Teaching*, Philadelphia: Caslon.

Stroud, C. and Wee, L. (2007) 'A pedagogical application of liminalities in social positioning: Identity and literacy in Singapore', *TESOL Quarterly*, 41: 33–54.

Sullivan, P. (2000) 'Spoken artistry: Performance in a foreign language classroom', in J. K. Hall and L. S. Verplaetse (eds), *Second and Foreign Language Learning through Classroom Interaction* (pp. 73–90), Mahwah, NJ: Lawrence Erlbaum.

Svalberg, A. (2009) 'Engagement with language: interrogating a construct', *Language Awareness*, 18: 242–258.

Swan, J., Scarbrough, H. and Robertson, M. (2002) 'The construction of "communities of practice" in the management of innovation', *Management Learning*, 33: 477–496.

Sweetman, P. (2003) 'Twenty-first century dis-ease? Habitual reflexivity or the reflexive habitus', *Sociological Review*, 11: 528–549.

Tajfel, H. and Turner, J. (1986) 'The social identity theory of intergroup behavior', in S. Worchel and W. Austin (eds), *Psychology of Intergroup Relations*, Chicago: Nelson-Hall.

Talmy, S. (2008) 'The cultural productions of the ESL student at Tradewinds High: Contingency, multidirectionality, and identity in L2 socialization', *Applied Linguistics*, 29: 619–644.

Tetreault, C. (2009) 'Cité teens entextualizing French TV host register: Crossing, voicing, and participation frameworks', *Language in Society*, 38: 201–231.

Tipton, S. (2005) 'Improving international medical graduates' performance of case presentations', *Journal of Applied Linguistics*, 2: 395–406.

Tomasello, M. (1999) *The Cultural Origins of Human Cognition*, Cambridge, MA: Harvard University Press.

Tomasello, M. (2000) 'Culture and cognitive development', *Current Directions in Psychological Science*, 9: 37–40.

Tomasello, M. (2001) 'Perceiving intentions and learning words in the second year of life', in M. Bowerman and S. Levinson (eds), *Language Acquisition and Conceptual Development* (pp. 132–158), Cambridge: Cambridge University Press.

Tomasello, M. (2003) *Constructing a Language: A Usage-Based Theory of Language Acquisition*, Cambridge, MA: Harvard University Press.

Tomasello, M. (2006) 'Acquiring linguistic constructions', in R. S. Siegler and D. Kuhn (eds), *Handbook of Child Psychology: Cognitive Development* (pp. 255–298), New York: Wiley.

Toohey, K. (1998) ' "Breaking them up, taking them away": ESL students in Grade 1', *TESOL Quarterly*, 32(1): 61–84.

Torres-Guzman, M. (1998) 'Language, culture and literacy in Puerto Rican communities', in B. Perez (ed.), *Sociocultural Contexts of Language and Literacy* (pp. 99–122), Mahwah, NJ: Lawrence Erlbaum.

Tusting, K. (2005) 'Language and power in communities of practice', in D. Barton and K. Tusting (eds), *Beyond Communities of Practice: Language, Power and Social Context* (pp. 36–54), Cambridge: Cambridge University Press.

Tusting, K. and Maybin, J. (2007) 'Linguistic ethnography and interdisciplinarity: Opening the discussion', *Journal of Sociolinguistics*, 11: 575–583.

Unsworth, L. (2006) 'Towards a metalanguage for multiliteracies education: Describing the meaning-making resources of language–image interaction', *English Teaching: Practice and Critique*, 5: 55–76.

Unsworth, L. (2008) 'Multiliteracies, e-literature and English teaching', *Language and Education*, 22: 62–75.

Upton, T. and Cohen, M.A. (2009) 'An approach to corpus-based discourse analysis: The move analysis as example', *Discourse Studies*, 11: 585–605.

van Dijk, T. (1993) *Discourse and Elite Racism*, London: Sage.

van Dijk, T. (2008) *Discourse and Power*, Houndsmills: Palgrave.

van Lier, L. (2006) 'Foreword', in G. Beckett and P. Miller (eds), *Project-based Second and Foreign Language Education* (pp. xi–xiv), Charlotte, NC: Information Age Publishing.

Villegas, A. M. (1991) *Culturally Responsive Pedagogy for the 1990s and Beyond*, Washington, DC: ERIC Clearinghouse on Teacher Education.

Violin-Wigent, A. (2009) '"Un" revisited: Variation in the pronunciation of "un" in Southeastern France', *Journal of French Language Studies*, 19: 117–134.

Vygotsky, L. S. (1978) *Mind in Society: The Development of Higher Psychological Process*. Cambridge, MA: Harvard University Press.

Vygotsky, L. S. (1981) 'The genesis of higher mental functions', in J. V. Wertsch (ed.), *The Concept of Activity in Soviet Psychology* (pp. 144–188), Armonk, NY: M. E. Sharpe.

Vygotsky, L. S. (1986) *Thought and Language*, Cambridge, MA: MIT Press.

Vygotsky, L. S. (1994) 'The problem of the environment', in R. van der Veer and J. Valsiner (eds), *The Vygotsky Reader* (pp. 338–354), Oxford: Blackwell.

Wallace, C. (2006) 'The text, dead or alive: Expanding textual repertoires in the adult ESOL classroom', *Language and Education*, 17: 74–90.

Wallerstein, N. (1983) *Language and Culture in conflict: Problem Posing in the ESL Classroom*, Reading, MA: Addison-Wesley.

Walsh, D. (2004) 'Doing ethnography', in C. Seale (ed.), *Researching Society and Culture* (2nd edn, pp. 226–237), London: Sage.

Waring, H. (2008) 'Using explicit positive assessment in the language classroom: IRF, feedback, and learning opportunities', *Modern Language Journal*, 92: 577–594.

Watson-Gegeo, K. A. (1997) 'Classroom ethnography', in N. Hornberger and D. Olson (eds), *Encyclopedia of Language and Education, Volume 8: Research Methods in Language and Education* (pp. 135–144), The Netherlands: Kluwer Academic Publishers.

Watson-Gegeo, K. A. and Gegeo, D. W. (1986) 'Calling-out and repeating routines in Kwara'ae children's language socialization', in B. B. Schieffelin and E. Ochs (eds), *Language Socialization Across Cultures* (pp. 17–50), Cambridge: Cambridge University Press.

Waugh, L. (2010) 'Power and prejudice: Their effects on the co-construction of linguistic and national identities', *Critical Inquiry in Language Studies*, 7: 112–130.

Webb, N. and Mastergeorge, A. (2003) 'Promoting effective helping in peer-directed groups', *International Journal of Educational Research*, 39: 73–97.

Weedon, C. (1997) *Feminist Practice and Poststructuralist Theory*, Cambridge, MA: Blackwell.

Weedon, C. (1999) *Feminism, Theory, and the Politics of Difference*, Oxford: Blackwell.

Weigel, R., Wiser, P. and Cook, S. (1975) 'Impact of cooperative learning experiences on cross-ethnic relations and attitudes', *Journal of Social Issues*, 31: 219–245.

Wells, G. (1993) 'Reevaluating the IRF sequence: A proposal for the articulation of theories of activity and discourse for the analysis of teaching and learning in the classroom', *Linguistics and Education*, 5: 1–37.

Wells, G. (1996) 'Using the tool-kit of discourse in the activity of learning and teaching', *Mind, Culture and Activity*, 3: 74–101.

Wells, G. (1999) *Dialogic Inquiry: Towards a Sociocultural Practice and Theory of Education*, Cambridge: Cambridge University Press.

Wenger, E. (1998) *Communities of Practice: Learning, Meaning, and Identity*, Cambridge: Cambridge University Press.

Wenger, E., McDermott, R. A. and Snyder, W. (2002) *Cultivating Communities of Practice: A Guide to Managing Knowledge*, Boston: Harvard Business School Press.

Wertsch, J. V. (1991) *Voices of the Mind: A Sociocultural Approach to Mediated Action*, Cambridge, MA: Harvard University Press.

Wertsch, J. V. (1994) 'The primacy of mediated action in sociocultural studies', *Mind, Culture and Activity*, 1: 202–208.

Wertsch, J. V. (1998) *Mind as Action*, New York: Oxford University Press.

Wertsch, J. V., del Rio, P. and Alvarez, A. (1995) 'Sociocultural studies: History, action and mediation', in J. V. Wertsch, P. del Rio and A. Alvarez (eds), *Sociocultural Studies of Mind* (pp. 1–34), New York: Cambridge University Press.

Whorf, B. L. (1956) *Language Thought and Reality: Selected Writings of Benjamin Lee Whorf*, ed. J. B. Carroll, Cambridge, MA: MIT Press.

Widdowson, H. G. (1998) 'Skills, abilities, and contexts of reality', *Annual Review of Applied Linguistics*, 18: 323–333.

Widdowson, H. G. (2000) 'On the limitations of linguistics applied', *Applied Linguistics*, 21: 3–25.

Widdowson, H. G. (2003) *Defining Issues in English Language Teaching*, Oxford: Oxford University Press.

Widdowson, H. G. (2007) 'Un-applied linguistics and communicative language teaching', *International Journal of Applied Linguistics*, 17: 214–220.

Willett, J. (1995) 'Becoming first graders in an L2: An ethnographic study of L2 socialization', *TESOL Quarterly*, 29: 473–503.

Williams, G. (1992) *Sociolinguistics: A Sociological Critique*, London: Routledge.

Williams, G. (2008) 'Language socialization: A systemic functional perspective', in P. Duff and N. Hornberger (eds), *Encyclopedia of Language and Education: Vol. 8, Language Socialization* (pp. 57–70), New York, NY: Springer.

Williams, R. (1977) *Marxism and Literature*, Oxford: Oxford University Press.

Wittgenstein, L. (1963) *Philosophical Investigations*, trans. G. E. M. Anscombe, Oxford: Basil Blackwell.

Wittgenstein, L. (1980) *Remarks on the Philosophy of Psychology* (Vol. 2), Oxford: Basil Blackwell.

Wodak, R. and Wright, S. (2006) 'The European Union in cyberspace: Multilingual democratic participation in a virtual public sphere', *Journal of Language and Politics*, 5: 251–276.

Wodak, R., de Cillia, R., Reisigl, M. and Liebhart, K. (1999) *The Discursive Construction of National Identity*, Edinburgh: Edinburgh University Press.

Wolfram, W. (1974) *Sociolinguistic Aspects of Assimilation: Puerto Rican English in New York City*, Arlington, VA: Center for Applied Linguistics.

Wolfram, W. and Christian, D. (1976) *Appalachian Speech*, Arlington, VA: Center for Applied Linguistics.

Wolfram, W., Adger, C. and Christian, D. (1999) *Dialects in Schools and Communities*, Mahwah, NJ: Lawrence Erlbaum Associates.

Wong, J. (2000a) 'Delayed next turn repair initiation in native/non-native speaker English conversation', *Applied Linguistics*, 21: 244–267.

Wong, J. (2000b) 'The token "yeah" in nonnative speaker English conversation', *Research on Language and Social Interaction*, 33: 39–67.

Wong, J. (2002) 'Applying conversation analysis in applied linguistics: Evaluating dialogue in English as a second language textbooks', *International Review of Applied Linguistics*, 40: 37–60.

Wong, J. and Waring, H. (2010) *Conversation Analysis and Second Language Pedagogy*, New York: Routledge.

Woolard, K. (2007) 'Bystanders and the linguistic construction of identity in face-to-back communication', in P. Auer (ed.), *Style and Social Identities: Alternative Approaches to Linguistic Heterogeneity* (pp. 187–208), Berlin: Mouton de Gruyter.

Year, J. and Gordon, P. (2009) 'Korean speakers' acquisition of the English ditransitive construction: The role of verb prototype, input distribution, and frequency', *Modern Language Journal*, 93: 399–417.

Yont, K., Snow, C. and Vernon-Feagans, L. (2003) 'The role of context in mother–child interactions: An analysis of communicative intents expressed during toy play and book reading with 12-month-old', *Journal of Pragmatics*, 35: 435–454.

Young, R. F. (2000) 'Interactional competence: Challenges for validity', Paper presented at meeting of the American Association for Applied Linguistics, from www.wisc.edu/english/rfyoung/IC_C4V.Paper.PDF.

Young, R. F. and Nguyen, H. T. (2002) 'Modes of meaning in high school science', *Applied Linguistics*, 23: 348–372.

Zentella, A. C. (1997) *Growing up Bilingual*, Oxford: Blackwell.

Zhiming, B. and Huaging, H. (2006) 'Diglossia and register variation in Singapore English', *World Englishes*, 25: 105–114.

Author index

Subject index

Page numbers in **Bold** represent figures.